F. C. Happold was born at Lancaster in 1893 and educated at Rydal and Peterhouse, Cambridge. He served in the First World War and was awarded a D.S.O. while still a second-lieutenant. After the war he started his career as a schoolmaster at the Perse School, Cambridge, where the foundations of his reputation as an educational pioneer were laid. In 1928 he became Headmaster of Bishop Wordsworth's School, Salisbury, from which post he retired in 1960. In the midst of a very active life as a schoolmaster he has written a considerable number of books and articles on education, history, social studies, religion, and philosophy. These include *The Approach to History*, *Towards a New Aristocracy*, *The Adventure of Man*, and *Adventure in Search of a Creed*. He has also published a nativity play, *The Finding of the King*. In 1937, in recognition of his educational work, he was made an Hon. Ll.D. of the University of Melbourne. Since his retirement he has written three Pelican Originals, *Mysticism: a Study and an Anthology*, *Religious Faith and Twentieth-Century Man*, and *Prayer and Meditation* as well as *The Journey Inwards*.

Prayer and Meditation

THEIR NATURE AND PRACTICE

F. C. Happold

PENGUIN BOOKS

Penguin Books Ltd, Harmondsworth, Middlesex, England
Penguin Books Inc., 7110 Ambassador Road, Baltimore, Maryland 21207, U.S.A.
Penguin Books Australia Ltd, Ringwood, Victoria, Australia

—

First published 1971

—

Copyright © F. C. Happold, 1971

—

Made and printed in Great Britain by
Richard Clay (The Chaucer Press) Ltd,
Bungay, Suffolk
Set in Monotype Garamond

To

ARTHUR AND MARGARET

and to all those, many of them now dead,
who have played a part in my life,
I dedicate this book,
probably the last I shall write.

Contents

CONTENTS

Acknowledgements

IT would have been quite impossible for me to have written this study of prayer at all levels of spiritual development in all the higher religions had I not been able to draw on the work of others.

I should therefore like to acknowledge my indebtedness to the chief books on which I have relied, together with their authors and publishers. First to Miss Constance Padwick whose *Moslem Devotions* (Student Christian Movement Press) I have found especially illuminating; I am especially grateful to her for allowing me to draw freely on her truly brilliant piece of research in the popular Islamic devotions throughout the Moslem world. Next to Mohammad Zafrulla Khan's *Islam, its meaning for Modern Man* (Routledge and Kegan Paul) which I have found of great help. For the chapter on Buddhist prayer I am indebted to Christmas Humphreys, who has through the years guided my steps through the difficult paths of Buddhism, and especially in this study to his *Concentration and Meditation* (Watkins); to Pe Maung Tin's *Buddhist Devotion and Meditation* (Society for Promoting Christian Knowledge); to King's *Buddhism and Christianity* (Allen and Unwin); to the Lama Govinda's *Foundations of Tibetan Mysticism* (Rider and Co.), and to his article 'The Importance of Prayer in Buddhism' in *The Middle Way* (August 1964).

For the chapter on Jewish prayer I have relied mainly on my knowledge of the Old Testament and on the Authorized Daily Prayer Book of the United Hebrew Congregations of the British Empire. I have also found a book by W. A. Simpson, *Jewish Prayer and Worship* (Student Christian Movement Press) very valuable.

I wish also to acknowledge my indebtedness to Geoffrey Watkins of the publishing firm of Vincent Stuart and Watkins who has helped me so much ever since I started to write this trilogy, and has allowed me in this book to quote from the edition of *The Prayer of Jesus* published by his firm.

Special acknowledgements are also called for for permission to include certain copyright material in The Prayer Book, which forms the second part of this book. To the Executors of Alice Meynell for permission to print two of her poems, 'Christ in the Universe' and 'The Unknown God'; to Messrs Collins and to Harper and Row for permission to print two passages from Teilhard de Chardin's *Le Milieu Divin*; to Mrs Gillian Wilkinson for permission to make and print a long meditation from Evelyn Underhill's *The Mystery of Sacrifice* (Longman and Green) and to include one of her poems '*Corpus Christi*' from her volume of verse *Immanence* (Dent); to Darton, Longman and Todd for spontaneously agreeing to my reprinting in this book the 'theme' meditations which first appeared in my *The Journey Inwards* which they published in 1968; to the Lama Govinda for two invocations from *The Way of the White Clouds* (Hutchinson); to my friend Brian Moorhouse who gave me the 'Masonic Prayer at the Lodge Closing', and obtained permission for me to use it, and to W. L. Wilmhurst who wrote it (it is printed in his *The Meaning of Masonry*); to my former pupil, John Carol Case, who wrote the tune of the 'Dedication Hymn' for me, and to my former Director of Music, J. McN. Milne, who wrote the tunes of the 'Hymn of the Oblations' and the 'Morning Recessional Hymn'.

I should also like to express my debt to the various hymnals from which I chose most of the hymns included in The Prayer Book. Also to Trevor Beeson of Prism Publications, which first published my *A Cosmic Eucharist* (now out of print) from which I have taken 'The Eucharistic Action'; and to the Mothers' Union for the help I received in compiling the sections 'Prayers from the Ancient Liturgies' and 'Prayers of some Christian Saints' from a book *Unto the Perfect Day* published many years ago and long out of print.

And last, but by no means least, to those who have actually helped to write this Prayer Book. To my friends who composed the Prayers of Recollection for the section 'The Practice of the Presence of God', and who wish to remain anonymous; to the three poets who sent me the poems which I have printed among the group of Meditations; to Mrs Phyllis Campbell whose beautiful mystical poems I am privileged to present to the world for the first time; to L. E. Machin who sent me from South Africa the poem I have called 'The Spiritual Adventure'; and to the author of 'The Man Born Blind' who does not want his name to be revealed. Other books and authors to whom I am indebted are mentioned in the Notes to this Prayer Book.

I cannot end these acknowledgements without thanking my friend, Sir Robert Parr, for his very complimentary 'Letter to the Author', and for the sonnet which he has appended to it. I am indeed proud to be given, unworthy of it though I feel myself to be, the title, *Sapientiae Minister* (Servant of Wisdom).

I have done my best to avoid using copyright material without first asking permission. In a book of this scope it has been an onerous task and I may have erred. If so, will the owners of copyright please inform Penguin Books so that the failure may be rectified.

Letter to the Author

from Sir Robert Parr, K.B.E., C.M.G., D. ès L.,
Associate Member of the Academy of Lyon and of the
Academy of Macon.

Dudleston,
ce Jour des Rois, 1970

Monsieur mon Frère, – for such, assuredly, is the only correct
appel in a letter from one poet to another, – It is very good of
you to have let me read the manuscript of your third volume,
an opportunity which, for more than one reason, I particularly
value, and I am all the more grateful.

Finis coronat opus. Formally, this book concludes your
trilogy. By its character, it recalls a lifetime of service. In its
essence, it is a conception, rooted in that service, directly
relevant to the needs of the present day and to the personal
problems which they must involve.

You record that you entered on the project of this Trilogy
ten years ago. It is wholly proper, I think, to trace its inception
to that first experience in your rooms at Cambridge, one
February evening of 1913, and to its sequel, related in more
than one of your books, and notably in the prologue to the
anthology included in *Mysticism.* 'Those who sought the city
found the wood: and those who sought the wood found the
city' – words with a profound significance for our present
situation. Eighteen months later there followed the searing
and revealing lessons of the first war. Then, with your return
to Cambridge, where you became a university lecturer and
also an assistant master at the Perse, – to be one of Rouse's
young men was a distinction not easily earned, – you began to
develop that knowledge of many disciplines and that insight,
first into the teaching of history and subsequently into the
field of education in general, which has won you so wide a
reputation as an outstanding leader of thought in this sphere.
For more than thirty years you held the Bishop Wordsworth's

headmastership, a period that included the disaster of the second war, with its endurances, with its heroisms, with its bitter humiliations for the human conscience. You had set yourself to endow your pupils with those qualities Plato describes as the power and clarity of vision which enable a man to contemplate all time and all existence, in every circumstance to shape his course by the certainty which derives from an understanding of true reality, that reality of which he is, essentially, a part. So, for generation after generation, over more than thirty years, you formed your young men. Max would have taken pleasure in drawing you as Cheiron. He might well have inscribed the portrait, – in that small compelling hand, – 'a pupil of Apollo'.

Meanwhile you had been working at your various studies in education and, at the same time as the ranks of your pupils were being extended by the ranks of your readers, the content of what you had to say was evolving. Thus, *The Approach to History* led to *Citizens in the Making* and then to *This Modern Age*. Your 1943 *Towards a New Aristocracy* was followed fourteen years later by *Adventures in Search of a Creed*. The logical sequel was *Mysticism*, today in its third edition, the opening volume of the trilogy which you now complete. The very fact that your thought should have followed such a course is an index of its relevance to our present situation. Through the manifold confusions, the disruptive turmoils, of these past six decades, two factors, – two factors for which history can afford no guidance, – have become more and more insistent. They are complementary aspects of the same phenomenon, the one material and the other spiritual. On the one hand, the dense populations of the industrial countries, with the technical means now at their disposal, present problems before which established institutions, administrative, political, social and ecclesiastical, academic and military, have revealed themselves progressively helpless, alike on the material plane and on the moral. *Si testimonium requiris circumspice.* Only Mammon flourishes. On the other hand, individual man, in an ever increasing proportion, is deprived from infancy, – and, for all effective purposes, during the whole of his lifetime, – of that direct experience of the daily and hourly life of the countryside which is his proper environment, his First Sacrament, his earliest epiphany of grace. Unless, somehow, he can make good this loss of his natural birthright, he must go through life spiritually handicapped, perhaps not consciously aware of his lack but, nevertheless, an incomplete personality. Indeed, no earlier generation has lain so fast bound in the depths of Plato's cave as are the present prisoners of their own technology. It is the looming shadow of Huxley's *Brave New World*, of George Orwell's *Nineteen Eighty-four*. Let me quote Seyyed Hossein Nasr's introduction to his 1966 Rockefeller Lectures before the University of Chicago:

To be at peace with the Earth, one must be at peace with Heaven. There is no way for man to defend his humanity, and not be dragged through his own inventions and machinations to the infra-human, except by remaining faithful to the image of man as a reflection of something that transcends the merely human.

That young people should complain and protest and revolt is no matter for surprise. Some of their liveries one might wish different, some of their methods may prove ill-advised, but that the burden of their movement, the theme of their unrest, is abundantly justified, no clear-headed observer can doubt. They are looking for a new order of things, a new order which must involve a profound change of heart, a new order which organized society cannot give them. Many of them repeat, – in Lydian mode, – that compassion, – love, – is the key; the solution to the problem of the iniquities which weigh on their world. Some of them are groping towards, some of them will see clearly, the concept that love is a spiritual force of gravity; that all life is one; and that the words 'God is Love' mean that the power manifest throughout the universe is an active and self-conscious force for continuing unity to which we all belong; and more and more of them will come to understand that 'he loveth best who prayeth best'. They will come to understand that verse of Epimenides which, six hundred years later, Saint Paul was to quote on Mars' hill: 'In thee we too live and move and have our Being.'

Finis coronat opus. Where institutions fail the remedy is in the spontaneous attitude, the conviction, of individual men and women. You have completed a study through which the younger generations, perhaps in very great numbers, may attain to such a conviction, may reach a valid certainty by which they can shape their course, – 'a truth higher than experience, of which the mind bears witness to herself'.

*

Those who sought the City found the wood: and those who sought the wood found the City.

*

Here is a sonnet, composed more than a generation ago, which treats of the service of Wisdom, that service which you have made your own. I think that your countless friends, – comrades, pupils, and readers, – mustered across the years, – will find in it some echo of those sentiments which your work has evoked in their hearts. Let me then, *Monsieur mon Frère,* assume the mantle of their authority, and in their name ask your leave to append it to this letter a small token of gratitude for so many years of single-hearted devotion, a small stone set in the frame of your Trilogy which for so many, – and in more than one sense, – will remain a κτῆμα ἐς ἀεὶ, an abiding possession.

ROBERT PARR

Sapientiae Ministro

Because your vision has not flinched nor turned
Aside from truth, because no wind of fear
Has chilled your heart, because your hands have learned
In toil and patience to establish clear
The living word, your name shines like that spear*

* The reference is to the great statue of Athene, the patron goddess of Athens, on the Acropolis, which would be one of the first sights which mariners approaching Athens would see.

The sonnet was composed by the writer of this letter more than twenty-five years ago, but was only recently presented to Dr Happold.

Whose blade was lifted over Athens' height
To warn the stranger, while his ship drew near,
What presence dwelt thereon and what her might.
And we who love you, who have spelled aright
The message of your priesthood, shall at length
Win courage from your courage till our sight,
Cleansed by your truth, made stronger by your strength,
Pierces the mundane darkness to descry
The shape of that proud head against a starlit sky.*

*

O Sapientia; Quae ex ore Altissimi prodiisti; Attingens a fine usque ad finem, fortiter suaviterque disponens omnia; Veni ad docendum nos.

* See footnote on previous page.

THE STUDY

Introduction: The Completion of a Trilogy

WITH this study of the nature, significance and practice of prayer the Pelican trilogy which I commenced writing in 1960 is brought to a close. Since the theme of *the mystical* runs through all the three volumes, I have called it a 'mystical' trilogy.

It began with an objective study of mysticism with, as its second part, an Anthology of the writings of the great mystics. Not many years ago a book on mysticism would have had only a limited market. During the last decade, however, the spiritual climate seems to have changed and the book has had from the first, and still continues to have, a wide appeal. It has now gone into a third enlarged edition, to the Anthology of which sections on the mystical elements in ancient Chinese Taoist religious philosophy, in Buddhism and in the theology of the Eastern Orthodox Church have been added.

Mysticism was followed by a book of a different sort, *Religious Faith and Twentieth-Century Man*, in which I endeavoured to describe and analyse the spiritual crisis of our age. This analysis led me to the tentative hypothesis that our age is one of those *leap-epochs* in the history of mankind in which consciousness is passing into a new level of awareness and insight, in which the only acceptable religion is likely to be a 'mystical' one. Consequently I called this change in spiritual and intellectual awareness 'a movement into the realm (or orbit, sphere) of *the mystical*'.

The mystical? What do I mean by that term? Is it the best term to convey my meaning? In writing this book and also *The Journey Inwards*, to which I shall refer later, to choose terms which would not be misunderstood has been difficult; so much so that in *The Journey Inwards* I added an appendix, 'On Words and Meanings'.

What one is attempting to describe by the term, *the mystical*, is a particular type of inner experience, or perhaps better, particular types of inner experience which may or may not be called 'religious' or 'spiritual' according to how one interprets these words. Some of these experiences may rightly be called *mystical* in the fullest sense; some may be more exactly called *intuitive*; for instance, some of the insights of great scientists which led to important scientific discoveries were intuitive. One may, therefore, aptly speak of the intuitive/mystical experience. There is another term which one ought to consider, *numinous*, sometimes spelt 'numenous' or 'numenal' (the *Concise Oxford Dictionary* gives 'numenal' only). The *noumenon* is there defined as 'an object of intellectual intuition devoid of all phenomenal attributes'. The eighteenth-century philosopher, Kant, used it as the antithesis of *phenomenon*. The numinous experience is the same as or analogous to that which is the theme of Otto's *Idea of the Holy*, the experience of the '*mysterium tremendum et facinans*'. Both William James, in *Varieties of Religious Experience*, and the German mystic, Jacob Boehme, however, seem to equate this experience with a high form of purely mystical experience.

So I shall content myself in stating that all true religious experience, even the rather vague sense of 'something beyond', is numinous and beg leave to continue to use the term, *the mystical*, normally printed in italics, in the sense in which I first used it in the chapter, 'The Nature of the Mystical' in *Religious Faith and Twentieth-Century Man*, expanding and elaborating on what I wrote there.

I shall follow very closely, but shall add to, the text of an essay entitled *The Challenge of a Leap-Epoch in Human History*, I contributed to a *Festschrift*, to be presented to the scientist-philosopher, Professor Ludwig von Bertalanffy, to commemorate his sixty-fifth birthday.

The mystical is contained in the totality of perception and experience of the human race. It manifests itself, however, at different levels and in different ways.

(a) Throughout man's history, in all parts of the world, in all religions, and in every age, there have been those who have been endowed with a range of perception and awareness different from that of ordinary men. This expansion of perception and awareness enabled them to undergo experiences which, though interpreted according to different religious philosophies, have the same character and may be presumed to have the same origin. It also enabled them to enter into permanent states of consciousness variously called Illumination, Union with God, Enlightenment, Nirvana, etc. Further, these experiences resulted in an apprehension of reality, including the reality of the phenomenal world, more intimate and profound than is possible to the unaided rational, analytical mind. These men and women are recognized as the mystics in the fullest sense, as the true contemplatives and seers. In them, *the mystical* is manifested in its highest and most specialized form. Let us call this manifestation *the mystical in the first degree.*

(b) There is also a type of mystical experience, known to many in no sense contemplatives, which is clearly in the same continuum. It is, however, usually of a transitory nature, infrequent, occurring perhaps only once or twice in a lifetime. Yet such experiences are clearly recognizable by those who have experienced them. They have a unique quality; they stand out from every other experience; they have a particular sort of objectivity. Further, they carry with them a tremendous sense of certainty, a sure conviction that, as it were, a curtain had momentarily opened on a part of reality which had not been previously apprehended, or at least not with the same certainty and intimacy. In *Watcher on the Hills*, Dr Raynor Johnson describes and examines thirty-six cases of this type of mystical experience. They have been given a number of different names, a *peak experience*, the *timeless moment, illumination, intuitive enlightenment*, etc. Let us call this manifestation of *the mystical, the mystical in the second degree.*

(c) The experience of *the mystical in the second degree* is, however, comparatively – but only comparatively – rare. What we may call *the mystical in the third degree* is more common. It may take more than one form. A typical one is that described by T. S. Eliot in *The Dry Salvages*, the third of his *Four Quartets*:

                              the unattended
Moment, the moment in and out of time,
The distraction fit, lost in a shaft of sunlight,
The wild thyme unseen, or the winter lightning
Or the waterfall, or music heard so deeply
That it is not heard at all, but you are the music
While the music lasts.

Eliot continues:

                         These are only hints and guesses,
      Hints followed by guesses.

All these three experiences of *the mystical* must be described as 'feeling' states, in the sense that they convey a 'feel' about the nature of reality, rather than a rational apprehension of it. Nevertheless they have a definite noëtic quality; they reveal something of the nature of things; they may thus rightly be regarded also as 'knowledge' states.

(d) There is, however, a fourth manifestation of *the mystical*, in which rational and analytical thought plays a greater part. This manifestation may break through when what is primarily a process of rational thought culminates in a flash of *contemplative insight*. It is as if the pieces which have been moving about in a mental kaleidoscope suddenly fall into a significant and revealing pattern. For instance, one has been reading and brooding over a passage in a book or pondering on some scientific or other hypothesis. Suddenly, something in it is illuminated, is seen from a fresh angle, and takes on a new and vivid meaning. The *Is-ness** of things shows itself in a new guise. The rational and the non-rational, the analytical and the intuitive-mystical coalesce.

One ought perhaps to add a fifth degree of *the mystical*, though, since it can take different forms, it is difficult to describe it precisely. One may say that it opens up vistas of as yet not fully explored country, which lies beyond reason, and yet in no way conflicts with it.

For instance, L. P. Jacks in his 1922 Hibbert Lectures used these words:

* Meister Eckhart's word *Isticheit*, roughly equivalent to Buddhist *Tathata* (Suchness).

All religious testimony, so far as I can interpret its meaning, converges towards a single point, namely this: there is that in the world, call it what you will, which responds to the confidence of those who trust it, declaring itself to them, as a fellow worker in the pursuit of the Eternal Verities.

I knew L. P. Jacks and was deeply impressed by his immense intellectual and spiritual power, which showed itself in his piercing eyes.

This consciousness of the numinous, for that is what this experience clearly is, comes out very vividly in Beatrice Webb's autobiography, when she speaks of a communion with a super-human force, of the consciousness of experiencing a sense of reverence and awe (the *mysterium tremendum?*), the feeling of a power and purpose outside herself. In her this resulted in a religious interpretation of the universe; and that without compromising her intellectual integrity.*

Let us call this sense of the numinous *the mystical in the fifth degree*. It has close affinities with *the mystical in the fourth degree*.

To sum up, what one finds in *the mystical*, at whatever level it manifests itself, is consciousness and cognition operating in a particular way, a way in which, as it were, an inner, non-rational light is communicated, through which the mind is enabled to apprehend something which would otherwise remain in darkness. While the higher manifestations of *the mystical* are known to comparatively few, it is possible for one who is in no way a contemplative and who has never known any unique mystical experience, *to think and apprehend mystically*, and so to arrive at a *mystical* interpretation of the nature of things.

The ability to think *mystically* is thus to expand one's range of perception and to enable one to penetrate more deeply and fully into the ultimate truth.

We have now reached a point when it is possible to set out three, albeit tentative, interlocking definitions of *the mystical*:
1. *The mystical* is the complexion which reality, whether it be the reality of the That we call God or of the world, assumes

* I owe these two examples to Sir Alister Hardy.

when perception and thought have moved into a particular dimension of consciousness.

2. *The mystical* is the response to the disclosure of *Is-ness*, whether of God or the world, of one who has attained to some degree of mystical cognition.

3. *The mystical*, particularly in its manifestation in the fourth and fifth degrees, is the point of intersection of rational and non-rational thought and perception.

After the publication of *Religious Faith and Twentieth-Century Man* in 1966, I wrote for Darton, Longman and Todd a book entitled *The Journey Inwards*, with the sub-title, 'A simple introduction to the practice of contemplative meditation by normal people'. It was published in November, 1968. Intended at first to be little more than a small booklet on one aspect of the practice of prayer, it grew into a book of nearly 150 pages. It covered at greater length and in some detail part of the field which is surveyed in this more all-embracing study of prayer and may be usefully read in conjunction with it. To avoid unnecessary repetition I shall at times refer the reader to it.

Each volume in this trilogy is complete in itself and may be read without reference to the others. The whole trilogy has, however, an underlying unity. I am aware that throughout its composition I have often repeated myself. The subject with which it deals is not an easy one for the ordinary reader to understand. I have tried to assist him in every way I could. Further, there are, at least apparent, inconsistencies. During the years I have been writing it my thought has developed and expanded; new vistas have opened out; new and more refined forms of expressing the same fundamental ideas have suggested themselves.

This final volume of my trilogy falls into two distinct parts: a study of the nature of prayer and the forms it has taken at different levels in Christianity and the other higher religions; and a prayer book, designed for the use of 'all sorts and conditions of men'. Its title, 'Offices, Prayers and Meditations', indicates its character. It is intended to be used as a devotional manual by those who, in whatever form is in accordance with the inclination and temperament of each, desire to cultivate the life of prayer. It also serves the purpose of a sort of anthology of prayer, for the most part drawn from Christian, but also from non-Christian, sources. So as to keep The Study as objective and as little didactic as possible, practical advice on the way the offices, prayers and meditations printed in The Prayer Book might be used in the development of the spiritual life has, for the most part, been confined to the notes in The Prayer Book section rather than included in the text of The Study.

Before concluding this Introduction I must make clear what I mean by the word 'prayer' throughout this book. In her charming autobiography* St Teresa describes in detail the characteristics of *the four degrees or stages of prayer*. They range from the simplest form of prayer up to the high and rare state of divine union. In this study I use the term, 'prayer', in the same way that St Teresa uses it, i.e. to cover all types of prayer-activity, endeavouring to convey my exact meaning at each point by means of such adjectives as 'petitionary', 'verbal', 'contemplative', 'mystical', etc. To pray truly is nothing less than to live in the Mystery of God. The deeper a man is plunged and immersed in that Mystery, the higher his degree of prayer until, in the state of union, the Spiritual Marriage, though the distinction between creature and Creator remains, there is nothing left but God.

Secondly the word 'meditation' conveys different meanings to different people. There are various types which I have tried to classify in the Introduction to The Prayer Book. It is sufficient to say here

(a) It is unsound to contrast 'meditation' with 'prayer'; meditation is simply one expression of the life of prayer. One may aptly speak of the Prayer of Meditation or of meditational prayer.

(b) There are two main forms of 'meditation'. These I have called 'rational-reflective', or the Prayer of the Head, and

* A good translation is published by Penguin Books: *The Life of St Teresa of Avila.*

'intuitive-contemplative', or the Prayer of the Heart. In practice they overlap and coalesce. How this happens will be made clear in the course of this book.

At the beginning of *The Journey Inwards* I started with the question which is posed by so many in our own time: 'How it is possible to pray to a God, let alone a God who is said to be a personal God, in whom I cannot believe?' and attempted by a consideration of the meaning of the four words, 'God', 'personal', 'believe' and 'prayer', to resolve this very common dilemma. It will not be inappropriate in this fuller study of prayer to start by discussing, though in a somewhat different way, the issues which were discussed in the earlier book.

1. The Problem of Prayer

WHAT is prayer? How and why have men prayed in the past? What function has prayer for men of this modern age, conditioned as they are by circumstance, impelled to think and live within the thought patterns of an age in which for many the God-image has faded, the age of so-called secular man, who no longer needs to postulate the existence of a God to account for the facts of the universe? How is it possible to pray if there is doubt as to whether there is a God to whom to pray? That is the theme of this book.

Most of the books on prayer written in the past have been written against a particular cosmological background, a particular picture of the universe. That picture has been shattered by modern science. A new picture of the universe has emerged, which it is not easy to reconcile with any sort of belief in a God which can be thought of as *personal* in any way one can conceive personality, or with a *supernatural* or a *supersensory* world standing over against a *material* world.

> The cold universe,
> Boundless and silent, goes revolving on
> Worlds without end. The grace of God is gone.
> A vast indifference, deadlier than a curse,
> Chills our poor globe, which Heaven seemed to nurse
> So fondly. Twas God's rainbow when it shone,
> Until we searched. Now, as we count and con
> Gusts of infinity, our hopes disperse ...

So wrote Pieter Geyl, the historian, in his concentration camp.

> God is dead;
> And the sanctuary of man's heart is empty,
> A void place, through which blows a bitter wind,
> Rustling the worn leaves of a lost beauty,
> Stirring the barren twigs of a vanished peace.

So I myself tried to express the same sort of emotion, the

same sort of reaction to the disappearance of that comparatively cosy universe which was the universe of our ancestors.
Let us be quite frank. There are many in our age who have
been compelled by intellectual honesty to see the universe in
this way; and, if they are sensitive, it hurts. In a universe,
conceived in such a way, there seems to be no place for God,
no place for love, no place for prayer.

Such a picture may, however, only be a partial one. We
may have to acknowledge that we human beings are only
insignificant atoms, passing swiftly, O so swiftly, between
birth and death, on an insignificant planet of an insignificant
solar system. We may have to discover a new way of 'seeing'
the universe and a fresh image of God. We may have to discard a now outworn anthropomorphic image of God. We
need not, however, despair. Man's exploration of the universe
is strewn with discarded 'images' of its nature; the evolution
of religious insight is strewn with discarded 'images' of the
That which we call God. It is, however, possible, while still
preserving intellectual honesty, by throwing one's mind open
to all possible interpretations of the nature of reality to arrive,
with Pierre Teilhard de Chardin, at a mount of vision where
one is able to see and feel 'the diaphany of the divine at the
heart of a universe on fire' and a God, not dead, but radiant
in an all-pervasive splendour of creative love. It is not
necessary to cling to a 'Supreme Being' type of theology if it
is no longer a helpful 'model'. There have been, and are,
other 'models'. No image of God is an adequate or exclusive
image. God is, as spiritually developed men throughout the
ages have known, the Inexpressible, the Unknowable, the
Unconditional, the One 'before whom words recoil', un-
definable by word or idea. He has been called by a hundred
names; but has no name. He is manifested in a thousand
forms; but has no form. He is simply, as St Bernard said,
when asked, 'What is God?', *That which Is*, the Mystery which
it has been the eternal quest of men to try to penetrate.

How many of the difficulties which modern man finds when
he tries to think about God would disappear if it is realized
that one cannot think about God at all. All we can think about

is some idea of God in the mind, some picture of God in the imagination. But neither the idea nor the picture is remotely adequate. The That which we call God is above every idea and every image.

Let it not be thought that I am saying anything new or unorthodox. The doctrine of the unthinkability of God is present in all the higher religions, not least in the deepest spirituality of Christianity. In support of this one could quote passages from St Augustine and St John of the Cross, from Dionysius the Areopagite and from *The Cloud of Unknowing*. Let me be content with a passage from the *De Veritate* of the greatest of the Doctors of the Christian Church, St Thomas Aquinas: 'What God actually is always remains hidden from us. And this is the highest knowledge one can have of God in this life, that we know Him to be above every thought we are able to think of Him.'

The religious experience, the sense of the numinous, is, however, part of the total experience of mankind throughout the ages. At the heart of it there is a paradox, a paradox bound up with the very nature of the religious experience itself. In the innermost depths of the soul men of spiritual insight are conscious of a Power or Presence, more real than anything else in their experience. It cannot be known as other things are known, or described as other things are described; and yet it is so intimate that it is known better than anything else is known. Of God they are compelled to say: 'The One is unknowable', and yet at the same time their experience is such that they can also affirm with complete confidence: 'God is more inward to us than we are to ourselves'; 'Closer is He than breathing, nearer than hands or feet'.

That unknown author of the medieval treatise, *The Cloud of Unknowing*, expressed this truth as follows:

Of the works of God, and of the works of God's self, may a man through grace have fullness of knowing and well he can think of them: but of God himself no man can think. And therefore I would leave all things that I can think and choose to love that thing that I cannot think. For why; He may well be loved, but not thought. By love may He be gotten and holden; but by thought never.

So the That which we call God cannot be apprehended by the intellect. Nothing one can think or say about Him (or It) can go beyond symbols, images, 'models' (to adopt the term used by the scientist). These symbols, images, models, are all true up to a point. They are, human perception being what it is, necessary and helpful. Indeed they can be, in a real sense, illuminations, revelations, disclosures of reality.

One such symbol is that used by Jesus, that of Father. Dr Martin Johnson, until recently Reader in Astronomy at Birmingham University, in his Eddington Memorial Lecture, *Time and Universe for the Scientific Conscience**, called it 'the greatest of symbols', 'the greatest discovery of Christianity'.†
He wrote as follows:

I will venture to paraphrase the way in which the incomparable perceptiveness of Jesus releases us for all time from the impossible task of describing what or whom we meet in our experiences of worship. He said in effect: 'You all meet experiences which you cannot justify in ethical or aesthetic terms, still less in the quantitative language of science and meet a response which you call worship. You will be unable to turn this mystic experience into a rational account of God, a notion beyond your grasp. But I will tell you of a symbol which in your present state of intelligence will not be misleading and to which you can dedicate your behaviour; you may think of God as a Father, a relationship containing the most beloved of human contact but freed from individual deficiency.' Let no one impute irreverence to this circumlocution of the direct simplicity of the Gospel. The symbol made God accessible to the learned and unlearned, the former unable and the latter unwanting to penetrate beyond the symbol.

One must, however, realize the inadequacy and limitations of these symbols and images and not rest in them.

'We ought not to let ourselves be satisfied with the God we have thought of,' (wrote Meister Eckhart), 'for when the thought slips the mind, that God slips with it. What we want is the reality of God exalted above any thought or creature.'

* Published by Cambridge University Press.

† It has been pointed out to me that Dr Johnson is not strictly accurate. The symbol of the Father–God is a very ancient one. Jesus, however, uses it in a particular way.

God cannot be *thought*, but He can be *known*. He can be
known in the way a husband may know his wife or a man a
beloved friend. Such knowing passes beyond any rational
knowledge, beyond symbol and image. He may be known
in a yet more intimate way by 'becoming God'. Let not the
reader be misled by this word 'becoming'. One can never
become God in the logical sense of the word. One can,
however, 'become God' by taking Him into one's inmost
self as the fulfilment of that self; and it is only by 'becoming'
Him in this way that one can really know Him.

But how is this possible? Get rid of any preconceived idea
of God as someone standing over against man. That is not
so. As Meister Eckhart wrote: 'The knower and the known
are one. Simple people imagine that they should see God as
if He stood there and they here. God and I, we are one in
knowledge.'

The world that we know and the self that we know are only
partial realities. Both are manifestations, seen within the
bounds of human perception, of a Divine Ground, which is
the Totality of God, the *IS* which contains within Itself all
partial realities.

Now the nature of man is such that he is drawn towards
this Divine Ground of all existence. 'Thou hast made us for
Thyself,' wrote St Augustine, 'and our hearts are restless
until they rest in Thee.' There is an urge in man to enter into
the Divine Ground. Rational thought can take him part of
the way. The Divine Ground is, however, to adopt Gabriel
Marcel's distinction, not a 'problem' but a 'mystery'. It can
only be known fully by becoming *united* with It – there are
many degrees of this knowing and union – so that, in some
strange and inexplicable way, the knower and the known are
one, the subject–object relationship is transcended.

This union with, or participation in, the Divine Ground is
possible because the nature of man is a dual nature. He has
two selves, the self of which he is primarily conscious, his
phenomenal ego, and a Greater Self, of which he may be hardly,
or not at all, conscious. This Greater Self partakes of the
divine essence and is the eternal part of a man. His phenomenal

ego dies, his real Self cannot die. It is the chief object of man on this earth to realize and identify himself with his real Self. By so doing he will be identifying and uniting himself with the Divine Ground, the Totality of God Itself, and by this identification and union he will come to an intuitive knowledge of It. Within this knowledge he will see God, the universe and himself as they really are.

All this may sound strange to one familiar only with conventional religious thought and expression. Yet, though it is expressed in different ways according to different theologies and philosophies, the doctrine of the Divine Ground and of the inherent divinity of man's real Self is common to the deepest spiritual thinking of all religions.

This inner deity, which is man's real Self, is, however, a 'hidden' deity. At the level of normal human existence it exists rather as a potentiality than an actuality. For it to become actual a 'new birth' must take place in the soul; there must be a process of 'transformation', so that a new man arises from the ashes of the old man.

But men, being rational creatures, are compelled to 'think' about this highest Reality we call God. If one is compelled to discard all anthropomorphic images, all ideas of some sort of Supreme Being, how shall one think? What is the most potent and illuminating symbol for modern man?

When as a headmaster I taught what I called 'philosophy' to my sixth formers, I tried to find out what the effect of my teaching had been on these boys. I remember one boy telling me that he had found a great deal of the course beyond his comprehension. Out of it, however, he had got one thing which he regarded as valuable; he had learnt that he could think of God as Spirit. Had he not done so, he told me, he would have felt compelled to abandon any sort of religious belief. Now he felt he could *believe* in God. He had found the symbol which might lead him into the mystery.

One may think of God as Spirit. Spirit is not localized in a particular place. It is everywhere, outside and within one,

above, around, below. It blows as the wind blows and one
does not know whence it comes or whither it goes. In Itself
It is unknowable; one cannot say what Spirit is. One can only
know it by its effects.

This is the sort of thought transition which many modern
men may be compelled to make if they are to be able to
apprehend the Mystery. There is no need to think of God in
anthropomorphic terms. There is no need to place a 'supernatural' over against a 'natural' world. 'God is Spirit,' said
Jesus to the woman at the well of Samaria, 'and those who
would worship Him must worship Him in the spirit and the
truth.' Much earlier, the writers of the Hindu Upanishads had
written: 'There is nothing in the world which is not God.
He is Everlasting Spirit, from whom sprang the world and
all its creatures.'

When one has come to realize God as all-pervading Spirit,
present everywhere, when one has intellectually discarded all
'Supreme Being', all personal (at least in the usual limited
sense of the word) images of God, have such phrases as a
'personal God', a 'personal universe' ceased to have any
meaning? This is an issue which troubles many people. It is
highly relevant when one considers the nature and object of
prayer.

The issue is a difficult one and has three aspects: metaphysical, e.g. the nature of Ultimate Reality in itself; linguistic,
e.g. the way it is possible to speak of this Reality; and experiential, e.g. the mode in which this Ultimate Reality manifests
itself in religious experience.

Ultimate Reality, Spirit, God, Being (all the words have
meaning) in Itself is simply *That which Is*, the Inexpressible,
the Unknowable, the Unconditional. It (or He) cannot be
grasped by the intellect, It cannot be described in words; if
we are to try to describe It we must use such terms as *non*-
personal (which is not the same as *im*-personal) or, at most,
supra-personal. Within religious experience, however, something happens. Being-in-Itself becomes Being-for-us; Spirit
becomes, as it were, incarnate in order to reveal Itself. There

is, in inner experience, a self-giving of God to the human mind and soul, and, simply because we are human beings, God in this self-giving assumes our own image. He becomes a *personal* God.

The idea of personality, in its widest sense, does not involve the idea of individuality or egohood. The word derives from the Latin, *persono*, to sound through and through. *Persona* is the thing sounded through, i.e. through which the sound passes. The word came to be applied to the mask which was worn by the actors of the Classical stage, which covered the whole head and was varied according to the character to be represented. Thus we may say that Being-in-Itself, in order to become Being-for-us and so reveal Itself to us, assumes a mask, which, without abuse of terms, may be said to be a 'personal' mask. I say 'may be' since, at the highest level of inner experience, as we shall see, the mask is discarded.

Now the character of the inner experience which we have been attempting to describe must be bound up with the essential nature of that from which it originates. If the religious experience is a manifestation of something real, and those who have entered into the depths of this experience cannot doubt it, the highest Reality, God, Spirit, is not a mere abstraction. It must be a Power, a living force which is alive through and through with what, in our human language, we can only term thought, awareness and intelligence, above all with love, all purged, however, of every human limitation and defilement. To speak, therefore, of a personal God and a personal universe has profound meaning. Provided one understands the implications of what one is saying, it is a valid way of describing the nature of the Ultimate Reality which pervades all things.

Let me emphasize again the dual character of man's religious experience and his apprehension of That which he calls God. It is an experience of a God Without, the completely Other, who cannot be grasped by the intellect, the One 'before whom all words recoil', to whom no concepts can apply, an experience of God in His non-personal aspect. It is also the experience of a God Within, who is 'more intimate to me than

I am to myself', an intensely personal experience. No one has described the religious experience more succinctly than the Blessed John Ruysbroeck when he wrote: 'God in the depths of us receives God who comes to us; it is God contemplating God.'

But, while God gives and reveals Himself to mind and soul in a personalistic mode, there is a level of the interior life of which those far advanced in the spiritual path speak, a level which is also described by the Blessed John Ruysbroeck: 'Here he meets God without intermediary. And from out the Divine Unity there shines into him a simple light; and this light shows him Darkness and Nakedness and Nothingness.'

Here the self-disclosure in a personal mode has faded out. All there is is a bare awareness of the highest Reality, which is empty of all images and all concepts. There is a movement into imageless, modeless contemplation. This urge to move into a state of imageless contemplation, freed from symbols and words, is present in the prayer-life of many who are far from the highest degree of the interior life. Few can expect to attain to that bare awareness which is of the essence of true mystical prayer. There are, however, types of mystical prayer, or contemplative meditation, which are within the range of quite ordinary people, leading the active life. These will be considered at a later stage in this book.

2. Some Aspects of Prayer

ONE of the best descriptions of the objective of the prayer-life I have found is that given by John Wren Lewis in *Return to the Roots*.* There he describes the objective of prayer as an effort 'to raise the whole psycho-physical complex which is man as a biological entity to the level of the life of the spirit (*pneuma*) which is achieved by participation in the ever-flowing life of the Creator-Spirit, Love.'

Prayer for many people, however, is primarily thought of as asking for something for oneself or for other people, that

* Published by Modern Churchman's Union.

is as petitionary prayer. Such petitionary prayer is usually linked with thanksgiving for benefits received and with adoration of the Deity.

Even for those who have been able to pass on to the higher types of prayer, there will always be a place for this sort of prayer, even for those who have been compelled to discard any type of anthropomorphic Supreme Being theology. Prayer is, however, much more than this. It is essentially a discipline, a form of spiritual exercise, which is deliberately undertaken with a definite object, a technique of accomplishing something desirable, a way of developing that spontaneous sensitivity which is brought about when a man, as a mere biological entity, is transformed into something greater than his phenomenal self through entry into a new level of being, the level of spirit. This state is reached when he comes to participate more and more in the everflowing life of the Creator-Spirit, Love, the That which we call God.

Prayer is a movement of mind and soul into the Source of all being, the That which we call God. The pattern of this movement may be described by considering the Great Mantra of Buddhism, *Om mani padme hum*.

More will be written about mantras and their use in prayer later in this book. They are known to the Eastern Orthodox Church in the Prayer of Jesus. In Hinduism and Buddhism they have been used since very ancient times. They are a form of creative speech through which a connection is made between the conscious mind and the depth-consciousness, so that the one using them is raised to a different level of consciousness. Thus they are said to be words of power.

At this stage, however, all we are concerned with is the way this Great Mantra images the pattern of movement which takes place in the developed prayer-life. It has been translated: 'Honour to the Jewel in the Lotus'; but such a translation conveys only a fraction of its meaning; indeed, mantras are not amenable to translation. An analysis of its elements works out as follows: *Om* is the hidden name of God; *mani*, the Radiant Jewel, is thought of as the luminosity of Universal Mind, but may, also, be personalized and become, for the

Buddhist, the Buddha (or perhaps more accurately the Celestial Buddha), for the Christian, Christ, in whom the luminosity of Universal Mind was revealed and lived. *Padme* (*padma*), the lotus, is the symbol of the unfoldment of spiritual consciousness. The lotus grows from the darkness of the mud up to the surface of the water where it opens its blossom to the sun. So the mind, which has its seat in the human body, unfolds its true qualities when it has been raised out of passions and ignorance. The dark power of the depths is transformed into 'the pure nectar of Enlightenment-consciousness', (*bodhi-citta*). The Jewel takes its seat in the heart of the Lotus.

So in the developed prayer-life mind and soul endeavour to move into the experience of the sacred syllable, *Om*, into the inner experience of God, of universality, finding there the incomparable Jewel, a Serene Light shining in the ground of its being. The lotus centre of consciousness unfolds itself in that light and is illuminated by it.

The movement is, however, as yet incomplete. In the experience of *Om* a man opens himself, and strives to go beyond himself, to liberate himself by breaking through the narrow confines of his egohood; to become one with the All, with the Infinite. But he cannot, must not, remain there. He must come down from the Mount of Transfiguration into the noise and squalor of the work-a-day world. He must empty himself, putting on the pattern of the Christ.* The experience of *Om* and of the Radiant Jewel must pass into the experience of *hum*, the realization of the infinite in the finite, of the eternal in the temporal, the translation of spirituality into selfless action and an all-embracing charity towards everyone and everything.

Such is the type of prayer at which all who would grow in the prayer-life must aim.

Let us now expand and through a consideration of various aspects of prayer come to realize what prayer in all its fullness is.

* cf. Richard of St Victor's description of the *Four Degrees of Passionate Love*, where the highest degree is this 'emptying', in the Anthology of *Mysticism*, Section 12 (Section 15 in the third edition).

1. PRAYER AS THE WAY OF UNION WITH GOD AND THE REALIZATION OF THE REAL SELF

'Prayer oneth the soul with God.' So the medieval contemplative Julian of Norwich defined prayer. *Oneth*, makes one, unites, so that in the end the egohood is dead and only God remains; so that one veritably 'becomes' the God Within. 'I live;' wrote St Paul, 'but it is not I who live any longer; it is Christ who lives in me.'

What am *I*? What is this 'me' I call 'myself'; this psychophysical complex which is man as a biological entity? It is my phenomenal ego, not my real self. My real self is the potential hidden divinity within me. That is my real I, my real being, the deathless I of my essential nature.

'Our created being abides in the Eternal Essence,' wrote Ruysbroeck, 'and is one with it in its essential existence.'

Through prayer one may become more and more conscious of one's real Self, more and more drawn into the source of one's true being, more and more a participator in the divine nature.

As one moves more and more into this *oneness* with God – and there are many degrees of this *oneness* – a process of transformation, of rebirth, takes place. Not only is there a sudden or gradual transformation of the whole personality, but also an enlargement of vision, a shifting of the level of awareness.

It is necessary, however, to know the right prayer-techniques to use. In prayer one engages in various sorts of *spiritual exercises*; different ones have different objectives. In the East these spiritual exercises are called *yoga*.

The highest aim of *yoga* is union with the divine within oneself and in the universe. It is accepted, however, that any sort of complete union may be beyond the scope of most people. Lesser goals are therefore recognized, such as, peace of mind and heart; control of the emotions, e.g. the elimination of anger, fear, lust, pride, greed, and worry; power of the will; influence of the mind over the body.* Not only is the acquisition of these virtues necessary for one who strives for the fullest union with God which is possible for him, they are also of great practical value and result in greater harmony and balance of personality, better mental and bodily health and a more effective leading of the active life.

Thought of in this way, prayer becomes an activity in which one may deliberately engage in order that one may lead a happier, fuller and healthier life. To be able to control the emotions is of great importance. They are far more unruly and uncontrollable than thoughts. More than rational thought they determine attitude and action. It is very easy to be deceived by our emotions. We think we are acting naturally when in fact we are driven on by concealed emotional urges. Emotional sincerity, if it can be attained, is a great virtue. It is not easy, however, to reach a state when emotions are so refined that one is impelled spontaneously to think and act in the way one's highest instincts dictate. When emotions have been brought under control and become sincere, right thought and right action become spontaneous, no longer the result of hard, deliberate effort, but coming about naturally and inevitably. This sort of spontaneity is evident in the characters of Jesus and of St Francis of Assisi. St Augustine summed it up in the epigram: 'Love and do what you like.'

The more one is drawn into the Source of all being, the more clearly one has realized the nature of one's real Self, the more spontaneous and sensitive thought and action become.

2. THE PSYCHOLOGICAL ASPECT OF PRAYER

In its psychological aspect prayer is a way whereby the division between the conscious and the unconscious is overcome.

* Those who may wish to study this form of *yoga* in greater detail may care to read Fr Déchanet's *Christian Yoga* (Burns and Oates) and the section 'To Contemplative Meditation through *Ratha yoga*' in my *The Journey Inwards* (Darton, Longman and Todd). A good general account of the practice of *yoga* is Wood's *Yoga* (Penguin Books).

It is an exploration of the unconscious, or better, the super-conscious, by the conscious mind so that the superconscious may be taken into the conscious and there be realized. It is a descent into that universal depth (or store) consciousness, in which is gathered up the totality of the spiritual experience of the human race.

Modern psychologists stress the large part the unconscious plays in our lives in determining thoughts, attitudes, responses and actions in ways which are unrealized and sometimes frightening. While some, for instance Freud, have regarded the unconscious solely as a sort of cesspool, into which are pushed all the unpleasant things which the conscious mind wants to forget, Jung postulated the existence of not only an *individual* cesspool *unconscious* but also of a *collective unconscious*, which was the seat of the deepest inherited wisdom of the race. The more the unconscious can be drawn up into the conscious, where it can become articulate and controllable, the more balanced and integrated, he maintained, the personality becomes. The more the archetypes of the collective unconscious, super-conscious or depth-consciousness (all mean the same thing) are enabled to manifest themselves in consciousness the greater the spiritual illumination which may result.*

3. PRAYER AS A DIRECTION OF THE HEART

Rilke defined prayer in its widest sense as a direction of the heart. This definition presupposes a mental and spiritual polarity, a state of creative tension between the human and divine, not only in oneself, but also in the whole cosmos. This polarity, and the creative tension from which it arises, is felt as existing between God and man, or between the finite and the infinite, or between the individual and the universal or between the imperfect and the perfect. Different people feel

---

* The idea of the unconscious and the collective unconscious is not peculiar to modern Western psychology. It is found in the Buddhist conception of *alaya-vijnana*, i.e. universal store-consciousness, which originated in the Yogacara School of Indian Buddhism in the fourth century A.D.

it in different ways. They feel a consciousness of incompleteness or imperfection, and a longing for completeness and perfection, a consciousness of separateness and a longing for incorporation into wholeness.

The approach to this completeness, this perfection, this unity with the whole, is not something which is possible only in a future life. It is ever-present, ever-existent, in the universal depth-consciousness of each one of us. Eternal life is in the here and now. 'The kingdom of heaven,' said Jesus, 'is within you.' Prayer, especially when it passes into its higher stages of meditation and contemplation, is the consciously directed approach towards the vast storehouse of experience and truth which is present in the universal depth-consciousness.

'In prayer,' wrote Lama Anagarika Govinda,

we turn back to that source (of creative power), we re-establish the connection between it and the individual, focalizing surface-consciousness, so that the tension between surface and depth, like the tension of a cord, produces a pure sound, a higher vibration of the spirit. . . . Prayer becomes a source of strength and certainty and not a mere sedative and tranquillizer. The inner peace that comes from prayer is due to the establishment of a balance between the forces of our individual consciousness and the vast potentialities of our depth consciousness, in which the experiences of a beginningless past are stored and through which we participate in that greater life that encompasses the universe and connects us with every living being. . . . Prayer turns our conscious mind inwards and transforms the potential forces of the depths into active ones.*

When super-consciousness is made conscious, it transforms what was a mere idea into a potent, living experience, an experience of wholeness; for the theist, an experience of all-pervading Deity.

4. PRAYER AS MOVEMENT INTO THE REALM OF THE MYSTICAL

There is no need to discuss this aspect of prayer here. It is fully explained in the Introduction to this Study. All that

* *The Importance of Prayer in Buddhism*: printed in *The Middle Way*, August 1964.

need be emphasized is that there are many who have never had any uniquely recognizable mystical experience but have moved into the realm of *the mystical*. They are impelled to make a particular sort of mental and spiritual response to the spontaneous disclosure of the *Isness* (to adopt Meister Eckhart's term) of God or of the world. Their minds are able to stand poised at the intersection of rational and intuitive thought, with a resultant enlargement, intensification and unifying of vision of the nature of everything. They possess, in varying degrees, a faculty of what may be called mystical cognition.

Prayer is a way of developing, enriching and refining this faculty of mystical cognition, and thereby reaching a new vision of the nature of the universe and of the That we call God.

5. PRAYER AS A SOURCE OF POWER

Through real prayer, prayer in its fullest sense, a vast energy is generated which not only transforms and enriches the one who prays, but is capable of being radiated outwards and affecting others. Prayer is essentially a mature activity, indispensable for the fullest development of personality and of achieving a complete, harmonious integration of body, mind and spirit.

How is this possible? It is possible because through prayer our finite energy is harnessed to and augmented by the Infinite Source of all energy.

'When we pray,' once wrote that great pioneer of medical science, Alexis Carrol,

we link ourselves with the inexhaustible motive power which spins the universe. We ask that a part of this power be apportioned to our needs. Even in asking our human deficiencies are filled and we rise strengthened and refreshed. . . . True prayer is a way of life: the truest life is literally the life of prayer.

6. PRAYER AS EXPLORATION

True prayer is not only a source of energy and power, it has also a noëtic quality. It is thus a way of exploring the nature of the truly real. It is not the only way. It is not, for instance, the way of scientific thought. The function of the scientist is to explore one particular aspect of reality. For this purpose he has developed his own tested and effective methods. There are, however, aspects of reality which the scientist, *qua* scientist, does not regard as falling within his province. These other aspects may be explored by means of rational thought; but not fully. True prayer, particularly mystical prayer, by releasing and developing spiritual insight and vision, opens up aspects of reality which are beyond rational thought. The knowledge which comes through mystical prayer is intuitive rather than rational knowledge, the sort of knowledge which St Thomas Aquinas calls knowledge through connaturality. This knowledge is sometimes a *dark* knowledge, without form, and inexpressible in words; but it may, by a subtle interplay of intuition and reason, be intellectualized and given form, so that a new and expressible picture of the cosmos emerges. The phenomenal world is illuminated by a new light and is changed, as by an abnormal sharpening of the senses. 'All things were new,' wrote George Fox, the founder of the Society of Friends, in his Journal, 'and all creation gave another smell unto me than before.'

7. THE PRAYER-LIFE AND THE ACTIVE LIFE

When, in the *Bhagavad Gita*, Prince Arjuna asked Krishna to tell him one definite way of attaining to the highest good, Krishna replied that there is not one way, but two, for the contemplative the path of spiritual knowledge and enlightenment, for the active man the path of selfless action.

Prayer is a means of enriching and fructifying the active life, the life of earning one's living, of bringing up a family, etc., the sort of life which is the destiny of most of us, so that the active life may be a dedicated life.* It is an activity, not only for those who would essay the high adventures of the soul, not only for the 'religious', but for everyone. The form it takes, the time given to it, may rightly vary from person to person. It will be different, both in its objective and character, at different periods of a man's life. When he is at the height of his powers, deeply involved in the active life, his prayer-life may have as its chief aim the sanctification of the active life, so that it may be more dedicated, less self-centred, less inspired by desire for worldly success, more done in relation to its benefit to others. Later, when the active life is past its zenith, and there is leisure to sit back, the prayer-life may become more intense and withdrawn. There is no rule. Each one must discover the sort of prayer-life proper to himself. In it there is a place for corporate and private prayer, for petitionary and verbal prayer, for the combining of verbal prayer with various forms of meditation and the lower stages of contemplation, for the discarding of words and symbols altogether and entering into the silence of God.

Through prayer that psycho-physical complex which is man as a biological entity is raised to the life of the spirit; through prayer our finite energy is augmented and refined by the infinite Source of all energy; through prayer is given the power which transforms and sanctifies action.

'The world is imprisoned in its own activity,' said Krishna to Prince Arjuna, 'except when actions are done as worship of God.'

When action becomes 'worship of God' it is taken up into something greater than itself; it is transformed and redeemed.

3. The Use of Words and Symbols in Prayer

FOR the communion of the soul with God, words are a potent medium. If these words are time-honoured and well known and easy of utterance and comprehension the worshipper benefits by

* The relationship of the life of prayer and the life of action is more fully discussed in Chapter 17.

them all the sooner. For generations we have been initiated in the Gayatri mantra. It runs in our blood. I continued to worship Him daily by means of the Gayatri mantra. . . . And now I obtained this thing beyond all hope, that He was not far from me, not only a silent witness, but that He dwelt within my soul and inspired all my thoughts.*

So wrote the Hindu religious reformer, Maharishi Devendranath Tagore in his autobiography.

There are several levels of prayer and several types, distinct and easily differentiated, but interlocking and combining in different ways. We may list four main types:

1. *Verbal prayer*, i.e. prayer in which words in one way or another are used. The best known sort of verbal prayer combines the elements of Adoration, Thanksgiving, Penitence and Petition. It may be individual or corporate, and may be linked with ritual acts.

2. *The Prayer of Meditation.* The term, meditation, is a somewhat hazy one; it covers a number of spiritual exercises or activities. At the level of *reflective meditation* it is primarily a prayer of the *head*, prayer at the level of rational thought. In it words, concepts, symbols and images are extensively used, either spoken or thought. Most of so-called mental prayer is meditation at this level. Rising out of it, however, there may be moments of *contemplative insight*, flashes of intellectual or spiritual illumination, when, for instance, some thought or some sentence in the Scriptures lightens up, as it were, and takes on a new and more vivid meaning. The Prayer of Meditation passes into and interlocks with

3. *Mystical or Contemplative Prayer.* Words and symbols still have a part to play in at least the earlier stages of this type of prayer. They are, however, used primarily as a means of passing onto a higher level, which, in those who are able fully to develop the prayer-life, may occasionally become the Prayer of Simplicity and Simple Regard, when the mind becomes more and more stilled, intellect ceases to be a dominant element, and words, concepts and symbols gradually, though not entirely, fade away.

* Quoted by Tillyard: *Spiritual Exercises.*

4. *Contemplation.* In fully developed Contemplation a state of bare awareness is reached, words, concepts and symbols are there no longer; in deep communion mind and soul enter the silence of God.

The higher levels of the prayer-life will be described as this book proceeds. Before, however, we pass on to our study of the Prayer of Meditation and of Contemplation, let us give some space to a description of the forms of verbal prayer as they are found in different faiths. Prayer by means of words, combined with some sort of meditation, is the form of prayer most suitable for the majority. Though in the higher levels of prayer words fade away, they are, as Tagore rightly says, potent media for the communion of the soul with God.

The words and symbols used in the prayers of the different religious systems of the world are closely bound up with the tenets of these different faiths. This will be seen in the brief studies of Christian, Islamic, Jewish and Buddhist prayer which we shall make in the next chapters.

4. Christian Prayer

WHILE the majority of readers of this book may not be familiar with the prayer of Islam, Judaism and Buddhism, many are likely to be familiar, some perhaps intimately, with the prayer of Christendom. This study would not, however, be complete without a chapter on Christian prayer.

In the chapters on Islamic, Jewish and Buddhist prayer I have quoted freely; each chapter contains a miniature anthology. In this chapter, however, such quotation is unnecessary. Though not intended to be an anthology in the normal sense, but rather a Prayer Book for practical use, the second half of this book fulfils the function of an anthology of Christian prayer. We shall, therefore, in this chapter on Christian prayer, concentrate on a description of the common worship of Christendom and attempt to bring out its character and to show briefly how it has evolved during the two thousand years of the Christian era. We shall be compelled to be selective, since a full description of the development of the Christian liturgy would take far more space than is available. Further, its pattern varies considerably in the different branches of the Christian Church, ranging from the simplicity of a Quaker meeting, which consists for the most part of silent meditation, and a typical Free Church service to the splendour and elaboration of the High Mass of the Roman Catholic and the Eucharist of the Eastern Orthodox Churches.

From the beginning a special place in its worship has been given by the Christian Church to the Eucharist,* the gathering together of Christians for the 'breaking of bread' as a memorial (*anamnesis*) of Jesus Christ. From its beginnings in the simple Agape (Love Feast) of apostolic times it developed through the centuries into an elaborate liturgy, enriched by ritual acts, colour, music, incense and lights. We shall, therefore, devote the greater part of this chapter to the Eucharist. But let us first look at the other main type of common worship found in the Christian Church.

We have little exact knowledge of Christian prayer during the first two or three centuries of the Christian era. It is probable, however, that apart from the Eucharist, the only public services were those on the eve of Sunday and on certain special days. Daily services were, for a long time, family prayers. In the second half of the fourth century, daily morning and evening worship of set liturgical patterns came into use in the Eastern Church and the practice was shortly afterwards followed by the Church of Milan in the West.

With the growth of monasticism in the West and its formalization by St Benedict (480–543), the founder of the Benedictine Order, the number of daily services was increased

* The word Eucharist is the most primitive and general term for this *anamnesis* of Christ. The Roman Catholic Mass, the Eastern Orthodox Eucharist and the Anglican Holy Communion are all Eucharists. The Eucharist is also called the *Liturgy* with a capital letter to distinguish it from other liturgical services, such as the monastic Hours and the Matins and Evensong of the Anglican Church.

to eight, two of which, the night and dawn offices,* *Nocturns* and *Lauds*, were said together. These daily offices, or *Hours* as they are called, for which the monks assembled in the choir of their church were in addition to the night and dawn services. *Prime*, said on getting up in the morning, *Terce* at 9.00 a.m., *Sext* at noon, *Nones* at 3.00 p.m. and the two evening services, *Vespers*, the sunset office, and *Compline* (the completion of the day), said before going to bed. Thus the day of the Benedictine monk was an ordered sequence of work, prayer and sleep. These offices were in the Middle Ages recited by the clergy only. The normal service attended by the laity was the Mass.

Monastic offices also developed in the Eastern Orthodox Church, though with less uniformity than in the West. Among the laity, with the exception of Eucharist, the keeping of the *Vigil* on Saturday evening and on the eve of festivals, was the only other form of public worship. The Vigil consisted, for the most part, of psalms, other chants and litanies, similar to those used in the Eucharist, together with a lesson from the Gospels, and sometimes from the Old Testament. The keeping of the Vigil has continued in most parishes up to the present time.

At the time of the Protestant Reformation of the sixteenth century Cranmer adapted the Monastic Hours for the common use of lay folk. The Matins and Evensong of the Anglican Church are a telescoping of the monastic Hours to make two services; Matins being based on Nocturns, Lauds and Prime, Evensong on Vespers and Compline. In the centuries following the Reformation, Sunday Matins and Evensong became the most common form of public worship in the Anglican Church, the Eucharist (Holy Communion) becoming an occasional service only. At the time of the Oxford Movement led by Newman, Pusey and Keble, in the mid nineteenth century, a monthly celebration was the normal practice. The

* I have called The Prayer Book, which is the second part of this book, *Short Offices, Prayers and Meditations. Officium* (office) simply means a duty, something which it was binding on the monk to perform. It can be applied to any sort of set pattern of devotion.

regular Sunday and, in some Churches, daily celebration of the Eucharist is a later nineteenth-century development.

Nothing corresponding to the Protestant Reformation of the West took place in Eastern Christendom. Such sectarian revolts as there were were against unpopular innovations.

Let us now turn to our consideration of the evolution of the Eucharist. Though there are references to the Eucharist in earlier Christian writers, of the primitive Eucharistic rite we know little. It is not until the third century, in *The Apostolic Tradition* of Hippolytus, that we have a reasonably full account of the primitive Eucharist. This can, however, be said with reasonable certainty:

1. The Eucharistic Prayer, the Prayer of Consecration of the bread and wine, was probably a simple thanksgiving for redemption through Jesus Christ.

2. The service was in two parts, the *Mass of the Catechumens*, at which all believers were present, and the *Mass of the Faithful*, for which only those actually baptized remained. Later these two parts were merged.

3. The primitive Eucharistic rite was an *action* in which the offering or oblation by the people was an essential part.

In Hippolytus we have the first version of a definite Eucharistic Prayer. Since this Eucharist Prayer is the ancestor of all later Eucharistic Prayers, it will be useful to set it out in full.*

We give Thee thanks, O God, through Thy beloved Servant Jesus Christ, whom at the end of time Thou didst send to us as a Saviour and Redeemer and the Messenger of Thy counsel. Who is Thy Word, inseparable from Thee, through whom Thou didst make all things, and in whom Thou art well pleased. Whom Thou didst send from Heaven into the womb of the Virgin, and who, dwelling in her, was made flesh, and was manifest as Thy Son, being of [the] Holy Spirit and the Virgin.† Who fulfilling Thy will, and winning

* *The Apostolic Tradition of Hippolytus* by Barton Scott Easton (Cambridge).

† This opening section throws interesting light on the Christology of the early Church and on the relationship of the Incarnation of the Word, the Divine Logos and the Jesus of history. (For a discussion of this see my *The Journey Inwards*, pages 51–7.)

[having purchased] for Himself a holy people, spread out His hands when He came to supper, that by His death He might set them free who believed in Thee. Who, when He was betrayed to his willing death, that He might bring to nought death, and break the bonds of the devil, and tread hell under foot, and give light to the righteous, and set up a boundary post, and manifest His resurrection, taking bread and giving thanks to Thee, said: 'Take, eat, this is my body which is broken for you.' And likewise also the cup, saying: 'This is my blood which is shed for you. And as often as you perform this, perform my memorial.'

Having in memory, therefore, His death and resurrection, we offer Thee the bread and the cup, yielding Thee thanks because Thou hast counted us worthy to stand before Thee and to minister to Thee.

And we pray that Thou wouldst send Thy Holy Spirit upon the offerings (and Thy holy church), * that Thou, gathering them into me, wouldst grant to all Thy saints who partake to be filled with Thy Holy Spirit, that their faith may be confirmed in truth, that they may praise and glorify Thee. Through Thy Servant Jesus Christ, through whom to Thee be glory and honour, with [the] Holy Spirit in the Holy Church, both now and always and world without end.†
Amen.

This Eucharistic Prayer, in which to the original simple thanksgiving a number of additional elements are added, falls into five sections: (1) a Thanksgiving for Redemption through Jesus Christ, (2) a Narrative of the institution of the Eucharist at the Last Supper, (3) an offering of the bread and cup, (4) a prayer for the sending of the Holy Spirit upon the offering (*epiclesis*), (5) a concluding doxology.

By the fourth century of the Christian era set forms of service for use in the celebration of the Eucharist had taken definite shape in the various parts of the Roman Empire. In the East we find, at Jerusalem, the Liturgy of St James, in Egypt, the Liturgy of St Mark, in Constantinople, the Liturgy of St Chrysostom, and in the West, the Gallican Liturgy in

* Gregory Dix considers the words 'and Thy holy church' a later interpolation (see 'The Idea of the Church in the Primitive Liturgies' in *The Parish Commission*, Society for Promoting Christian Knowledge).

† Professor Edward Ratcliffe considers that this version of the doxology is not complete and that it ended with the *Sanctus*.

France, the Mozarabic Liturgy in Spain and the Ambrosian Liturgy, which survives until the present day, in Milan.

In course of time the Liturgy of St Chrysostom (or more exactly the Liturgy of St Chrysostom and St Basil) became the normal Eucharistic rite of the greater part of the Eastern Church, which accepted the Declaration of Faith of the Council of Chalcedon. Orthodox Eastern Christendom, however, has been tolerant towards branches of the Church which did not adhere to the Chalcedonian Confession, and among these are found a considerable variety of liturgical forms.

In the West the local liturgies were absorbed by that of Rome, a *Use** which had developed gradually through the sixth-century Leonine, the seventh-century Gelasian, and eighth-century Gregorian Sacramentaries, and was influenced and enriched not only by the Western liturgies of France and Spain but also by those of the Eastern Church.

To try to write a full and balanced description of the development of the Eucharistic rite throughout the whole of Christendom in a small space is to attempt the impossible. This may, however, be said. The particular pattern which the rite has taken in the different branches of the Christian Church is, in part at least, the result of the particular theological presuppositions of that branch of the Christian Church and its social and political environment. Because the theology of the Eastern Orthodox has been more mystical than, and its environment different from, that of the Roman Catholic Church, the pattern and feel of its Eucharistic rite are different. For the same reason, the Eucharistic rites of the Reformed Churches of the West took on different shapes from that of the Roman Mass.

In what immediately follows I shall confine myself to the departure from the more primitive conception of the meaning of the Eucharistic Action and consequent changes in the shape

* By the *Use* of a particular branch of the Church is meant its ceremonial and liturgy. Since Cranmer used it as the basis of his Service of Holy Communion, it is interesting to note here that, during the Middle Ages, England developed its own particular Use, the Use of Sarum, based on the Roman Liturgy.

of the Eucharistic rite as they are seen in the Roman Mass and in the service of Holy Communion of the Anglican Church.

1. The idea that a 'sacrifice' and 'offering' were made in the Eucharist was present from very early times. Their nature was not, however, precisely defined. The simple oblation of the bread and cup of Hippolytus: 'We offer Thee the bread and the cup yielding Thee thanks [making eucharist to Thee] because thou hast counted us worthy to stand before Thee and to minister to Thee' has become in the Ambrosian Liturgy: 'We offer Thee this spotless offering, reasonable offering, unbloody offering, this holy bread and cup of eternal life: and we pray Thee that Thou wouldst receive this oblation at Thine altar by the hands of Thine angels.' It was further elaborated in the Roman Mass.

2. In the early Church the rite was understood eschatologically, i.e. as the ascent in the Eucharist of the whole Church into the timelessness of God, where redemption is complete. The Thanksgiving was a solemn recalling before God of the whole work of redemption through the Incarnation, Passion and Resurrection of Jesus Christ, a redemption which was both in and outside time.

As the centuries passed, however, this timeless conception tended to be supplanted by a preoccupation with the historical aspect of the Passion. Instead of looking forward the Church looked backward; it became 'earthbound'.

Further the idea of sacrifice became despiritualized and formalized into a doctrine which was precisely and unequivocally defined in the sixteenth century in the Confession of the Council of Trent:

I profess likewise that true God is offered in the Mass, a proper propitiatory sacrifice for the living and the dead and that in the Holy Eucharist there are truly, really and substantially present the body and blood, together with the soul and divinity of our Lord Jesus Christ, and that a conversion is made of the whole substance of bread into His body and the whole substance of wine into His blood, which conversion the Catholic Church calls transubstantiation.

3. The primitive Eucharistic rite was an *action* in which the offering or oblation by the people was an essential part.

The way this offering was made by the people is of interest. Each brought his little loaf and tiny flask of wine which, in the West, were received by the deacon, the bread either in a linen cloth or a silver dish, the wine poured from the flask into a two-handled cup. In the East the bread and wine were brought at the beginning of the service and placed on a special table, and were carried with singing by the deacon to the altar at the *Great Entrance*. This is still the custom in the Eastern Orthodox Church.

In course of time, however, the Eucharist, especially in the West, though not to the same extent in the East, ceased to be an action of the whole people and became something *said* by the priest. With the substitution of wafers for ordinary bread, the offering of bread and wine by the laity disappeared; their offering became one of money, the 'Mass Penny' of the Middle Ages. Though the offering of bread and wine still remained, it was made by the priest alone.

There are considerable differences in the Eucharistic rites and the interpretation of the Eucharistic Action among the different national Churches which came into existence as a result of the Protestant Reformation. There is only room here to describe very briefly what took place in this country. The author of the Anglican Prayer Books of 1549 and 1552 was Thomas Cranmer, Archbishop of Canterbury. A few more or less significant changes were made in the Prayer Books of 1559 and 1662. The 1662 Prayer Book has been for centuries the beloved Prayer Book of the Church of England. Cranmer was a master of English prose and his Prayer Books are among the literary treasures of the English language.

The need of a reform of the Eucharistic rite was obvious to many in Cranmer's time. The corrupt ideas and practices of the Catholic Mass of the later Middle Ages were manifold. Cranmer set himself the task of, in a phrase used at the time, 'turning the Mass into a Communion'. In the Eucharistic rite contained in his First Prayer Book of 1549 he closely followed the pattern of the Mass; in that of his Second Prayer Book of

1552 he moved much further in a Protestant direction. In the pattern of the Eucharistic Action in this Prayer Book, Cranmer broke with the previous patterns of both the Western and Eastern Churches.

Any form of offertory* has disappeared. The word 'oblations' in the phrase, 'our alms and oblations', in the Prayer of Intercession, though in the seventeenth century the words came to be interpreted as referring to the bread and wine, originally meant an offering of money for purposes other than the alms intended for the relief of the poor. The *epiclesis*, i.e. the prayer for the hallowing by the Holy Spirit of the bread and wine, 'that they might be for us the Body and Blood of Christ', though it is found in the Eucharistic Prayer of the First, disappeared in the Second Prayer Book. The long established pattern of the Eucharistic Prayer, which starts with the *Sursum corda* (Lift up your hearts) dialogue, though followed in the First, in the Second Prayer Book is mutilated by the insertion of the Confession and Absolution in the middle of it.

Cranmer was a man of his age and his rite, despite its beauty, now dates badly. We no longer think and believe in the thought and belief patterns of the sixteenth century. Many of Cranmer's concepts and symbols no longer appeal; some of them definitely alienate. At the present time, in both the Roman and Anglican Churches, there is much discussion on the reshaping of the Eucharistic rite so that it may better meet modern needs and conform more adequately to modern thought and belief patterns.†

* The word 'offertory' strictly means something said or sung at the offering, or oblation, of the bread and wine. It is, however, commonly used to refer to the offering of the bread and wine itself. The complete pattern of the offering and consecration of the bread and wine is called the Eucharistic *Action*, the Eucharistic *Prayer* is the Prayer of Consecration of the offering.

† Indeed the discussion has been going on for some time and there have been a number of recastings of Cranmer's rite already, for instance in the various Liturgies of the different Churches of the Anglican Communion scattered throughout the world. An amended Prayer Book for use in this country, which was presented to Parliament for approval in 1928, was re-

As we have seen, the word, Eucharist, simply means thanksgiving; to 'make eucharist', to use the old phrase, means to give thanks. The earliest Eucharistic Liturgy was thought of primarily as a gathering of Christians in order to make a thanksgiving for creation and redemption through Jesus Christ. Very early, however, it became more than a thanksgiving; into it was introduced the idea of an 'offering' and a 'sacrifice'. Round the conception of the Eucharist as an 'offering' and 'sacrifice' violent controversies have raged. What was it that was offered? What was the nature of the sacrifice? What, if anything, happened when the priest pronounced the words of consecration over the bread and wine? These controversies have not only divided Christendom but have also resulted in cruel persecutions of Christians by Christians.

When they are studied these controversies are seen to have been the result of trying to understand and define at the level of rational thought something which can only be understood mystically in the light of contemplative insight and cannot be either understood or defined in rational terms.

Controversy as to the exact nature of the offering and the sacrifice, or as to whether what happens in the Eucharist works *ex opere operato*, i.e. through something inherent in the Eucharistic Action itself, or *ex opere operantis*, i.e. through the release of something latent in those who celebrate it, is a sterile occupation. To attempt to comprehend or define at this level is not only to be imprisoned in a world of polar opposites, where there can be no reconciliation, but also to fail to grasp the essentially mystical nature of the Eucharist. What is important is the inner realization, through the Eucharist, of that Centre, which is man's eternal quest, 'where day is not nor flow of any tide'.

Much can be learnt from the profound insights of the early Church of which we have already written.

We may with advantage push back through the theologies of the Reformation and the Counter Reformation, back

jected. As this book is being written, two experimental Eucharistic rites are in use, side by side with that of 1662, in the Church of England.

through the scholastic thinking of the Middle Ages to these more profound insights of the early Fathers of the Church. We may also allow our understanding to be enlarged and refined by that picture of the nature of cosmic reality which has come out of that transformation of the scientific world-view which has occurred in our time. It has become more and more difficult to avoid the conviction that we live in a universe which can only be called a spiritual universe, that the distinction, still not uncommon, drawn between objective and subjective knowledge has become meaningless. Can the formulations of Einstein mean anything except that space and time are forms of intuition, which can be no more divorced from our consciousness of them than can our concepts of colour or shape or size, that space has no objective reality except as an order or arrangement of the objects we perceive in it, and that time has no independent existence apart from the order of events by which we are compelled to measure it? The universe of the scientist is no longer thought of as being made up of solid, indestructible 'matter', but rather as consisting of some sort of undefined 'energy', which cannot be known of itself but only by its effects. His knowledge has become no longer a knowledge of things themselves, but of 'a structure or pattern of operations', of (to quote Sir Richard Eddington) 'unknowable actors executing unknowable actions'. He now realizes that scientific knowledge is not purely objective; that it is not possible for the observer to separate himself from that which he is observing; and that a great deal of his knowledge is, therefore, the creation of his own mind. Indeed, in a recent radio broadcast one scientist – I have forgotten his name – said that all his scientific knowledge was forcing him in the direction of the apparently impossible hypothesis that there was nothing in the universe except something which can only be called Mind. The Hindu Upanishads and some of the Buddhist scriptures said very much the same thing more than two thousand years ago. Further, the advance of scientific knowledge has forced on the minds of men a sense of the infinite series of interactions and interlockings which bind together the whole universe. The words of the mystical poet, Francis Thompson:

> All things by immortal power,
> Hiddenly,
> To each other linked are
> That thou can'st not stir a flower
> Without troubling of a star.

seem no longer mere poetic fancy, but a particular way of stating a scientific truth.

As one allows old and new insights to meet and unite in one's mind it becomes possible to apprehend the Eucharist as an *action* through which there is an *ascent* not only of the whole Church but also of the whole of mankind into the timelessness of God, a movement of the temporal into the eternal, and an *offering* of the total, cosmic Christ, the Christ who is the All-in-everything, in whom is the whole of mankind, as a living *sacrifice* to God most high.

As one learns to understand mystically, so many things that were once dark become luminous and clear, so many of the intellectual difficulties which are the result of the polar nature of human perception fade away. This is true of the understanding of the nature of Jesus Christ, of His Incarnation, of His Passion, of His Resurrection. They are seen not only as events in time but also contained in the Eternal Now, where time is not. One understands what Meister Eckhart meant when, in a Christmas Day sermon, he said: 'Here we make holiday because the eternal birth which God the Father bore and bears eternally is now born in time, in human nature. St Augustine says this birth is always happening. But if it happens not in me what does it profit me? What matters that it should happen in me.'

So it is of the Eucharist. Within the Eternal Now in every Eucharist Christ is born again; in every Eucharist He ascends the wood of the Cross; in every Eucharist He is resurrected and ascends. But what does it profit you or me unless it happens in us?

In a verse sequence on the *Passion of Christ*, which is printed in full as a meditation in the second half of this book, I wrote:

> Why must Thou suffer thus, deserted One?
> Why have we broken Thee, pitiful, ruined Love,
> Who on this Tree
> Art dying? Word Incarnate, sole-begotten Son
> Of God, why hast Thou put thyself
> Beneath the feet of Thine own creation,
> That it might trample Thee?
> Answer, O sharer and victim of our destiny.

The answer comes:

> Here is a Mystery,
> Not to be understood save in the darkness,
> Which is the darkness of God.
> Here is an Act without ending or beginning,
> Luminous, mysterious, unpriced,
> Co-mingling with another, timeless, incomprehensible,
> Where Love attains the apogee of love,
> And God bows down before God sacrificed.

If you ask me to explain in the language of reason and commonsense what this (particularly the last three lines) means, I cannot do it. I only feel, deep down in me, that it is eternally true, and that if I could fully understand the last line of all I should know not only the mystery of the Eucharist, but also the mystery of the universe.

5. Islamic Prayer

In orthodox Islam the nature of God is expressed in essentially personalistic, one might even say anthropomorphic, terms. He is the omnipotent Creator before whose Majesty man is nothing, before whom man must bow in absolute submission, the Almighty One, the All-wise, All-knowing, All-hearing, All-aware. Between God and man there can be no intermediary; Islam does not acknowledge any Incarnation of the Supreme Being. Mohammed is the Prophet of God and so honoured in prayer, but he is not accorded any sort of worship. At the very centre of Islamic worship is the Witness of the Unity:

There is no god but God and we are His surrendered ones.
There is no god but God and none but Him will we worship.
There is no god but God, our Lord and the Lord of our fathers.
There is no god but God, He alone, He alone!

The creed of Islam is epitomized in the *Azam*, the Call to Prayer:

Allah is Great; I bear witness that there is no being worthy of worship save Allah; I bear witness that Mohammed is the Messenger of Allah; come to Prayer; come to Salvation; Allah is Great; there is no being worthy of worship save Allah.

Though in Islam God is the Omnipotent One before whom man is as nothing, He is also a God who hears and answers the prayers of His servants, with each of whom He has a personal relationship. Islamic devotion assumes such a relationship; it is a direct pouring forth of aspiration and desire before the Divine Majesty.

At the centre of Muslim devotion is the *Salat*, the congregational services of the mosque. The *Salat* is made up of five services, each taking from fifteen to thirty minutes, said daily, at dawn, noon, in the afternoon, after sunset and at nightfall. The pattern of these five services is one of congregational, preceded or followed by individual devotions.

Before each service the worshippers cleanse mouth and nostrils and wash face and hands and, if uncovered, the feet. The service then begins with the recitation, either aloud or silently, by the Iman, of the *Fatiha*, the opening chapter of the Koran:

In the name of Allah who sustains us and has made all manner of provision for us in advance, and who rewards righteousness with beneficent results. All worthiness of praise belongs to Allah, the Sustainer of all the worlds, who leads them stage by stage towards

perfection; the Gracious, the Merciful, the Master of the Day of
Judgement. Thee alone do we worship, and from Thee alone do
we implore help. Guide us along the right path – the path of those
on whom Thou hast bestowed Thy blessings, those who have not
incurred Thy displeasure, and those who have not gone astray.

The congregation recite the *Fatiha* silently after the Iman.
Then, in silence, all bow and make two prostrations, glorifying and praising God. The rest of the service consists of
periods of silent prayer, separated from each other by *rakas*,
i.e. postures or prostrations. The change from one section of
the service to the next is made by the Iman's reciting: 'Allah
is great', or 'Allah hastens to him who utters His praise'. The
prayers used in these periods of silent congregational worship
may be Allah's blessing on the Prophet, prayers from the
Koran or prayers chosen by the worshipper. Constance
Padwick, in *Islamic Devotions*, has collected a large number of
these prayers. The service concludes with the blessing, 'Peace
be on you and the blessings of Allah'.

Compared with the congregational worship of other faiths,
the congregational worship of Islam is austere, as befits a
Creed which is, at least formally, an austere one. Much of it
is carried out in silence; there is no singing or music; no
offering of flowers, lights or incense at an altar; except for
the use of prostrations and postures, there are no ritual acts.

Throughout Muslim devotions there is a continuous insist-
ence on the uniqueness, majesty and remoteness of God:

> Glory to Him who girds Himself with might!
> Glory to Him who wraps Himself in greatness!
> Glory to Him who is unique in His soleness!
> Glory to Him who is veiled in light!
> Glory to Him who quells His servants with death!

This feeling in the Muslim religious consciousness of the
uniqueness of God and the utter littleness of man before Him
inevitably gave rise to a sense of sin and unworthiness. The
expression of penitence and the plea for forgiveness is a
constantly recurring motif in Muslim prayer. Three particularly vivid examples of this may be quoted:

I have lost my purpose. I am stripped of will, lacking strength and power. . . . O God, my soul is a ship wandering in the seas of [her own] will where there is no refuge and no shelter from Thee but in Thee. Appoint for her, O God, in the name of God, her course and her harbour.

> O Thou who forgiveth sinners,
> One who confesses his sin is at Thy door.
> O most merciful of the merciful,
> He who has erred is at Thy door.
> O Lord of the worlds,
> He who has wronged is at Thy door,
> The lowly, fearful one is at Thy door.
> Have mercy upon me, my Lord.
>
> I have nought but my destitution
> To plead for me with Thee.
> And in my poverty I put forward that destitution as my plea.
> I have no power save to knock at Thy door,
> And if I be turned away, at what door shall I knock?
> Or on whom shall I call, crying his name,
> If Thy generosity is refused to Thy desolate one?

But Allah is not only the Almighty One, He is also the Merciful, the Compassionate, who answers the prayers of his servants. Islamic devotion is full of a sense of gratitude for His compassionate care. One of the most beautiful Muslim Acts of Praise runs:

Praise be to Him who when I call on Him answers me, slow though I am when He calls me.

Praise be to Him who gives to me when I ask Him, miserly though I am when He asks a loan of me.

Praise be to Him to whom I confide my needs whenever I will and He satisfies me.

My Lord I praise, for He is of my praise most worthy.

The same element of gratitude and trust comes out in this little prayer:

Thou hast given me of Thy Providence widely, abundantly of Thy free will and Thy good pleasure,

And Thou hast asked of me in return the easy task of thanking Thee.

While it is true to say that, in general, Islamic devotion is objective, the Call to Prayer, Adoration and Praise of Allah, Thanksgiving, expressions of penitence, Refuge-taking, Witness to the Unity of God, the calling down of blessings on the Prophet, recitations from the Koran, this is not the complete picture.

In Sufism* there arose in Islam one of the most beautiful and profound expressions of mystical consciousness. Not only that, Sufism had a wide influence on all classes of people and consequently on the character of their devotions. As one studies Constance Padwick's collection of prayers contained in the numerous Manuals of Prayer used by Muslims in different parts of the Muslim world, one cannot but be impressed by the frequent emergence of a mystical element.

Consider, for instance, this Act of Praise, which has assumed a mystical form:

> Praise be to God, abundant praise, in this present state.
> Praise be to God in all states.
> Praise be to God before all states.
> Praise be to God when all states shall be cut off
> [i.e. in the ultimate union with changeless Reality].

And this Witness to the Unity in which the absolute uniqueness and unity of God is asserted, but in terms of a mystical theology which reminds one of that of Dionysius the Areopagite:†

There is no God but Thee who art transcendent of embodiment or division or appellation.
There is no God but Thee who art exalted beyond kind or similitude or locality or direction.
Who art not perceived by imagination or supposition of the mind, nor grasped by thought or sight.

* There is no space to describe Sufism in detail. The reader is referred to Arberry's *Sufism* (George Allen and Unwin), Nicholson's *The Mystics of Islam* (Routledge and Kegan Paul), Margaret Smith's anthology *The Sufi Path of Love* (Luzac) and the section, 'The Sufi Path of Love', in the Anthology of my *Mysticism* (Penguin Books).

† *The Mystical Theology* of Dionysius the Areopagite is printed in full in the Anthology of *Mysticism*.

Thou art the One, the Permanent, Transcendent of mate or off-
springs or partnership or comparison or localization or modality.

One finds, too, a widespread cult of stillness and a longing
for that tranquillity of heart and mind through which one may
enter into the peace of God. The reader will already have
noted how very small an amount of spoken prayer takes place
in the services of the mosque as compared with, for instance,
the services of a Christian church. Consider these two
prayers:

Bestow on me tranquillity. That is, let me realize in my heart
peaceful stillness till I do not turn to any movement of created
things. Bring this about by the recollection of Thyself granted to
hearts, whence comes their tranquillization.

O Lord, I ask Thee for a soul tranquillized by Thee, believing
that it will meet Thee . . .

And this meditation:

Requests break off in the presence of His bounty, and needs fade
away as the soul finds support in Himself. The need of the creature
is not satisfied by the whole of created things, rather it is necessary
for its infinite need to be met by infinite generosity and power, that
is to say, by none other than the Truth Himself; praised and exalted
be He.

The mystical element is clearly present in this spiritual
prayer of light of Ahmad al-Tigani:

O Light of Light, who dost illumine the obscurity of non-being
with the effulgence of Thy Light, make Thy Light the lamp of my
subconscious being and of my mind and my soul and spirit and
heart and body and of all of me and each part of me, till I shall be
only light and flooded with the Light of Thy Unity.

And in this lovely evening prayer:

My God and my Lord, eyes are at rest, stars are setting, hushed
are the movement of birds in their nests, of monsters in the deep.
And Thou art the Just who knoweth no change, the Equity that
swerveth not, the Everlasting that passeth not away. The doors of
kings are locked, watched by their bodyguards; but Thy door is

open to him who calls on Thee. My Lord, each lover is now alone with his beloved, and Thou art for me the Beloved.

Finally let this beautiful little prayer of old age be the epilogue to this brief survey of Islamic devotion:

O Lord may the end of my life be the best of it, may my closing acts be my best acts, and may the best of my days be the day when I shall meet Thee.

6. Jewish Prayer

JEWISH prayer and worship have close resemblances to the prayer and worship of Islam. Both are desert religions; both stress the transcendence and unity of God and deny any possibility of an Incarnation of the Divine Being.

Further, Jewish prayer and worship is of particular interest to Christians, for it was in Jewish prayer and worship that Christian prayer and worship had its origin. Though Christian prayer branched out on lines particularly its own, bound up with its particular theological pattern, it has up to the present day retained many elements of this origin, for instance, in the use, as in Jewish prayer, of the Psalms and of numerous passages and phrases from the Old Testament. Indeed the Lord's Prayer itself is said to be a mosaic of phrases of the Jewish liturgy which were known to Jesus. This point is emphasized by Dr Israel Abrahams in his *Studies in Pharisaism and the Gospels*, in the following reconstruction:

Our Father, who art in Heaven, Hallowed be Thine exalted Name in the world which Thou didst create according to Thy will. May Thy Kingdom and Thy Lordship come speedily, and be acknowledged by all the world, that Thy Name may be praised in all eternity. May Thy will be done in Heaven, and also on earth give tranquillity of spirit to those who fear Thee, yet in all things do what seemeth good to Thee. Let us enjoy the bread daily apportioned to us. Forgive us, our Father, for we have sinned. Forgive also all who have done us injury; even as we also forgive all. And lead us not into temptation, but keep us far from all evil. For Thine is the greatness and the power and the dominion, the victory and the majesty, yea all in Heaven and on earth. Thine is the Kingdom and Thou art Lord of all beings for ever.

Were there any mystical elements in the Jewish faith? If so, were they mirrored in Jewish prayer as they were, as we have seen, in some of the prayers found in the Manuals of Prayer used by Mohammedans?

There has been a good deal of, I think, sterile controversy as to whether there is any relation between the religion of the Old Testament and the experience of the Hebrew prophets and the faith and experience of the mystics. It has been maintained that the stress on the utter transcendence of the Divine Being allowed no scope for the growth of mysticism with its tendency to stress the divine immanence. A sharp contrast has been drawn between the religion of the Hebrew prophets and the religion of the mystic.

While it is true that mysticism does not occupy in Hebrew religion quite the place it occupies in all the other higher religions, it is clear that mystical experience was known both in the age of the Old Testament and throughout Jewish history up to our own day. Nor is the distinction between the mystic and the prophet really a useful one. 'Prophetic' mysticism is a particular sort of mysticism, a variety of that immediate, experiential knowledge of God which all types of mystics claim, different from what may be called 'contemplative' mysticism, where the main quest is union with God regarded as an end in itself. What one finds in the Old Testament prophet is a compelling numinous experience of a holy transcendent Deity, summoning to action.*

In general, however, the mystical element is absent from Jewish prayer, unless it be in the hymn called the Hymn of Glory which is chanted at the Opening of the Ark in the Morning Service, and which begins as follows:

I will chant sweet hymns and compose songs; for my soul panteth after Thee.

* For a good analysis and description of Jewish mysticism see Spencer's *Mysticism in World Religion* (Penguin Books).

My soul hath longed to be beneath the shadow of Thy hand, to
know all thy secret mysteries.

Even whilst I speak of Thy glory, my heart yearneth for Thy love.

Therefore will I speak glorious things of Thee, and will honour
Thy Name with songs of love.

I will declare Thy glory, though I have not seen Thee; under
images will I describe Thee, though I have not seen Thee.

By the hand of Thy prophets, in the mystic utterance of Thy servants, Thou hast imaged forth the grandeur and glory of Thy
majesty.

Thy greatness and Thy might they described in accordance with
the power made manifest in Thy acts.

In images they told of Thee, but not according to Thy essence;
they but likened Thee in accordance with Thy works.

They figured Thee in a multitude of visions; behold Thou art One
under all images . . .

Jewish prayer and worship express the four main elements
of Jewish religion:

1. The Oneness and Transcendence of God.

2. The binding force of the moral law, regarded as revealed
by God.

3. The Hebrew sense of historical continuity and destiny,
of being the chosen people.

4. The sanctity of every aspect of life.

Judaism is essentially a religion of the home and the family.
The Synagogue may be the centre of Jewish worship; it is,
however, not the only place of corporate prayer. It is not
only on the door post of the synagogue that the *Mezuzah* is
nailed; it is also fixed on the right-hand door post of a Jewish
house. It is a small wood or metal container, in which is
placed a small scroll on which is written those verses of the
sixth chapter of Deuteronomy, known as the *Shema*, which
express the essence of the Jewish religious faith:

Hear, O Israel, the Lord is our God.
The Lord is One.
And thou shalt love the Lord thy God
With all thy heart,
With all thy soul and

With all thy might.
These words which I command thee this day
Shall be upon thine heart:
And thou shalt teach them diligently to thy children
And thou shalt talk of them when thou sittest in thy house,
And when thou walkest by the way,
And when thou liest down,
And when thou risest up.
And thou shalt bind them for a sign upon thine hand.
And they shall be for frontlets between thine eyes.
And thou shalt write them upon the door-post of thy house,
And upon thy gates.

For one who would get a clear idea of the character and
feel of Jewish prayer and of the pattern of Jewish liturgy no
better way could be found than to browse through the book
found in every Jewish home in the English speaking world,
the Authorized Daily Prayer Book of the United Hebrew
Congregations of the British Empire. It is in Hebrew, which
still remains the liturgical language of the Jewish Church,
with, on the opposite page, an English translation. It contains
the daily morning and evening services, the services for the
Sabbath, the services for the joyous and solemn festivals and
prayers for numerous other occasions.

There is no space or need to examine all these services and
prayers in detail. In them there are constant echoes of passages
in the Old Testament familiar to Christians and in them too
the Psalms occupy a prominent place. Not all the Psalms are,
however, used – only seventy-three out of one hundred and
fifty – as they are in some at least of the Christian liturgies; the
imprecatory Psalms have little or no place. The most favoured
Psalms are 24 ('The earth is the Lord's and the fullness
thereof'); 29 ('Give unto the Lord, O ye sons of the mighty;
give unto the Lord glory and strength'); 91 ('He that dwel-
leth in the secret place of the most High'); 93 ('The Lord
reigneth; He is apparelled in majesty'); 128, the psalm of
home life ('Blessed is everyone that feareth the Lord'); and
145 (of which see below).

As one reads through this Daily Prayer Book one is forcibly
struck by the constant repetition of the words 'Blessed be

Thou, O Lord our God'. The Blessing of God is not only used in the actual services of the synagogue and the home, but on every conceivable occasion, for instance, on washing the hands before meals, on smelling fragrant spices, at the sight of the sea, on seeing trees blossoming for the first time in the year, etc. etc. Fifteen blessings, one after the other, are said in the daily morning service. Some are rather amusing; for instance, 'Blessed art thou, O Lord our God, King of the universe, who hast given to the cock intelligence to distinguish between day and night', and the double one, the first part said by the men, the second part by the women: *Men:* 'Blessed art thou, O Lord our God, King of the universe, who hast not made me a woman.' *Women:* 'Blessed art thou, O Lord our God, King of the universe, who has made me according to Thy will.'

Some of these blessings are of great beauty. These are both from the evening service for weekdays:

Blessed art Thou, O Lord our God, King of the universe, who at Thy word bringest in the evening twilight, with wisdom openest the gates of the heavens, and with understanding changest the times and varies the seasons. . . . Thou createst day and night; Thou rollest away the light from before the darkness, and the darkness from before the light. . . . The Lord of Hosts is Thy name; a God living and enduring continuously, mayest Thou reign over us for ever and ever. Blessed art Thou, O Lord, who bringest in the evening twilight.

Blessed be the Lord by day; blessed be the Lord by night; blessed be the Lord when we lie down; blessed be the Lord when we rise up. For in Thy hands are the souls of the living and the dead. . . . Into Thy hands I commend my spirit; Thou hast redeemed me, O Lord God of truth. Our God, who art in heaven, assert the unity of Thy name, and establish Thy kingdom continually, and reign over us for ever and ever.

Three elements of Jewish liturgy are of particular interest. The first of these is the *Hallel.* The word Hallel, i.e. praise, is the root of the word Hallelujah (often spelt Alleluja) meaning 'Praise ye the Lord', familiar in Christian liturgy. The Hallel consists of a group of Psalms, Nos. 113 to 118. It came to be called the Hallel of Egypt, for it commemorates the deliverance of Israel from Egypt. It is thus especially connected with the Feast of the Passover, and was probably the hymn which Jesus and his disciples sang at the conclusion of the Last Supper.

In his *Modern Reader's Bible*, Professor R. G. Moulton groups Psalms 145 to 150 under the title of the Great Hallel. The Great Hallel opens with a sort of preparatory meditation (Psalm 145). Then follows a series of psalms of praise, ending with the well-known Psalm 150 ('Praise God in his sanctuary; praise him in the firmament of his power').

Another interesting element is the prayer known as the *Amidah* or the Eighteen Benedictions. It is a long prayer, found in most of the principal services of the Jewish liturgy, too long to quote. It opens with three great ascriptions of praise, passes on to petition, and then ends with a very impressive act of thanksgiving for the mercies of God.

The third of these particularly interesting elements is the prayer called the *Kaddish*, particularly in its use by mourners for one who has died, when it is said by the mourner and the congregation reply. It opens as follows:

Mourner: Magnified and sanctified be His great Name in the world which He has created according to His will. May He establish His kingdom during your life and during your days, and during the life of all the house of Israel, even speedily and at a near time, and say ye, Amen.

Congregation and Mourner: Let His great Name be blessed for ever and to all eternity.

Mourner: Blessed, praised and glorified, exalted, extolled and honoured, magnified and lauded be the Name of the Holy One. Blessed be He: though He be high above all blessings and hymns, praises and consolations, which are uttered in the world; and say ye, Amen.

Congregation: Amen . . .

Mourner: He who maketh peace in His high places, may He make peace for us and for all Israel; and say ye, Amen.

It is noteworthy that in this Mourner's Kaddish there is no reference to the departed, no *Requiem eternam dona ei Domine*;

it is entirely a hallowing of the Name of God and concentrates not on the one who is no more but on those who still live.

Is then a belief in the immortality of the soul not an article of Jewish faith? To make such an assertion would be quite untrue; though it is difficult simply from a study of the several liturgies of the dead, the home service prior to a funeral, the Divine Service itself, the prayer in the house of mourning, and the memorial service for the dead, to decide in what form some sort of after-life is envisaged. The Home Service prior to a Funeral includes this beautiful prayer:

O Lord, who art full of compassion, who dwellest on high, God of forgiveness who art merciful, slow to anger and abounding in loving kindness, grant pardon of transgressions, nearness of salvation, and perfect rest beneath the shadow of thy divine presence, in the exalted places among the holy and pure, who shine as the brightness of the firmament to — who has gone to his eternal home. We beseech Thee, O Lord of compassion, remember unto him for good all the meritorious and pious deeds which he wrought on earth. Open to him the gates of righteousness and light, the gates of pity and grace. O shelter him for evermore under the shadow of Thy wings; and let his soul be bound up in the bond of eternal life. The Lord is his inheritance; may he rest in peace. And let us say, Amen.

The Burial Service contains the following:

He maketh death to vanish in life eternal; and the Lord God wipeth away the tears from all faces; and the reproach of the peoples shall be taken away from off all the earth; for the Lord hath spoken it.

While the Memorial Service for the Dead includes this prayer:

My God, remember the soul of my reverend father [mother] who has gone to his [her] repose. May his [her] soul be bound up in the bond of life. May his [her] rest be glorious, with fullness of joy in Thy presence, and bliss for evermore at Thy right hand.

There is also another version of the Mourner's Kaddish, said by children after the burial of their parents, which opens as follows:

May His great name be magnified and sanctified in the world that is to be created anew, when He will quicken the dead, and raise them up unto life eternal; will rebuild the city of Jerusalem, and establish His temple in the midst thereof; and will uproot all alien worship from the earth and restore the worship of the true God. O may the Holy One, blessed be He, reign in his sovereignty and glory during your life . . .

When one compares these several prayers an interesting point emerges. While in the Home Service before a Funeral and in the Memorial Service for the Dead there is present the idea of an enduring life in some spiritual realm, in the Mourner's Kaddish some sort of resurrection on this earth, when the glory of Israel shall be restored and the Jewish Faith shall triumph, seems to be envisaged. The reason for this incompatibility of conception is probably due to the fact that the Jewish Prayer Book, as we now have it, is the result of a very long evolution and contains conceptions which belong to different stages of development.

In conclusion, Jewish prayer and worship are a perfect expression of those four basic elements of the Jewish faith which have been set out above. In no prayer is the union of these four elements more fully expressed than in the prayer which concludes the service at the dedication of a house:

Sovereign of the universe! Look down from Thy holy habitation and in mercy and favour accept the prayer and supplication of Thy children, who are assembled here to consecrate this dwelling, and to offer their thanksgiving unto Thee for all the loving kindness and truth Thou hast shown unto them. We beseech Thee, let not Thy loving kindness depart, nor the Covenant of Thy peace be removed from them. Shield this their abode that no evil befall it. May sickness and sorrow not come nigh unto it nor the voice of lamentation be heard within its walls. Grant that the members of the household may dwell together in this their habitation in brotherhood and fellowship, that they may love and fear Thee, and cleave unto Thee, and may meditate on Thy Law, and be faithful to its precepts.

Bestow Thy blessing upon the master of this house. Bless, O Lord, his substance, and accept the work of his hands. Keep him far from sin and transgression. Let Thy grace be upon him, and

establish the work of his hands. May Thy loving kindness be with
her who looketh well to the ways of her household, and may she
be mindful that the woman who feareth the Lord, she shall be
praised. Bestow upon their sons and daughters the spirit of wisdom
and understanding. Lead them in the path of Thy commandments,
so that all who see them may acknowledge that they are offspring
blessed of the Lord, blessed with a knowledge of Thy law and with
the fear of Thee. Preserve them from all evil; preserve their lives.
May Thy gracious promise be realized in them: Blessed shall Thou
be when Thou comest in, blessed when Thou goest out. And even
as we have been permitted to consecrate this house, so grant that
we may together witness the dedication of Thy great and holy
temple in Jerusalem, the city of our solemnities, speedily in our days.

Amen.

7. Buddhist Prayer

BUDDHISM has been called a spiritual or religious atheism, a
system of psychology rather than a religious faith, not a
religion at all, and the most profound and mystical of all
religions.

There is an element of truth in all these descriptions,
however much they seem to contradict each other. It is
practically impossible to describe the tenets of Buddhism
simply and precisely. There are so many schools of thought
in it that, though all have a common foundation in the Pali
Canon, what one may say of one school may not be true of
another. As a general statement, however, it may be said that
there is no 'God' in Buddhism as a Christian, Jew or Moham-
medan understands 'God', no 'Creator' or 'First Cause' or
'Supreme Being'. While a profound luminous experience is
known to spiritual Buddhists, an experience which is not
dissimilar to the luminous experience which the mystics of all
religions have known and described, it is not thought of as
the experience of a Divine Presence, as the phrase is normally
understood. A Buddhist does not pray *to* God; there is no
God of that sort to pray to.

The Buddhist intellectual 'faith' becomes clearer when one examines the experience and teaching of the Buddha himself. He knew the truth which the most highly developed spiritual insight of other religions has known, that the intellect cannot know the That which we call God. It is not possible to demonstrate *logically* that God 'exists' at all, whatever the word 'exist' may mean when applied to God. Nor, he maintained, is it possible to demonstrate logically that man has an 'immortal soul'; which must be 'saved'. All that can be found intellectually about the make-up of a man is a perpetual changing flux of bodily and psychological states. The Buddha, therefore, discouraged all theological and metaphysical speculations and statements on the ground that no satisfactory and demonstrable answers were possible and that it was not necessary to enter into such speculations in order that man's main purpose in this life might be achieved. On such matters he recommended a 'noble silence'.

What, in effect, the Buddha said was:

Do not waste your time trying to do something you cannot do. Concentrate on the practical problems of human existence and human living. Look around you; what do you find? Everywhere suffering, ignorance and pain. Analyse their causes; they all stem from *desire*.* Therefore eliminate desire, for it is in desire that all the woes and disharmonies of the world have their source.

Out of this analysis came the extremely practical and scientific Buddhist 'faith', embodied in the teaching on the three Signs of Being, the Four Noble Truths, the doctrine of Causation or Conditioned Genesis and the Noble Eightfold Path. The teaching of the Buddha may be summed up in a single sentence: 'Do not waste your time on the sort of unprofitable *thinking* which will get you nowhere; concentrate on *being*.'

As the deepest insights of all religions, Christianity included, tend to lead to a position of *intellectual* agnosticism, so while a religion may appear on the surface to be atheistic, it inevitably contains what may be called its 'God-idea'.

* Perhaps a better word to express the Buddha's meaning would be *craving*, craving for fame, riches, comfort, etc.

In his book, *Buddhism and Christianity*,* King describes the Buddhist 'God-idea' as a 'four-fold reality complex'. The first element of this four-fold reality complex is the orderly universe of *Dharma*, translated 'teaching' or 'law' or 'norm', but also containing the idea of cosmic order. The second element is *Karma*, the moral order within the universe. The third is *Nirvana*, the supreme Buddhist goal and heaven, an indescribable state, the nature of which is hinted at in such descriptions as deathless, peace, release, the disappearance of greed, hatred and delusion, unutterable bliss. The fourth element is *the Buddha*, the supreme revealer and exampler.

King considers, I think rightly, that the essence of the 'God-furation' in the Buddhist four-fold reality complex is Nirvana. For the Buddhist the realization of Nirvana is an existential experience, which experientially is not dissimilar to – it may be the same as – what other religious faiths describe as 'knowing', 'entering into', 'being united with' God. For him Nirvana is the synthesis of ultimate reality and values. It is an inexpressible existential experience, which, because it is inexpressible, is assumed by the Buddhist to be the ultimate metaphysical reality. And Nirvana, like the kingdom of Heaven, is in the here and now, a state of being which is potentially present in every man and may by strenuous spiritual effort be attained in this life.

The idea of 'God' in Buddhism can be expressed in other ways. For instance, when I put to an eminent Buddhist the question: 'Is there a God in Buddhism?' he replied: 'What about the Void, the Dharmakaya? Words, words!'

Buddhism is difficult for the Westerner to understand, particularly since so many of the Buddhist sacred writings are written in paradoxical language, in the language of nonduality. What one finds in them is an attempt to express the fact of an inexpressible Ultimate Reality, not in the language of metaphysics, but of a living experience of it. One may say that while the Buddhist is reluctant to speculate about a 'God Without', he acknowledges, a 'God Within' which can be *realized* by man.

* Published by Allen and Unwin.

Since in this chapter our primary concern is with Buddhist 'prayer', instead of attempting a fuller explanation here, may I refer the reader to the much fuller discussion in the Anthology, Section 5 in the third edition of my *Mysticism*.

We have already written of prayer as a direction of the heart, presupposing a mental and spiritual polarity between God and man, the infinite and the finite, the universal and the individual, the perfect and the imperfect. While in Christianity, Judaism and Islam the individual human pole is expressed as the soul, the divine pole as the Creator-God, and in Hinduism as *jivatman*, the divine spark in man in its individual aspect, and Brahman (or *Paramatman*), which is both Ultimate Reality and Universal Soul, in Buddhism the two poles are conceived as a limited mundane self-consciousness and a potential universal consciousness, latent in all men, which is experienced and realized by one who has attained a state of enlightenment.

'Prayer,' writes Lama Anagarika Govinda, in the illuminating essay on the 'Importance of Prayer in Buddhism' (already quoted),

arises from a state of tension between the human and the divine, the consciousness of incompleteness [or imperfection] and the ideal of completeness [or perfection], between the present state of ignorance and delusion and the longed-for future state of liberation, the awakening from the illusion of separateness to the wholeness of life.

Prayer, particularly when it passes into meditation, is, for the Buddhist, a consciously directed drawing upon the treasure-house of universal experience in the depth-consciousness, not in order that the riches of this treasure-house may be submitted to any sort of intellectual analysis, but, as the conscious mind turns inward, the potential forces within the depth-consciousness may be made active ones, so that they may be used in the quest of completeness, by being transformed into a living, potent reality.

This is not the complete picture. In the same essay Govinda writes:

Prayer is an act of opening heart and mind; and while we open ourselves we not only allow the light to enter, but we make the first breach in the walls of our self-created prison, which separates us from our fellow beings. Thus, in the same measure in which the light streams in and makes us recognize our true universal nature which connects us with all that exists in the infinity of space and time, our love and compassion for all living and suffering beings wells up and streams from us like a mighty current that embraces the whole world. In this way prayer becomes an act of devotion in a two-fold way: to the forces of light as well as to our fellow beings. The forces of light are not, however, an abstract ideal but a living reality, embodied in those great leaders of humanity, whom we venerate as Enlightened Ones.

The two passages of the Lama Govinda quoted are worth pondering on. Not only do they bring out all-important aspects of Buddhist devotion, but also of the nature of all true prayer.

In Buddhist spirituality meditation is regarded as more important than verbal prayer. Indeed verbal prayer is regarded as a prelude to meditation. More will be written later about forms of Buddhist meditation. Let us here look at some examples of verbal prayer.

There is, as we have seen, no belief in Buddhist theology in a Creator Deity, nor indeed of a separate egohood, i.e. a continuing individual 'soul' which has to be 'saved'. The Buddha (as are all the other Buddhas and Bodhisattvas) is the model of the complete and perfect man, who has become conscious of his universality and released the divine within him. He has thus become an example and light to struggling humanity, one in whom they can 'take refuge'. The devotion called The Three Gems, which is used as an act of veneration before the altar of the Buddha, runs as follows:

> I take refuge in the Buddha, the Enlightened One.
> I take refuge in the Dharma
>   [i.e. the Sacred Law kept by the Buddha and the
>   other Enlightened Ones].
> I take refuge in the Community
>   [i.e. those who have realized the Teaching in
>   themselves].

A more elaborate form of the veneration of the Buddha is found in the devotion known as the Buddha Homage:

Honour to Him, the Blessed One, the Saint, the Buddha supreme!
Well-farer well-farer the Best, the merit – the merit winner!
The deathless deathless Peace, the peerless peerless Gem,
The World of refuge refuge, the Leader the Leader I worship.

Home of pity, Doer of all hard things,
Who has gone the gait crossing the life ocean.
Lord of the three worlds, mind well composed, beneficent,
To the all-seeing Eye, I bow, to Him I bow.*

[Note the pairs of words, which are in the original]

What is known as the Common Prayer (*Okasa*) begins as follows:

I beg leave! I beg leave! I beg leave! In order that any offence I may have committed either by deed or by mouth or by thought may be nullified, I raise my joined hands in reverence to the forehead and worship, honour, look at and humbly pay homage to the Three Gems, the Buddha, the Law and the Order once, twice, three times, Lord.†

Thus, what one finds in Buddhism is not a transcendent God to whom it is possible to pray, but what may perhaps be called an 'immanent deity', an unborn spark of light (*bodhi-citta*), which, in some schools, is thought of as the 'Holy Ghost' of the Buddha, and which, for instance among the Shin Buddhists of Japan, is to all intents and purposes 'worshipped' as Amida Buddha. This divine principle in man manifests itself, not in terms of a personal God, but as a yearning towards perfection, completeness and that enlightenment which comes when a man becomes fully conscious of his own divine essence. Further, this realization is a continuous process in the spiritual history of mankind. There is a perpetual birth of God, manifested in a continuous succession of enlightened beings, in each of whom the totality has become

* Printed in Pe Maung Tin: *Buddhist Prayer and Meditation* (Society for Promoting Christian Knowledge).
† Printed in Pe Maung Tin: op. cit.

conscious. This 'birth of God' has its fullest and most complete manifestation in the numerous Buddhas and Bodhisattvas, the Enlightened Ones of Mahayana Buddhism, who, because of their attainment, have become active forces of light and power which are able to help others towards the goal of perfection, completeness and enlightenment.

And as the pious Buddhist moves forward along the path of devotion and realization, he becomes capable of making in complete sincerity of heart this lovely prayer which Govinda quotes in his essay:

Wholly and without reserve I dedicate myself to the Enlightened Ones and their spiritual sons. Take possession of me exalted beings. Filled with humility I offer myself as your servant. Having become your property, I have nothing more to fear in this world. I will do only what is helpful to other beings. I will give up any former wrong doings and not commit further wrong deeds. I did not realize that I was only a traveller, passing through the world. Day and night, without cessation vitality decreases and death approaches. This very day, therefore, I will take my refuge in the great and powerful protectors of the world. From the bottom of my heart I take refuge in the doctrine – and likewise on the multitude of Bodhisattvas. With folded hands I implore the Perfect Enlightened Ones in all the regions of the universe: may they kindle the light of truth for all those who on account of their delusions would otherwise fall into the abyss of misery.

Whatever merit I may have obtained, may I become thereby the soother of every pain for all living beings. The merits which I have acquired in all my rebirths through thoughts, words and deeds, all this I am giving away without regard to myself in order to realize the salvation of all living beings. Nirvana means to give up everything: and my heart desires Nirvana. If I must give up everything, is it not better to give everything to living beings. I have dedicated myself to the welfare of all living beings; may they beat me and abuse me and cover me with dust. May they play with my body and make me an object of their ridicule. I have abandoned my body to them; why should I worry about it? Those who abuse me, or others who treat me badly, or those who jeer at me, may they all attain enlightenment.

Though some of the phrases may not be phrases a Christian

would use, how truly 'Christian' this prayer sounds. One is reminded of the prayer of St Francis: 'Make me, O Lord, an instrument of Thy Peace. . . . May I seek to comfort rather than to be comforted, to understand rather than to be understood, to love rather than to be loved . . .' And of the words of Jesus Himself: 'Love your enemies, bless them that curse you, do good to them that hate you, and pray for them which despitefully use you and persecute you.' Indeed how many Christian prayers show forth an equal charity and selflessness? Can one, reading such a prayer as this, remain any longer exclusive in one's religious sympathies or feel that all truth and virtue is limited to one's own faith?

8. The Prayer of Meditation

WE are now ready to move on to a study of the Prayer of Meditation. The difficulty in writing about the various stages and levels of meditation and contemplation, indeed about all levels of the spiritual life, is a threefold one. First, there are so many schools, with different methods and with different objectives; secondly, the stages of the prayer-life overlap and merge into each other and they are different for different people; and, thirdly, terms are used with different meanings. What is impressive and significant, however, is that the descriptions of actual experience in all schools and in all religions at the higher levels have a striking similarity.

The techniques of meditation have been more fully explored in the East than in the West, and are there more widely used by ordinary people. In the pages which follow we shall, therefore, draw freely on this age-old experience of the East. For those who want to advance in the life of prayer, the chief objective is to discover the way of prayer most appropriate to their own circumstances and spiritual stature.

In his book, *The Graces of Interior Prayer*, one of the standard works of Christian spirituality, Father Poulain classifies the four degrees of prayer before it passes on to the level of the fully developed mystical Prayer of Contemplation as follows:

1. Vocal prayer, prayer by means of words, primarily in the form of adoration, thanksgiving, confession and petition.

2. Meditation, in the sense of methodical and discursive prayer, in which considerations, arguments and resolutions play a large part, i.e. meditation at the level of the intellect.

3. Affective prayer, in which acts of affection and aspiration rather than of petition play the predominant part.

4. The 'Prayer of Simplicity and Simple Regard', in which spiritual intuition and 'a simple seeing' replace the intellectual.

This is a useful scheme if it is not understood too rigidly. It describes four *types* rather than four *stages* of prayer. I would add the following comments at this point:

1. Experience indicates that one should envisage two types of meditation. They may be called *thought* meditation and *intuitive* meditation, or *rational/reflective* meditation and *mystical/contemplative* meditation. In practice they tend to intermingle. The one meditating passes backward and forward from one to another; one may say that he engages in *mixed* contemplative prayer.

2. Meditation, even when it reaches the stage of contemplative meditation, does not necessarily involve the abandonment of words, symbols and concepts. Though the petitionary element is to a great extent discarded, much meditation is prayer through and with the aid of words and symbols.

3. Among many Catholic writers on mysticism and mystical prayer a distinction is drawn between *acquired* contemplation and *infused* contemplation. The first is an experience or state which is the result of a man's own efforts, assisted by divine grace; no effort on man's part can necessarily result in the onset of infused contemplation; it is solely and entirely *given* by God. Nor are some writers prepared to call any sort of prayer before Contemplation proper, e.g. the level of the Prayer of Quiet, mystical. The Prayer of Simplicity and Simple Regard is considered as the gateway to mystical prayer rather than as true mystical prayer. As the reader will have gathered from what I have already written, I am not prepared to limit the

word, mystical, in this way. I would call all prayer which is, or is designed to result in, 'a movement into the realm of *the mystical*' mystical prayer.

The Prayer of Meditation is, in essence, a form of spiritual exercise designed to achieve a specific purpose; the purpose may vary in different types of meditation. When deliberately carried out as a spiritual exercise it commonly contains the following elements:

(a) The quieting of the emotions. In Eastern types of meditation a common method is by rhythmic breathing.

(b) The banishing of intruding thoughts.

(c) The concentration of the mind. An effective way of achieving this concentration is by the repetition of some sacred sentence or mantra. The nature of the mantra has already been touched on and will be further expanded later.

(d) Very often the taking up of some particular posture, such as kneeling or sitting in a relaxed position. The greatest measure of relaxation is desirable so that the body intrudes as little as possible. In the East one of the favourite postures is the 'lotus seat'. Some, however, find that they can meditate most effectively while walking up and down.

In the manuals of meditation much is written about concentration and many exercises for developing mindfulness, as it is sometimes called, are described. In itself concentration is not 'spiritual' or 'religious' at all. It is a form of mental gymnastics used for the purpose of learning to fix the attention on a particular object or idea without allowing it to wander from it. It is very easy to describe, but how few people have any power of deliberate concentration. Try it for yourself and see. Place a watch with a second hand in front of you. Take some object or idea and see how long you can hold your thought on it without some other thought intruding. You may be surprised at the failure to hold your mind fixed for more than a few seconds. Yet some degree of concentration, of mental 'one-pointedness', is necessary if a person is to make progress in the art of meditation.

I do not propose to describe the various ways used to develop a capacity for concentration. A good deal has been written on it and I would refer the reader to such books as Humphrey's *Concentration and Meditation* (Watkins) and Wood's *Yoga* (Penguin Books), particularly Chapter 4, 'Yoga and the Intellect'.

Two things may, however, be said. There is a danger in intense concentration on, say, a physical object, that one may slip into a state of self-hypnosis. When concentration is practised as a form of mental gymnastics the mind must, all the time, remain active. Secondly, while for effective meditation the mind must be kept 'one-pointed', there are times when it should be allowed to drift, so as not to dam the onset of contemplative insight. As one becomes practised in the Prayer of Meditation, one will learn when this is desirable.

Thus, when deliberately undertaken as a form of spiritual exercise the Prayer of Meditation, at the level of reflective meditation, is the concentration of the mind upon a particular spiritual object or idea and, while holding it there and, as far as possible, not deviating from it, examining it in its various aspects. This is an intellectual process, an adventure of the mind, an exploration, frank, searching and humble, into the nature of reality, both of the self and the cosmos. At a higher, or perhaps it is better to say a deeper, level it becomes more spiritualized, more intuitive in character. While words and symbols are still used, it draws closer and closer to contemplation.

'Closer to contemplation'. Before we examine the practice of the Prayer of Meditation in greater detail, it may be desirable to explain what is meant by 'contemplation', since the word may be used in two main senses, and, in order to distinguish these two uses, is often spelt with either a capital or small letter.

In the first place Contemplation is a word used to describe that stage of the Mystic Way which is also called Illumination. When used in this way the word is spelt with a capital letter. Those who have reached this stage are called contemplatives, or contemplative saints. In the true contemplative, consciousness moves on to a higher level as the result of the emergence and deliberate cultivation of powers which in most are latent or possibly absent altogether. In the true contemplative is found a complete withdrawal of attention from the sensible world and a total dedication of action and mind towards a particular interior object. In him consciousness is transformed and remade, the individual self is well-nigh lost and he lives in a state of permanent illumination.

The word is, however, used in a less limited sense, to describe a particular way of 'seeing' and 'knowing', a particular way of apprehending the nature of things.

One view of the world and the way that it can be apprehended is that it is spread out before us for our detached and dispassionate rational examination, that its nature can be fully grasped by rational thought, analysis and classification. Another view, however, is that the world is in its essence a *mystery*, the secret of which can only be partially apprehended by thought, analysis and classification. In order to probe into its deepest secrets, to see it as it really is, one must not stand over against it as a dispassionate observer, but try, as it were, to 'feel' it in one's innermost being, to become part of it. To feel the world intuitively, to become part of it by 'participation' in its essential nature is what is meant by 'contemplating' it. In contemplation one not only 'thinks' the world, one tries to 'know' it as it really is, not as a collection of parts, each one of which can be examined separately, but as a unity, as a whole.*

To make this clear let us take two examples. One may look at a picture, analysing the technique of its arrangement, colour and brushwork, examining its several elements. But one may also try to grasp it as a whole, not as a collection of parts but as a unity, and allow it to work on one. Similarly with a

---

* cf. Gabriel Marcel's distinction between a *mystery* and a *problem*. A problem is tackled from outside and the solution is capable of empirical verification. A mystery, on the other hand, cannot be apprehended from outside; one must be involved in it in such a way that the subject–object relationship is transcended, (see *Religious Faith and Twentieth-Century Man*, page 78).

piece of music. Here again one may analyse and examine all its parts. One will not, however, truly appreciate its beauty and significance until one hears and feels it as a unity in which the parts are lost. In both these instances the faculty of contemplation is employed.

Contemplation, in the less limited use of the word, thus embraces all those forms of reflection which call for a recollected frame of mind and have in them the quality of intuitive vision. It comes into play not only in the mental attitude necessary for apprehending spiritual truth, but also in the understanding of deep scientific and philosophical theories, and in originating new ways of thinking in philosophy and science. Indeed it can be said that most great innovations in the active and practical sphere have their roots in contemplation.

Contemplation is a method of apprehending the nature of things which is not antagonistic to rational, analytical thought, but is complementary to it. Nor is the contemplative vision of the advanced contemplative different in kind from that of one who contemplates at a lower level. The difference is rather one of degree, clarity and intensity.

In *Religious Faith and Twentieth-Century Man* I quoted the 'confession' of an eminent scientist, Ludwig von Bertalanffy. May I quote some sentences from it, which illustrate what I am trying to say:

I certainly had 'peak experiences' in the sense of Maslow, with self-transcendence, experience of a greater unity, liberation from the ego boundary. In moments of scientific discovery I have an intuitive insight into a grand design. I found this part of experience a complement to the rational and scientific way of thinking. ... Cusa, Spengler and others introduced me into what I call a 'perspective' philosophy, in which different forms of experience mirror, as it were, different aspects of reality.

This seems to me to show that there is not a necessary opposition or enmity between the rational way of thinking that finds its clearest expression in scientific empirico-deductive thought, and intuitive experience culminating in what the mystics, in necessarily insufficient language, tried to express.*

* Quoted in *Religious Faith and Twentieth-Century Man*, pages 120–21.

These things are not easy to write about. They become clear, however, to one who is willing to follow the sometimes laborious path of meditative prayer. They will I hope become more luminous as we proceed to describe the various ways of meditation in detail. Some sort of summing up may, however, be useful here.

1. A distinction may be made between *casual* and *deliberate* meditation. The latter is a deliberate spiritual exercise, the setting aside of a definite time for meditation in which a definite pattern is followed. The former can take place at any time; indeed one may simply slip into it. For instance, one is reading a book. Some passage, some idea strikes one. One places the book on one's knees and starts to think about it. It starts to become luminous, revealing, even exciting. One ceases merely to think about it; there is an intuitive realization of its deeper meaning; instead of thinking about it, one contemplates it. One may say that one passes into a contemplative state.

2. A distinction may also be drawn between *reflective/rational* meditation and *contemplative/intuitive* meditation. The distinction is an important one and will determine the form the meditation takes. This distinction will become clearer by the accounts of various types of meditation which will be described later.

3. Each person must discover the forms of meditation most appropriate to his own urge, needs, temperament and stage of life. Some form of deliberate meditation, however brief, is desirable for everyone. One who is getting on in life, who has retired from an active career and for whom the humdrum problems of ordinary living are no longer pressing, will possibly tend to use casual meditation very much more than one deeply absorbed in his active career. He has a great deal more time and inclination to stretch out to the eternal things. The young, active man, if he does not set aside some time for deliberate meditation, may never meditate at all.

4. The prayer-life, whatever form it may take and with whatever objective, is rather like the work of a carpenter making some article of furniture. In his task he uses a set of

different tools, each designed for a particular purpose. As we have seen, there are a number of types of prayer and a number of different prayer-elements. They can be combined in any way each individual likes and finds most suitable for himself. The repetition of some mantra or sacred sentence, reflective and contemplative meditation, petitionary and meditative prayer etc. may be combined in all sorts of ways.

5. Meditation is not easy, particularly if one has not become practised in it. Group meditation, under a competent leader, is much easier for most people than private meditation, at least at first. Meditation groups, however, are not so common as they ought to be; competent leaders are sometimes hard to find.

6. The Prayer of Meditation, indeed the whole of the practice of prayer in all its forms, has two main objectives, to find God and to be transformed into the pattern of the Christ, and to be thus enabled to lead the active life more effectively, which can only be when action is taken up into something greater than itself.*

7. Finally, what is within the reach of the ordinary person who is not over-gifted spiritually but who is prepared to make the necessary effort? What should be his aim? Few are called upon to enter the full Contemplative life or are able to do so. There is no reason, however, why the ordinary person should not develop himself by the regular practice of meditative prayer to pass at times into the Prayer of Simplicity and Simple Regard, the prayer in which one is no longer 'praying' in the usually accepted sense, no longer carrying out any sort of deliberate spiritual exercise of reflective or contemplative meditation, but simply 'looking at', communing with the Source of all being, simply, as it were, 'wooing' God, quietly, serenely, without words, simply waiting on Him.

For one who follows the Way of the Prayer of Meditation, in whatever form it may take, it is impossible to say what may happen, what form the vision will take, whether it will be some flash of contemplative insight, whether it will be one

* A Buddhist would not express himself quite in this way and there are types of Hindu *yoga* which do not have these objectives.

of those 'slips' of consciousness into a new wave-length or dimension of reality, perhaps of the reality of the everyday world, perhaps of a supersensory world, which impress those who have known them as more real than normal vision, or whether it be that experience of 'the timeless moment', which is, in the fullest sense, a true mystical experience, standing out in all its uniqueness and power. One does not know. 'When,' wrote a master of the spiritual life, 'the servant is ready, then is the Master present.'

Among the collection of lovely poems, coming out of deep spiritual experience, which Phyllis Campbell has sent to me, is this one. With it I will end this chapter:

> Seek not His gifts, the more to be
> made one with Him who gives to thee;
> No gift can fill the heart as He.
>
> And when no light illumines prayer,
> Then through the darkness grope and dare
> unseeingly to find Him there.

9. Reflective Meditation

WE have classified the Prayer of Meditation as falling into two main types, reflective rational meditation and contemplative intuitive meditation, at the same time pointing out that in practice these two main types not seldom merge into each other. In this section we shall consider some types of reflective rational meditation.

In his excellent book, *Concentration and Meditation*,* Christmas Humphreys, writing as a Buddhist, divides meditation into higher and lower meditation and lists and describes seven types of lower meditation. They are: on 'passing through the bodies', on things as they really are, on dispassion, on motive, on the doctrines of religion, on the self, and on analogy. We cannot do better than use this scheme as our basis.

* Published by John M. Watkins.

I. ON THE NATURE OF THE SELF

This is of supreme importance. The masters of meditation recommend that at an early stage of the meditative prayer-life one should enter on this meditation. Not only have I discussed it in both the previous books of this trilogy and in *The Journey Inwards*, but have also written something on it earlier in this book. Let us, however, consider it more fully at this point.

Self is a mystery. 'Myself', as known to myself, is bound up with my physical body, my feelings, emotions and mental processes. I am aware, however, dimly perhaps, of something else, something which, while in this earthly existence it is yoked to my physical body, my sensations and my mind, and which cannot function without them, yet is not of them. It is greater than the elements which are its instruments.

Examine this self of which one is aware. It is a human being among other human beings, placed without any volition of its own, by divine providence or by mere chance, at a particular point in space and time, a point which is its individual and inescapable destiny.

This I know; but that I know it surely means that there is a part of me which can stand aside, another *I* which can observe and interpret this externalized *I*. This other *I* cannot be regarded as synonymous with my mind, for my mind is one of the things it can observe and examine. Let us call this other *I*, so closely bound up with, yet in some ways so distinct from, the externalized *I*, the *non-objectivized self*.

Look a little closer. One perceives the self as both subject and object; as observing itself and as also observed by itself; as the knower and a part of that which is known; as belonging to a world outside itself and yet, at the same time, distinct from that world.

Further, this non-objectivized self is aware, not only of its objectivized self, not only of a world of material objects, but also of other selves, akin to itself, with which it can establish relationships, different from the relationships it has with the world of things.

The wholeness of my experience does not end here. In addition, I am aware of a world which is not one of things nor of other selves, and with this world I also feel I have kinship. It is an inner world, a world of ideas and values, a world in part of mind, but also of spirit.

However deeply one delves into the nature of self one never strikes bottom. It is not possible to demonstrate rationally the existence of 'mind' or 'soul' or 'spirit', nor to say precisely what they are, or how they are interrelated. It is possible to argue that they do not exist at all, that all that exists is a material brain, which is a part of the body, of the same physical character as heart or liver, but designed to perform a different function in the physical economy.

Yet somehow that does not ring true; it leaves too much unexplained. One is conscious in one's experience of this other self, which is not the phenomenal self of which one is mainly conscious.

When some three thousand years ago those spiritual explorers of India retired to the forests to meditate on the nature of God, of the world and of man, they concluded that the self of which a man is mainly conscious and which he thinks is himself, is only a phenomenal self, not the real self at all, destined to be dissolved at death. Man's real and enduring self, his Greater Self, is not this phenomenal self. His real self is bound up with the Divine Essence, a spark of divinity within him. This Greater Self they called the Atman. The Atman alone is immortal and unchanging. It is a divine light, an unsleeping seer, present in all, yet distinct from all, a Universal Self and at the same time a personal Self.

The Hindu formula of faith is *Tat twam asi*, translated, 'Thou [your real Self] art Brahman [the Ultimate Reality]'. This formula uses the *mystic copula*. It does not state a logical identity but an identity of essential being. The same sort of insight, expressed in different ways, is found in all religions. In Genesis it is written, 'God created man in His own image:

in the image of God created He him.' But God-as-He-is-in-Himself, the Ultimate Reality, has no 'image'; It is the Unexpressible. The Hindu and Hebraic insight is clearly the same.*

Man has within him the possibility of contact and communion with that Ultimate Reality he calls God because his essential being is linked up with Divine Being. Though in this life the union may be potential – as Ruysbroeck says, the essential union between man and God is passive until it is made actual – the Greater Self partakes of the divinity of the Divine Self. It is the chief object of man on earth to realize this truth in his own inner experience.

2. ON PASSING THROUGH THE BODIES

Some teachers of meditation recommend that one who would become proficient in meditation should start by examining those three vehicles of consciousness through which contact is made with the three spheres of activity, the physical, the emotional and the mental; and then try to realize that none of these, either alone or combined, is the essential, the true, Self.

The spiritual exercise used to effect this realization is called 'the passing through the bodies'. It may take the following form:

I, i.e. my real I, am not my physical body
I am not my emotions
I am not my mental processes

The exercise can be carried out in several ways; by, as it were, *rising* through the bodies to a higher level of consciousness, or by *moving inward* through the bodies to the deep centre of one's being, or by *moving forward* through them towards that universal consciousness, which is also one's own personal consciousness. The exercise is both a mental and psychological

* The superb myth with which the Book of Genesis opens is of later composition than the rest of the book, possibly not until after the Captivity, when other religious insights influenced the earlier Hebraic ones.

process. What one is trying to do is to realize one's own essential nature by raising the level of consciousness from a lower to a higher plane.

A similar spiritual exercise is used by the Sufis of Islam. Here the 'disciplined student of philosophical mind' is bidden to ask himself the question: What am I? and then to pass through a series of five meditations:

I am not body,
I am not the senses,
I am not the mind,
I am not this,
I am not that

What then am I? What is the Self?

It is in this body.
It is in everybody.
It is everywhere.
It is the All.
It is Self. I am It. Absolute Oneness!

'I am not the mind.' It may be useful to say something here about the concept of Mind. It is a difficult one, for the word, 'mind', carries a number of meanings. We shall find ourselves using it with more than one meaning in the course of this book. In the phrase above it is used in the sense of the thought-machine, which creates and uses concepts, including the concept of 'mind' itself. In 'the passing through the bodies' the essential I is dissociated from this thought-machine which forms the continuous series of mental images which is the material of so much of our thinking.

The Hindu religious philosophy of the nature of man aims at a greater precision. The only absolute reality is Atman, which might be roughly translated 'spirit'. 'Mind' is envisaged as of a three-fold nature: spiritual mind (buddhi), which could be called 'soul', the higher part of the personality, from which proceeds inspiration, religious, artistic, etc.; higher manas, i.e. intelligence and reason; and lower manas, the unconscious mind which directs the operations of the body. In

Buddhism a distinction is made between 'mind', in the sense of a thought-machine, and the *Essence of Mind*, which is a non-rational spiritual reality.*

For our purpose it is not necessary at this point to say more. The concept of Mind is a difficult and confusing one.

3. ON DISPASSION AND THINGS AS THEY REALLY ARE

Most of us live in a state of perpetual deception. We tend to see what we want to see and to believe what we want to believe. We are not entirely responsible for this, for each one of us is deeply conditioned by our own heredity, environment, education, etc., which create in each a mass of prejudices and predispositions. Consequently it is only too easy to spend our lives in blinkers, never being able to see objectively, living always in a fantasy world, which is not the world as it really is.

It is, therefore, salutary at times to meditate, so far as we are able, on things as they really are and not what we imagine them to be. There need not be anything formal in a meditation of this sort. It is really an exercise in clear thinking, the cultivation of a particular attitude to ordinary living and of the habit of pulling oneself up and asking oneself the question: 'Are things really like that or am I letting my imagination run away with me?'

The objective of this meditation is to be able to lead one's life dispassionately, not unduly worried or affected by outward circumstances. Let me try and make clear the meaning of dispassion by narrating an experience in my early life as a headmaster. My task at the time was not an easy one; I was faced with innumerable difficulties and life was very frustrating. It happened after a very difficult Governors' Meeting. Everything had gone wrong. When I got to bed I was so worried that I could not sleep; my mind was going round and round in circles. I could stand it no longer. I got up and pulled back my bedroom curtains and looked out on a clear night sky, studded with stars. And I saw my own particular little life and my own particular little problems in a new light; and

* See Section 5 of the Anthology of *Mysticism* (third edition).

I said to myself: 'What a silly little creature you are! What a fuss you are making about nothing! What do all your little worries matter in the face of this immensity? Get back your sense of proportion, little man.' I closed the curtains, got back to bed, and peacefully fell asleep. I had learnt the meaning of dispassion. This is, of course, a very simple example. There are times when it is much more difficult to be dispassionate and detached.

To live, think and feel dispassionately does not mean sitting back and doing nothing. Each one of us, as we pass through the brief span of our existence between birth and death, has his particular function to fulfil. This function will call for dedication and effort if it is to be done well. It does, however, mean that one maintains not only one's sense of proportion, but also one's sense of humour, that one does not allow oneself to be unduly affected by frustration and failure, or allow oneself to be worried by trifles, that one sees one's actions in their proper setting, in the setting of the immensities of space and time, and of the eternal world.

4. ON MOTIVE

Not only is it salutary to consider things as they really are, it is also equally salutary to meditate on one's motives, to endeavour to know oneself. Everyone ought deliberately to ask himself at intervals questions such as these: 'Why am I performing this or that action in this or that particular way? What motive impels me? Is it really what I want to think it is? Why do I think on this or that question as I do? Why am I living my life in the way I am living it? What is the purpose of life, anyway? For me? For the world?' And then may come the crucial question: 'Am I doing what I should about it? Or am I merely drifting?'

I warn the reader that this meditation on motive, if it is really carried out objectively, can be painful. It is a self-stripping which can reveal all sorts of hidden things in yourself which will hurt. If you are frank with yourself, you will realize that you may not be such a nice person as you

thought you were, that a great many of the actions which you
thought were selfless and altruistic were not pure, but were
in part dictated by less worthy motives, by the desire to be a
'big noise', to be well spoken of, or were an expression of
the desire, which in varying degrees we all have, to impose
ourselves and our ideals on other people.

If this should happen you need not be unduly perturbed.
We all have what Jung calls 'the dark shadow', which we
must accept and learn to live with. Looking back on my own
life work I am bound to acknowledge that, though I think I
was driven on by high ideals, there was a strong strain of
egoism in me. Not only that, I also feel that it was this
egoistic drive, this urge towards self-expression, which was the
impulse which enabled me to do what I was able to do.

5. ON THE NATURE OF FAITH AND KNOWLEDGE

Let the reader carry this form of meditation further and put
these questions to himself: 'What is the basis of my philosophy
of life? What, if I have one, is the basis of my religious faith?'
And the more-embracing question: 'Why are there different
religious faiths, different philosophies, different values?'

There are significant things within our experience, for
instance, the love of goodness, beauty and truth, and the
inspiration which leads to the composition of great works of
art, which reason cannot explain. As one writer has put it:
'Reason may help to discover truth but it cannot explain the
hunger of men to discover it.' Where have these significant
things their origin?

There is a faculty of knowing which men possess in varying
degrees of development and intensity and through which they
have found an immediate, direct intuitive awareness of truth,
or some fragment of it. Let us, borrowing a term from the
Wisdom of Solomon in the Apocrypha, call this faculty, *wisdom*.*
One may, if one wishes, call it by the roughly equivalent Buddhist word, *buddhi*; *buddhi* is the human faculty of *Bodhi*, i.e.

* See the 'Hymn to Wisdom' in The Prayer Book.

Wisdom, Enlightenment, Awakening; it is an essentially intuitive, not a rational, faculty.

At the *wisdom* level of awareness, while the knowledge is real knowledge, what is known is without *form*. In order to be made capable of communication and rational apprehension at the level of ordinary experience, this knowledge must pass through some medium, whereby it is given intelligible form, through words, concepts, music, colour etc. This medium of transformation we shall, without defining its nature too exactly, here call *mind*. Now – and this is the important point – *mind* is conditioned by such factors as heredity, history and environment. Thus the direct, clear vision of truth, perceived at the *wisdom* or *buddhic* level of perception, is, as it passes through and is given intelligible form through the medium of *mind*, distorted and coloured. The result is different schools of thought, different theological and philosophical systems, different value judgements, different forms of art. So what at the *wisdom* or *buddhic* level of perception is the same truth may be given a variety of forms as it passes through minds differently conditioned and at different stages of development.

Here is an hypothesis, an hypothesis to account for what is known through experience, an hypothesis which can be reached by a process of rational thought. When one arrives at this hypothesis, what follows? One becomes capable of what, in *Religious Faith and Twentieth-Century Man*, I have called *Intersection*. When one becomes capable of Intersection, two things happen. One sees things in a different light and, because of that new vision, one is oneself changed. There is a vast increase in charity and humility, both in general and also on the intellectual plane. One is no longer irritated because people are different from oneself, that they think and see things differently. One's own particular religious faith does not become any the less real, the truth it enshrines any the less luminous; indeed it takes on an even greater radiance. One no longer assumes, however, that one is God's particular little white-headed boy, more spiritually illuminated than those who express their religious faith in different concepts and images. Tolerance, charity and humility become steady

tempers of mind, determining all one's outlook. And not in
the domain of religious faith only does this new capacity of
Intersection operate. It gradually permeates all one's physical
and intellectual activities, including one's relations with other
people. One increases in love and cleary realizes what St Paul
meant when, at the end of his great Hymn to Love, he wrote:

When I was a little child I talked and felt and thought like a little
child. Now that I am a man my childish speech and feeling and
thought have no further significance for me.

At present all we see is the baffling reflection of reality; we are like
men looking at a landscape in a small mirror. The time will come
when we shall see reality whole and face to face! At present all I
know is a little fraction of the truth, but the time will come when
I shall know it as fully as God now knows me!

In this life we have three great lasting qualities – faith, hope and
love. But the greatest of these is love.*

6. ON THE DOGMAS OF FAITH

That a man of religious temperament, whatever form his
religious faith may take, should meditate on the particular
doctrines enshrined in his faith is natural and inevitable. They
express his image of God and eternal truth. There are some
who regard dogma as not only unnecessary but also definitely
undesirable. Rightly seen, however, dogma has not only
immense value, but also great beauty. It is the translation into
symbols and concepts of truths apprehended at the *wisdom* or
buddhic level of awareness, the taking of form of mystical
vision and insight, so that they may be perpetuated and
passed on to following generations. This is true of the dogmas
of all religions.

One must not, however, rest in dogma. Dogma is a means
not an end. In order that the illumination which is present in
dogma may take place, it is necessary to move from both
unthinking acceptance and mere intellectual comprehension

* I Corinthians, Chapter XIII, as translated by J. B. Phillips: *Letters to
Young Churches* (Bles).

to spiritual understanding. For it is only when a truth is intuitively assimilated that it is truly understood. When this process of intuitive apprehension takes place, the dogmas of the Faith cease to be static and lifeless formulae and become dynamic and revealing. The great dogmas of the Christian Faith, the Incarnation, Passion, Resurrection and Exaltation of Christ, take on a luminous quality and a penetrating beauty. They cease to be things that a Christian is expected to 'believe'. There is no longer any need to 'believe', for they are 'known' intuitively in the innermost being. They grip and convince in their essential rightness. Through them it is possible to contemplate the intersection of time and eternity, the marriage of history and that which is not history.

Not only that, but also in this sort of meditation sayings enshrined in the Christian Scriptures, for instance the sayings of Jesus and of St Paul and the writer of the Fourth Gospel, become luminous. As a man meditates on them, there are leaps of understanding and flashes of contemplative insight. Suddenly the significance of such cryptic sayings of Jesus as 'He who shall lose his life shall save it', or 'Unless a man eat the flesh of the Son of Man he has no part in Him', become crystal clear to him, though, if he is asked to express what he has grasped in words, he might be inadequate and confused. And so it is with the sayings found in the scriptures of other religions, in the Upanishads and the Bhagavad Gita, scriptures, like the Christian ones, redolent with wisdom and light.

In meditations on the dogmas of the Faith one may rightly include the whole of knowledge, striving to unify in the mind the 'truths' of science, the 'truths' of history and the 'truths' of religion, letting the insights of each play upon the others, until they intersect and thereby illuminate each other. The thoughtful modern man cannot live in an uncomfortable thought-world in which there is a clash of 'truths'. By an inner compulsion he is forced to strive to move forward from fragmentation to unity, to endeavour to draw all knowledge, spiritual and material, into one. How may he do this?

In that Perennial Philosophy, which is expressed in different ways in all the higher religions, everything is regarded as the partial manifestation of one Divine Ground, of one Ultimate Reality. From it originate and are gathered together all those fragmentary realities of which, in our present existence, we are mainly conscious. All separate 'truths' are thus facets of one all-embracing Truth, fragments of one pure light which comes to us, owing to the nature of our perception, in the separated colours of a spectrum. May we not then expect that each 'truth' will illuminate and in part explain every other 'truth'? Further, would it not be reasonable to assume that when one is able to glimpse the same principle operating in a number of different fields, appearing in similar forms in different settings, that what one has glimpsed is indeed an ultimate principle, which may rightly be allowed to influence one's thinking in all fields of knowledge, and that through it one has penetrated more deeply and more surely into the heart of the Real? And is it not also reasonable to assume that a principle, apprehended at first perhaps in a leap of contemplative insight or a flash of mystical intuition, if it is also found in approximately the same guise, appearing in widely separated places, at different times in history and in different spheres of knowledge, is a true principle, in which one can place one's trust?

Let me explain what I mean by drawing on my own experience. In *Religious Faith and Twentieth-Century Man* I told how, as a young man, in what I can only regard as a flash of mystical intuition, I glimpsed the truth of what Nicholas of Cusa called 'the coincidence of contradictories [or opposites]', and how over the years I found the same truth expressed in different ways in a variety of settings: in the Creation Myth of the Book of Genesis, in the Taoist philosophy of ancient China, in the non-dualistic thought of Hinduism and Buddhism, in the Greek philosopher-scientist, Heraclitus, in the writings of the fifteenth-century Cardinal, mathematician and mystic, Nicholas of Cusa and, at length, in the complementarity of the twentieth-century quantum physicists.

What is meant by the coincidence of contradictories or opposites? In ancient Taoist philosophy the doctrine takes this form: the phenomenal world is envisaged as coming into existence by the splitting up of *Tao*, the Primal Meaning, the undivided Unity of everything, into the polar opposites of *yang* and *yin*, which are evident in all phenomena and are a characteristic of all human perception. We are unable to conceive anything except in relation to its opposite. The concept of light, for instance, can only be grasped in relation to its opposite, darkness. Yet these polar opposites only operate in the world of phenomena. They merge and are resolved in that Primal Meaning, that Undivided Unity, from which they spring. To find the ultimate Truth, therefore, it is needful to pass through the polar opposites into the Unity which they manifest.

Nicholas of Cusa writes in this way:

> I have learnt that the place where Thou art found unveiled is girt round with the coincidence of contradictories and this is the wall of Paradise wherein Thou dost abide. . . . 'Tis beyond the coincidence of contradictories that Thou mayest be seen, and nowhere this side thereof.

Had the mystical experience I have described remained isolated I might, despite the intense feeling that what I had glimpsed was very important and contained the key to a profound secret, have been tempted to distrust it. When I discovered that many others, in many places, at many times, had penetrated to the same secret, then my belief that I had indeed had a clear vision of the reality of things was confirmed. This revelation, for such it was, has throughout my life affected all my thinking and removed many difficulties.

10. Christian Meditation

BEFORE we pass from our study of reflective meditation to that of contemplative meditation, it will be useful to fill out our picture of the Prayer of Meditation in general by describing and contrasting some aspects of Christian, Hindu, Buddhist and Islamic meditational practices and noting where they seem to differ in the particular stresses they lay on the objective of these practices.

First Christian meditation. While the practice of meditation has always been present in Christianity, objectives at different periods have not always been the same, nor has the same weight been given to the practice of meditation as a spiritual activity for ordinary people as is given to it in Hinduism and Buddhism.

In Hinduism and Buddhism, and indeed among the Sufis of Islam, the chief object of the spiritual exercises of the Prayer of Meditation at all levels is the deliberate raising and enlargement of consciousness and the cultivation of that super-conscious, whereby enlightenment can alone be found. In Christianity, on the other hand, there has been a tendency, particularly since the sixteenth century, to assess the value of meditation practices by the extent to which they are con-ducive to an increase in holiness, whether they make the one who meditates morally a better man or woman. Progress in meditation has tended to be assessed on a criterion of growth in humility and the moral virtues. There has been a tendency among some spiritual directors and writers on meditation to frown on any sort of spiritual exercises which aim at produc-ing mystical states of mind, which are deliberately intended to enable the aspirant to pass into a state of Contemplation. If God leads him into such a state well and good. It must not, however, be sought or expected. This is clearly evident in such classic examples of formal meditation as the Ignatian and Sulpician methods. There does not seem to be any intention that one undertaking the very complicated Ignatian Spiritual Exercises should rise to the heights of Contempla-tion; rather their object seems to be that the sense of sin should be increased. Some of the ways used, for instance meditation on the tortures of hell, in the Ignatian Spiritual Exercises, seem to the present writer truly horrible. One is tempted to wonder what this sort of meditation has to do with the religion of a God of Love. In this criticism I would like to avoid any accusation that I do not realize the immense and beneficial effect the practice of the Ignatian Spiritual

Exercises has had on men of particular temperament, fitting them for the particular tasks they were called upon to do. There is evidence of their profound spiritual effect on St Francis Xavier and his companions; and anyone who has read Pope John XXIII's *Journal of a Soul* cannot but have been impressed by the part they played in preparing that saintly man for the great work which fell to him to do at the end of his life. In any case, St Ignatius Loyola did not design them for the use of ordinary folk.

Now, while in any comparative study of meditation objectives as found in the religious faiths we are considering, it is necessary to stress this particular bias found among Christian spiritual directors of the West in recent centuries, it would be entirely misleading to create the impression that this bias has been in any way characteristic of all periods of Christian history or is in any way universal. Among the apophatic theologians and spiritual directors of the early Christian Church of the East not only was the objective of spiritual exercises regarded as the attainment of states of illumination and 'deification', but also it was believed that by means of these spiritual exercises these states could be reached. Further the Prayer of Jesus, the 'Prayer of the Heart', typical of the deepest meditational practice of the Eastern Orthodox Church, has, as its objective, that enlargement and elevation of spiritual consciousness which is characteristic of Hindu and Buddhist meditation.

We have noted in some types of Christian meditation the stress laid on the sense of sin. It is desirable to discuss this more fully, since a too great emphasis on, and obsession with, sin can not only be unhealthy but can also lead to mental disorders.

There is a true and healthy sense of sin of the sort which comes to those to whom in one form or other has come the kind of vision of the Holy which came to the prophet Isaiah.

In the year that King Uzziah died I saw the Lord sitting upon a throne, high and lifted up, and his train filled the temple. . . . Then said I, Woe is me for I am undone! Because I am a man of unclean lips and dwell in the midst of a people of unclean lips: for mine eyes have seen the King, the Lord of hosts.

Or when it has come as the result of an experience such as that which Warner Allen describes in *The Timeless Moment* and which called from him these words:

Something has happened to me – I am utterly amazed – Can this be that? (*That* being the answer to the riddle of life) – but it is too simple – I always knew it – like coming home – I am not 'I', not the 'I' I thought – there is no death – peace passing understanding – *yet how unworthy I.* [The italics are mine.]

There is also a healthy sense of sin which arises through the realization of the 'fallen' state of mankind and of oneself, of all the cruelty, greed, hatred, intolerance and consequent misery in the world, the result of ignorance, pride, and pre-occupation with self. Or when it arises out of that state of 'anxiety' and 'guilt', consciously or unconsciously felt by so many in our age and which is characteristic of so much modern literature, both in prose and poetry. For it is only when men feel the sense of alienation, discord and loneliness that they realize the need of repentance (*metanoia*, a turning round of the mind), redemption and deliverance from self-centredness and separation.

Sin, and the feeling of guilt and alienation bound up with it, are realities in human existence, realities not to be shirked.

It is, further, a good and salutary experience to realize one's own littleness and insignificance in face of infinite time and space. Go out on a starlit night. Gaze up at the heavens, studded with stars. Bring to your mind all that modern astronomy has to say about the vast extent of the universe. However much it may hurt, however much you may feel lost and annihilated, let that immensity sink into you, even though it overwhelms and crushes you, and you cry with the Psalmist: 'When I consider the heavens, the work of thine hands, and the firmament which Thou hast made, what is man that Thou regardest him and the son of man that Thou visitest him?'

What you are doing is meditating on things as they really

are. If it ended there, however, it would not be complete. Carry the meditation further and ask the question: 'What is there in the nature of man, an insignificant atom of an insignificant planet in an insignificant solar system, that enables him to comprehend this vast universe, to hold it all in his mind?' And then pass on to the consideration of another not conflicting but complementary aspect, also within the totality of human experience, the sense of some Power upholding it all, a Power which he cannot know through his intellect, but with which man may have intimate communion, and whose nature is Love.

When one has, deep down, realized that the Power behind the universe is Love, one is no longer lonely and afraid. One can trust oneself to it with the sure conviction that upholding it and each one of us are the Everlasting Arms. The sense of insignificance, inadequacy, sin and utter unworthiness remain but the balance has changed.

Above all it is necessary to keep a right balance and a sense of proportion. Not only that; it is desirable also to keep a sense of humour. There is a vast difference between a healthy conviction of sin and inadequacy and that scrupulosity which solemnizes and magnifies every trifle.

> Once in a saintly passion
> I cried with desperate grief,
> 'O Lord my heart is black with guile,
> Of sinners I am chief.'
> Then stopped my guardian angel
> And whispered from behind:
> 'Vanity, my little man;
> You're nothing of the kind.'*

Perhaps too much space has been given to this obsession with sin that one finds in some types of Christian spirituality. While one of the objectives of Christian meditation is the transformation of character and progress in the way of holiness, it is equally, indeed more so, communion with God through Jesus Christ, the Redeemer, Mediator and Exemplar;

* Quoted in Jessop, *Law and Love* (Student Christian Movement Press).

so that one may be able to 'put on' Christ, to participate in His Risen Life, to so die to self that one can say with St Paul: 'I live, but it is no longer I, my own little self, but Christ who lives in me.' Some have described the objective of the true Christian life as one of becoming 'another Christ (*alter Christus*)': and St Athanasius (in his *De Incarnatione*) penned the words: 'God became man that man might become God.'

Let us consider some forms which are characteristic of Christian meditation.

I. THE VALUE OF VISUALIZATION

The Christian Faith centres round the Incarnation of Divine Being in a human person, Jesus Christ, and the Christian image of God tends to be expressed in personalistic terms. Consequently one type of Christian meditation makes considerable use of visual imagery. This type of meditation is also found in other religions. While such meditation may perhaps be labelled 'lower' meditation, it is of great value and particularly suitable for certain temperaments. Further it has real value as the beginning of a meditation which gradually transcends imagination and visualization and passes into what is essentially contemplative meditation. Types of this sort of meditation are meditations on the Sacred Heart of Jesus, meditations before the Crib or the Holy Child, meditations before the crucifix, icon or picture, and meditations before the Reserved Sacrament.

2. COLLOQUY AND AFFECTIVE PRAYER

Colloquy and affective prayer, which is very much of the same character, are two of the most natural types of meditation for ordinary people, and, indeed, for many who have made definite progress in the spiritual life, but who are not able to pass into imageless meditation. In essence, both are a personal conversation with God or with Christ. In them, words, symbols, thoughts and aspirations combine. They are of value in the simpler forms of contemplative meditation, leading up

to the stage when talking stops and one becomes silent, doing
nothing except waiting for the still voice of God, speaking in
the depths of the innermost being. St John of the Cross
described real prayer as 'the privilege of listening for the
delicate voice of God'.

Nor are colloquy and affective prayer, despite their personal
character, bound up with any particular image of God. God
may have become the Inexpressible, ungraspable by the
intellect, all-pervading Spirit. Yet this Unknowable One,
'before whom words recoil', is by a process of strange,
spiritual alchemy, still the Father and the dear Comrade of all
our ways. One may say:

You are the Eternal One, Creator and Sustainer of all life, unchanging, unfathomable, beyond human thought and conceiving.
Yet I may call You Father and Your Spirit speaks to my spirit. The
pure in heart may see You and You reveal Yourself to those who
seek You in humility.

A colloquy may spring spontaneously out of a discursive
meditation, in which a complex of ideas is intellectually
examined. There are a number of colloquies of this sort in
the writings of Pierre Teilhard de Chardin. For instance, in
*Le Milieu Divin**, Part III, Section 2, 'The Nature of the Divine
Milieu, the Universal Christ and the Great Communion', a
piece of sustained argument culminates in a petition:

Grant, O Lord, that when I draw near to the altar to communi-
cate I may henceforth discern the infinite perspectives hidden
beneath the smallness and the nearness of the Host in which You
are concealed.

And then passes into a long colloquy:

I am beginning to understand; under the Sacred Species it is
primarily through the 'accidents' of matter that You touch one. . . .
What can I do to gather up and answer that universal embrace? . . .
To the total offer that is made me, I can only answer by a total
acceptance. I shall therefore *react* to the eucharistic contact with the
entire effort of my life – of my life of today and my life of tomorrow,
of my personal life and of my life linked to all other lives. . . .

* Published by Collins; also issued as a Fontana Book.

Because You ascended into heaven after having descended into hell, You have so filled the universe in every direction, Jesus, that henceforth it is blessedly impossible to escape You. . . . What I cry out for, like every being, with my whole life and all my earthly passion, is something very different from an equal to cherish: it is a God to adore. To adore: that means to lose oneself in the unfathomable, to plunge into the inexhaustible, to find peace in the incorruptible, to be absorbed in immensity, to offer oneself to the fire and the transparency, to annihilate oneself. . .

The colloquy ends with a final petition:

Disperse, O Jesus, the clouds with Your lightning! . . . And so that we should triumph over the world with You, come to us clothed in the glory of the world.

Father Teilhard's *The Mass on the World** is also a sustained colloquy, not coming out of a rational demonstration of a sequence of ideas but out of a particular situation: he found himself in the Ordo Desert without the means of saying Mass. It is one of the most beautiful and moving examples of sustained meditation in the whole of the religious literature of Christendom.

3. THE PRACTICE OF THE PRESENCE OF GOD

Yet another form of meditation typical of the Christian attitude is the Practice of the Presence of God. The standard book on it is, of course, the one with that title by the little monk, Brother Lawrence, who spent most of his time in the monastery kitchen. It may be defined as the carrying of meditation into the active life, as the holding of the mind, as the duties of ordinary life are carried out, so fixed on God that one is living the whole time in His presence, performing every duty as an offering to Him,† in the spirit of the principle so clearly expressed in the Hindu *Bhagavad Gita*:

The world is imprisoned in its own activity except when actions

* Printed with other pieces in *The Hymn of the Universe* (Collins).

† A number of prayers for this purpose, written by my friends, are printed in The Prayer Book.

are performed as worship of God [i.e. *done in relation to something higher than themselves*]. Therefore you must perform every action sacramentally, and be free from any attachment to results.

4. RECOLLECTION

The Practice of the Presence of God is the same as Recollection or the Prayer of Recollection, so well described by Father Thomas Merton:*

Recollection makes me present to myself by bringing together two aspects, or activities, of my being as if they were two lens of a telescope. One lens is the basic semblance of my spiritual being, the inward soul, the deep will, the spiritual intelligence. The other is my outward soul, the practical intelligence, the will engaged in the activities of life . . .

When the outward self knows only itself, then it is absent from its true self. It does not know its own inward spirit. It never acts in accordance with the need and measure of its own true personality, which exists where my spirit is wedded with the silent presence of the Lord's Spirit and where my deep will responds to his gravitation towards the secrecy of the Godhead.

11. Hindu, Buddhist and Islamic Meditation

IN a study of Hindu and Buddhist spirituality one finds oneself in a different atmosphere and a different thought-world. Far from the moral element being absent from Hindu and Buddhist spirituality, one has only to read, for instance, the Yoga Sutras of Patanjali to realize how great an importance is attached to the moral and social virtues. They are, however, regarded as a beginning rather than as an end, an essential prerequisite for entry on the path of deeper meditation. Meditation and Contemplation are regarded primarily as spiritual exercises deliberately undertaken to create in those undertaking them desirable states of mind, which will

* *No Man is an Island* (Hollis and Carter).

eventually lead to illumination, escape from ego-consciousness, and the destruction of the illusion of individuality. Though there are similarities between Hindu and Buddhist meditation there are also certain differences. The Buddhist approach is, in some schools at least, very much more intellectual; this is particularly true of Theravada Buddhism, much less so in Mahayana Buddhism; the Hindu approach is more abstract, mystical and rarefied. The differences should not, however, be stressed too much. In both one finds deep psychological insight; indeed Buddhism has been called more a system of spiritual psychology than a religion in the normal sense of the word.

I. HINDU MEDITATION

The main objective – there are lesser objectives – of Hindu *yoga*, the path, through spiritual exercises, to union with God, is the realization of the true nature of self and of the world. As we have already seen, according to Hindu religious philosophy, the self of which we are mainly conscious is not the real Self. It is only a phenomenal self, destined to disappear at death. Man's true self is his Greater Self, the Atman, which is both an individual and universal Self, a Divine Indwelling, which is of the same essence as Brahman, God, Spirit. It is the chief object of man on this earth to realize this truth, not as an intellectual proposition, but in his inherent being; a realization which is accomplished through the spiritual exercises of concentration, meditation and contemplation.

Great importance is attached to these spiritual exercises, not only for the few but also for as many as are fit to undertake them. A comment on the lack of attention given to spiritual exercises in the West made by a famous *guru* (spiritual director) to Edward Carpenter is interesting:

You in the West say 'O God, O God!' but you have no *definite* knowledge or methods whereby you can attain to see God. . . . It is only in India that complete instruction exists on this point – by which a man who is 'ripe' can systematically and without fail attain the object of his research.*

Though not completely correct, the comment contains an element of truth.

The forms of yoga have been classified in various ways. The main types are:

1. *Bhakti yoga*, the way to union through faith in and love towards God.

2. *Karma yoga*, the way to union through selfless, dedicated action.

3. *Jnana yoga*, the way to union through spiritual knowledge.

4. *Raja* (or royal) *yoga*, the yoga of will. The term, *raja* (king), carries the idea of self-mastery of mind over body and will over mind. It aims at the mountain top, the experience of inward illumination beyond all sensation, the attainment of a complete state of super-consciousness.

5. *Hatha yoga*, has, as its objective, the good health of the body and the awakening of latent powers. In Hindu spirituality great attention is paid to correct breathing and bodily posture. Both are regarded as of immense value in successful meditation, not only in the attainment of bodily well-being, peace of mind and poise, but also as ways of reaching the higher levels of meditation.†

These different ways should not be regarded as mutually exclusive. For instance, a man of active disposition may primarily follow the way of dedicated action (*karma yoga*) but the urge to follow this way may be grounded in a deep faith in and devotion to God (*bhakti yoga*). The man of philosophical mind, intent on penetrating the most profound recesses of reality (*jnana yoga*), may combine this way to knowledge and unison with those of *bhakti* and *karma yoga*.

The first requisite for progress in the spiritual life is goodness in personal character and in social relations. In view of

* From *Adam's Peak to Elephanta*, quoted by Tillyard: *Spiritual Exercises*.

† See Father Déchanet's *Christian Yoga* (Burns and Oates) where the exercises of *hatha yoga* are described in detail and their combination with breath-control, mental discipline and silent meditation.

the impression given by some who have written on Hindu and Buddhist spirituality, it is necessary to emphasize this. It is not, however, the end.

The Yoga Sutras of Patanjali* lists eight 'limbs', i.e. tools or aids to progress. They are (1) Abstention, (2) Observance, (3) Posture, (4) Breath control, (5) Sense-withdrawal, (6) Concentration, (7) Meditation, (8) Contemplation (*samadhi*). The first two of these are concerned mainly with morality and ethics.

By *Abstention* is meant the avoidance of evil in thought and deed.

Observance is described as five fold: (a) *Cleanliness*, not only in body but in mind; (b) *Contentment*, in the sense of equanimity or dispassion; (c) *Austerity*, not in the sense of self-mortification, but of moderation, the avoidance of excess in such things as eating, sleep etc.; (d) *Self-study* of one's own being and nature, the oft reiterated 'Know thyself'; and finally (e) *Attentiveness to God*. This does not involve the acceptance of any particular 'image' of God. It is rather seeing God, the That which is the ultimate source of all knowledge, in everything. Of posture and breath-control it is neither possible nor necessary to write here. Any attempt at a summary would give no idea of the immense variety of postures or the elaborations of breath-control which are described. Two useful books are Ernest Wood's *Yoga* (Penguin Books) and Father Déchanet's *Christian Yoga* (Burns and Oates). There are many others.

Sense-withdrawal virtually explains itself. It is the elimination from the mind of all intruding thoughts and influences, the bringing of the senses under control and the calming of the mind, so that it is in a fit state for fruitful meditation.

Concentration has the same object, to attain 'onepointedness'.

Contemplation (*samadhi*) has more than one meaning. The

* These Sutras are very ancient. They consist of a series of often puzzling aphorisms and are usually published with explanatory notes. They are very difficult to translate meaningfully, and I do not think that any really satisfactory translation has yet been made. The one I know best is that published by John M. Watkins, *The Yoga Sutras of Patanjali; The Book of the Spiritual Man*, an interpretation by Charles Johnston.

word may be used to describe not only a spiritual state, but also a particular way of the functioning of the mind, when that which is meditated on is seen not as a combination but as an integration of particulars, when it is seen in its wholeness, in its unity. Any aspect of reality may be contemplated in this way.

There are various types and levels of *samadhi*. The two main types are *samadhi-with-seed*, i.e. contemplation at the level of thought, and *seedless-samadhi*, which is a level not of thought but of vision, inner experience and intuition. In its fully developed form all images and concepts have faded out and the contemplative enters an indescribable state of naked awareness. The experience of what the Hindu calls *seedless-samadhi* is known in the highest spirituality of all religions.

2. BUDDHIST MEDITATION

Speaking in very general terms, Buddhist religious philosophy differs from that of Hinduism in that Hinduism contains the idea of a God, who has close affinities with the ineffable, attributeless God-head of such Christians as the Pseudo-Dionysius, Eckhart and Ruysbroeck, and of an enduring self, Atman, the Greater Self, which continues to exist amid the slow changes of the organism, the flux of sensations, the dissipation of ideas and the fading of memories. Buddhism, if it does not reject the idea of God, at least gives it a form different from that found in Hinduism. Further, in the doctrine of *anatta* (no soul) Buddhism *appears* to reject a belief in any permanent, enduring self. The *anatta* doctrine is, however, a difficult one to interpret and some schools of Buddhist thought incline towards a teaching very similar to the Hindu teaching on the Atman. There is neither need nor space to discuss it here.

Nevertheless, despite these differences in religio-philosophy, Buddhist spiritual exercises have many similarities with those of Hinduism. Indeed early Buddhism took over many of the yoga practices of Hinduism. Both have, to a great extent, the same objective, the creation of desirable states of mind, which

will lead not only to enlightenment, but also to a high degree
of moral conduct; for how one acts is dependent on one's
state of mind and one's belief in what constitutes the Real.
In both Buddhism and Hinduism meditation is conceived as
a consciously directed drawing upon the treasure house of
universal experience in the depth- (or super-) consciousness,
a turning inward and a transforming of the potential forces
of the depth-consciousness into active ones, so that one can
use them in the quest of completeness and enlightenment.

Two things particularly impress one as one studies Buddhist
spiritual exercises. The first is their deep psychological insight;
Buddhism had discovered long ago many of the truths about
the psyche which Western psychologists are only now
beginning to discover.

The second is the widespread emphasis placed in Buddhist
spiritual exercises on not only the engendering, but also the
radiation, of love and compassion. This is clearly evident in
the practice of the radiation of the four *Brahma Viharas*: love,
compassion, sympathetic joy and equanimity. One Buddhist
has stated that love and compassion for all sentient beings is
the chief motive of Buddhist meditation, while another said
to Aelfrida Tillyard: 'He who has not sympathy with all
living things, and with Nature cannot even begin to be a
Buddhist.' The Buddha himself called a sustained attitude of
love towards all sentient beings, 'dwelling in God'.

What, however, is needed in order to love one's fellows, a
Buddhist would maintain, is not any sort of vague altruism,
but a profound realization of the essential unity of life and the
mutual relationship which exists between all human beings.
The driving force must be more than mere altruism, it must
be much more akin to the spontaneous and selfless love of a
mother for her child, based on the essential oneness between
them. According to the Buddhist point of view, in order to
love a man must *become* love.

The virtues of love (*metta*), in the sense of kindliness,
friendliness; compassion (*karuna*), equivalent to the Christian
agapē, the virtue extolled by St Paul in his Hymn to Love
(I Corinthians, XIII); and sympathetic joy, i.e. joy in the

happiness and well-being of others, are virtues to be culti-
vated through spiritual exercises. They are called Sublime
Moods or Divine States of Mind.*

The cultivation of equanimity is regarded as of equal
importance. By equanimity the Buddhist means detachment,
in the sense of dispassion, not being affected by outward
things, indifference to everything that may happen to one, a
permanent calmness and serenity of mind. It may be doubtful
whether Rudyard Kipling was influenced by Buddhist religious
philosophy when he wrote the lines:

> If you can meet with triumph and disaster,
> And treat these two impostors just the same,

He was, however, expressing, reasonably faithfully, at least
part of what a Buddhist understands by equanimity.†

Not all types of Buddhist meditation are equally attractive.
The point of some of them is difficult for the Westerner to
understand. Some are definitely unattractive and stem not
merely from a mood of world-negation but of what looks like
a real hatred of life and of the body. Is it really necessary, in
order to impress on oneself the impermanence of all earthly
things, to meditate on the Ten Foul Things, e.g. the swollen
corpse, the discoloured corpse, the worm-fouled corpse etc.?
It is not unreasonable, surely, to feel that it is more spiritually
healthy to meditate in the mood of a St Francis of Assisi or a
Teilhard de Chardin.

In conclusion, while great stress is laid on love, compassion,
sympathetic joy and equanimity, the ultimate goal of Buddhist
meditation and contemplation is release from that state of
sorrow, ignorance and frustration which is the result of desire
and the illusion of egohood; the attainment of that freedom

* See 'The Radiation of Love' meditation in The Prayer Book. The
Metta Sutra and the Brahma Viharas are printed in the Anthology of the
third edition of my Mysticism, Section 5.

† One of my friends who read this and knows something of Rudyard
Kipling told me that Kipling was very interested, indeed influenced, by
the religious thought of India. He drew my attention to the concluding
chapters of his novel, Kim, where this interest is evident.

which comes when the illusion of individuality is overcome,
since consciousness has so expanded that it is able to participate in the consciousness of the whole; eventually to enter the
bliss of Nirvana.

> He goes
> Unto NIRVANA. He is one with Life,
> He lives not. He is blest, ceasing to be.
> OM, MANI PADME, HUM! the Dewdrop slips
> Into the shining Sea!*

3. ISLAMIC MEDITATION

We have already made a brief study of Islamic devotion as it
is found in the services of the mosque and in its numerous
Prayer Manuals in many languages. We saw there signs of the
widespread influence of Sufism, the mystical movement within
Islam.

While the techniques of Sufi spirituality, and the experiences
which spring out of them are similar to those found in the
mysticisms of other faiths, Sufism has an attractive quality
all its own.

Self-renunciation is preached as necessary for progress in
the spiritual life. It is not, however, a renunciation of the
world, in the sense of turning the back on the world. Rather
it is a plunging into the world, a merging of oneself in it.
Thus one may come not only to see reality as it truly is, but
also one may thereby reach union with God. Before that can
happen, however, the senses must be purified, the organs of
perception must become clear and limpid, affections and will
must be subjugated, the I-hood surrendered. Only thus is the
aspirant able to become in tune with the Universal Life; only
in so far as he is lost in God can he see the world as it is seen
by God.

This doctrine of self-mergence in both God and the world
resulted in a spirituality in which the vision is one of God as

---

* Sir Edwin Arnold: *The Light of Asia*. This long poem is based on the
Lalita Vistara, a work of the Mahasanghika School of Buddhism. It is
published by Routledge and Kegan Paul.

Absolute Beauty and Absolute Love, and of earthly beauty and love as revelations of the Divine Beauty and the Divine Love, a vision of God in Everything. This vision was given expression not only by great philosopher-mystics but even more by a galaxy of poet-mystics. Islam can claim a greater number of eminent mystical poets than any other faith.*

There is no need to describe Islamic spiritual exercises in detail. One finds the mantra used in somewhat the same way as elsewhere. Three features of these Islamic spiritual exercises which stand out may, however, be mentioned:

1. The importance attached to music as a means of arousing longing for, and love of, God.

2. The practice of using beautiful objects or thoughts as subjects of meditation. The aspirant is bidden to meditate on, for instance, a beautiful material object, or a beloved relative, or a tree springing up from him and giving shade to the whole world.

3. The use of symbolic language. Some of the Sufi mystical poems are full of it. For instance, the well-known *Rubaiyat* of Omar Khayyam employs an understood symbolic language. In it the tavern symbolizes the soul, wine, mystical ecstasy; the rose, the desert and the book, each have spiritual meanings. One finds a similar use of symbols in the poems of Hafiz of Shiraz.

Some features of Sufi practice are unlikely to have much appeal for the Western temperament, for instance the sort of wild dances used by the dervishes to induce a state of ecstasy. Such features one may, however, neglect, and concentrate on those which have real beauty and appeal.

12. Contemplative Meditation

THROUGHOUT this study we have been trying to show why throughout the ages men have prayed, and how they have prayed. We have examined the nature of prayer and the

* For some examples see the Section in the Anthology of *Mysticism*.

prayer-life and described the forms it has taken in the different world religions. We have considered the value of concepts, symbols and words and the part they inevitably play, not only in petitionary prayer, but also in that type of the Prayer of Meditation, which, though it may result in flashes of contemplative insight, is carried out primarily at the 'head' centre of personality. As, in the last chapters, we have gone on to describe some aspects of meditation as they are found in Christianity, Hinduism, Buddhism and Islam, we have at times been describing meditational prayer at a different level, that level when it passes from the 'head' to the 'heart' centre, becoming less reflective/rational, more contemplative/intuitive.

The level of the prayer-life which we shall try to describe and explain in this chapter may be called contemplative meditation, contemplative prayer, mystical prayer, or provided it is recognized as a lower level of contemplation than that of the advanced contemplative, simply contemplation. All of these terms have approximately the same meaning and I shall for the sake of variety sometimes use one, sometimes another. I shall also use the phrase, 'the way or path of contemplation'. We may also call this level of the prayer-life a deep movement into the realm of *the mystical*, in the sense I have used that phrase in *Religious Faith and Twentieth-Century Man*, and further elaborated in the first chapter of this book.

This contemplative level of the prayer-life, though it is known to increasing numbers, is not easy to describe to those who have not yet entered on this path. It is more difficult to write about it than to write about the higher levels of contemplation, those levels of spiritual awareness, of which there are numerous descriptions in the literature of mysticism, that state in which, to quote one writer, 'the psychology of man mingles with the psychology of God'. I can only do my best to write as clearly and vividly as possible.

Throughout the countless ages during which life has evolved on this planet, life has passed from its purely physical phase to the phase of *the psychical*.* *Homo sapiens* has not only

* This is the theme of the first part of Teilhard de Chardin's *Phenomenon of Man*.

a physical nature but also a psychical one, in which he has become more and more centred. Within this psychical realm he has created for himself a picture of the world. It is a world of images, of things seen, heard and felt. These images are gathered together in the mind in a complex of memories and are there measured, compared, classified and co-ordinated. Out of this process there emerges that pattern of general ideas and concepts which make up man's mental life and give him his picture of what he regards as real. For all practical purposes this imaged world, this creation of a world-picture by the human mind, is a real world. Nevertheless it is fundamentally an imagined world in the sense that it is the product of a particular, limited range of perceptions. That is what Eastern thinkers meant when they called the world perceived by the human mind and senses *maya*, or illusion. It was what St Paul meant when he said: 'The things which are seen are temporal; it is the things which are not seen that are eternal.'

Nor is it the great religious thinkers only who have reached the conclusion that our world, the world that we think we know so well, is an imagined world, a world in part at least of our own creation. One writer, commenting on the significance of the formulations of Einstein has said that they made clear that our concepts of space and time are particular forms of intuition. They can no more be divorced from our consciousness of them than can our concepts of colour or shape or size. Space has no objective reality except as an order or arrangement of the objects we perceive in it. And the same is true of time. It has no independent existence apart from the order of events by which we measure it.

That is as far as the scientists, *qua* scientists, are prepared to go. The great spiritual pioneers throughout the ages are prepared to go further. They say that the veil of *maya*, the world perceived by psychical man, can be penetrated by the development of powers inherent in him, that the psychical man is only the veil and the prophecy of the spiritual man.

The birth of the spiritual man from the psychical man, and how it may be brought about, is the theme of *The Yoga Sutras of Patanjali*, already referred to, which has been given the sub-title of 'The Book of the Spiritual Man'. In it Patanjali sets out the practical means whereby this birth can be brought about.

It is also the theme of the most profound teaching of St Paul, in whose writings it is intertwined with the theme of Jesus Christ, the Incarnation of the Divine Logos, as the supreme manifestation of the Spiritual Man in history, the divine Mediator, who is the firstborn of many brothers, and through participation in whose spirit the great regeneration can be accomplished. Consider such sayings as 'As many of you as have been baptized into Christ have put on Christ'; 'Ye are dead and your life is hid with Christ in God'; and 'I am crucified with Christ; yet I live, but it is no longer I [the psychical man] who lives; it is the Christ [the Spiritual Man] who now lives in me'.

Nowhere is the idea put more vividly than in the striking phrases in I Corinthians, Chapter XV. 'There is a natural body, and a spiritual body. And so it is written: The first Adam was made a living soul; the second Adam a quickening spirit.' 'The first man is of the earth, earthy; the second man is the Lord from heaven.' 'For as in Adam all die, even so in Christ shall all be made alive.'

And finally in the great passage on the redemption of the whole creation in Christ in the Epistle to the Romans: 'The whole creation groaneth and travaileth in pain until now. And not only they, but ourselves also, which have the first fruits of the Spirit, even we ourselves groan within ourselves, waiting for the adoption, to wit, the redemption of our body.'

This is not the same language as that of Patanjali, but anyone who has studied the writings of both cannot but feel that the Indian sage and the Christian apostle are speaking of the same thing, the transformation of the psychical man into the spiritual man.

The essential stages which every religion teaches must be passed through in order that the spiritual man may rise out of the ashes of the psychical man are the cleansing and subduing of that complex of passions: desire, hatred, ambition, envy, self-interest and self-will: which are part of the make-up of the psychical man, and the cleansing of perception, so that the veils of *maya* may be penetrated and reality seen as it truly is.

Every type of prayer, sincerely followed, is an instrument of this purpose. All the longings and aspirations of intense petitionary prayer, all those meditations on things as they really are, on motive, on dogma, etc., described earlier, are rungs in that ladder of prayer which psychical man must climb in order to attain the stature of spiritual man.

That form of prayer which we have called contemplative meditation or prayer is a further rung in this ladder. It is the attempt to penetrate more deeply into that secret place within oneself, where perhaps we may find, shining in the ground of our being, the Serene Light, the indwelling Christ, not a Christ standing over against ourselves, but the true Self of each one of us, the Buddha who dwells within, the Atman.

In all religions this sense of a divine indwelling is known, though it is conceived and spoken of in different ways.

Of the nature of contemplation and the two ways in which the term may be used I have written in Chapter 8. There is no need to repeat what was said there. Nor is this the place to describe the techniques of contemplative prayer. That I tried to do in *The Journey Inwards*, and more will be said in the Introduction to the second part of this book. So that my readers may get as clear an idea as possible of what contemplative prayer is, let me, however, end this chapter with a number of general observations.

1. The way of contemplation is like a high mountain which has to be climbed. Some, the great mystics, the contemplative saints, the cragsmen of the life of the spirit, have been able to reach the summit. They are, however, few. The less spiritually endowed must be content with ascending, so far as each is able, the lower slopes. Even that demands great effort and self-sacrifice. The majority never leave the valleys.

This ascent may also be conceived as a descent, an ever deeper descent into the depth-consciousness, in which is stored up the collective wisdom and insight of the human race and where the inner deity is enthroned; as a journey inwards into the innermost depths of personality.

2. The way of contemplation is not one way but many. The great pioneers describe a state of contemplation in which all concepts, all symbols and all images disappear in a *Void*, a state of pure intuitive awareness.

Eckhart calls this Void 'the central silence, the pure peace and abode of the heavenly birth'. He, and other mystics, have also called it 'a desert', 'a barren wilderness' or 'a waste'. It is a state of *sunyata* (emptiness) in the sense that consciousness is stripped of all its empirical contents and has discarded all ideas of multiplicity. St John of the Cross calls it a state of 'dim' Contemplation. Yet this Emptiness is full of life, illumination and an activity, which is different in kind from the activity of the senses; it is a *Plenum* – Void.

3. At this point we are, however, chiefly concerned with lower contemplation. It is a mistake to suppose, as some do, that in the practice of lower contemplation one should try and make the mind a blank. This is quite wrong. It is, however, true to say that one should try, so far as one is able, to rise above normal sense consciousness by disidentifying oneself with the body, senses and lower mind, but without losing awareness and consciousness of them. This is brought out very clearly in Phyllis Campbell's prayer to the Serene Light, used in contemplative prayer at this level:

> Serene Light, shining in the ground of my being,
> Draw me to Yourself!
> Draw me past the snares of the senses,
> Out of the mazes of the mind;
> Free me from symbols, from words,
> That I may discover
> The Signified,
> The Word Unspoken,
> In the darkness which veils the ground of my being.

Another aspect is brought out in this prayer from the Upanishads:

> May quietness descend upon my limbs,
> My speech, my breath, my eyes, my ears;

May all my senses wax clear and strong;
May Brahman [God] show himself unto me.

In practice what happens at this stage of contemplative prayer is that, of deliberate intent, we employ two types of perception, the intellectual-rational and contemplative-intuitive, which intermingle in various ways, sometimes one, sometimes the other, predominating. One passes backward and forward between the two. This is clearly evident in the meditations (or spiritual exercises) which are printed in *The Journey Inwards* and are also included in The Prayer Book which forms the second half of this book.

4. Meister Eckhart once said: 'The seed of God is in us. Given an intelligent and hard working farmer it will thrive and grow up to God, whose seed it is, and accordingly its fruit will be God-nature. Pear seeds grow into pear trees, nut seeds into nut trees, and God seed into God.'

The whole of the prayer-life sincerely followed is simply this, the cultivation and bringing to fruition of that seed of God which is present in everyone. As the intelligent farmer knows, successful cultivation depends on doing the right and appropriate thing at the proper time. So it is in the cultivation of the God-seed. Contemplative prayer is one process in this cultivation of the God-seed.

5. Out of the That we call God, who is Himself the Supreme Light, there streams forth a pure white light which vitalizes and illuminates the ego-consciousness. Functioning at its normal level of perception, the ego-consciousness is like a prism; it splits up the pure white light into a number of different colours which give it its picture of the phenomenal world. Thus it perceives a world of multiplicity. The ego-consciousness of man, however, is such that it stands at a point where, if it wishes, it can look out not on one but on two worlds, the multiple world of sense-perception, and also a world of pure light which reveals to it another world, not of multiplicity but of oneness. In contemplation one strives to enter as far as possible into this realm of pure light, so that one may apprehend the world and oneself as they really are.

6. The result of sincerely following the way of contemplation is both a gradual transformation of the personality, or, perhaps better, the selfhood, and also a new vision of the nature of Reality. As the Quaker, George Fox, said, 'The world smelt different.' The psychical man, slowly and laboriously perhaps, grows into the stature of the spiritual man, through the *realization* in direct experience of the presence of a Someone, or Something, within him which is not the phenomenal ego. It is an inner deity, which he may apprehend as Spirit, God, Self, the Christ (or the Buddha) Within, or the Atman, a Greater Self which is and is not him-self. It is not the self of which he is for most of the time conscious; yet he recognizes it as his real, his essential Self, the being he essentially is.

This realization of deity and of the true Self may take a personal or a non-personal form, and may be described in personalistic or non-personalistic terms.

In Eastern spirituality the realization is more often non-personal than in the West. In the experience of the great Christian contemplatives, however, this sense of a divine indwelling seems, the further they have advanced in the spiritual life, to become more and more non-personal. For instance, this is how in *The Adornment of the Spiritual Marriage*, the Blessed John Ruysbroeck describes the highest stage of what he calls the superessential or God-seeing life:

And here there is death in fruition * and a melting and dying into the Essential Nudity,† where all the Divine names, and all the living images which are reflected in the mirror of Divine Truth lapse in the Onefold and ineffable in waylessness and without reason. For in this unfathomable abyss of the Simplicity,‡ all things are wrapped in fruitive bliss; and the abyss itself may not be comprehended unless by the Essential Unity. To this the Persons § and all that lives

* Total attainment or complete and permanent possession.

† Roughly equivalent to the Buddhist Void or Emptiness.

‡ A word frequently found in the literature of mysticism, meaning wholeness, completeness, synthesis, a total undifferentiated act of spiritual perception.

§ i.e. of the Blessed Trinity.

in God, must give place; for here there is nought but an eternal rest in the fruitive embrace of an outpouring Love. And this is that wayless being which all interior spirits have chosen above all other things. This is the dark silence in which all lovers lose themselves.

7. Finally it must be emphasized that to follow the path of contemplation is not necessarily to try to escape from the world in order to dwell in some sort of nebulous pietistic state, remote from the activities of everyday life. In most ordinary folk the life of contemplative prayer and the life of action can be harmoniously combined. Each fertilizes and enriches the other. And indeed some of the greatest Christian contemplative saints were men and women who led very full lives of unselfish action.

In that beautiful manual of the spiritual life, *The Four Degrees of Passionate Love*, Richard of St Victor writes of the third degree of love:

> The third degree of love is when the mind of man is ravished into the abyss of divine light so that the soul, having forgotten all outward things, is altogether unaware of itself and passes out completely into its God. . . . The third degree hinders action, so that a man cannot be occupied about anything unless the power of the divine will draws or drives him.

In one who has reached this third degree the psychical man has been transformed into the spiritual man. But he cannot stay there. He must descend from the Mount of Transfiguration to the dusty market place.

In the third degree the soul is glorified, in the fourth she is humbled for God's sake. In the third she is conformed to the divine light, in the fourth she is humbled for God's sake. In the third she is conformed to the divine light, in the fourth she is conformed to the humility of Christ. And though in the third she is in a way almost in the likeness of God, nevertheless in the fourth she begins to empty herself, taking the form of a servant.

The time has come to pass on to describe the higher levels of prayer, the way of higher contemplation. But first, let us pause and devote a chapter to the nature of *mantras* and their use in contemplative meditation.

13. Mantras: Their Nature and Use in Contemplative Meditation

THOUGH the mantra is extensively used and occupies an important place in the spiritual exercises of Hinduism and Buddhism and is known to the Eastern Orthodox Church in the Prayer of Jesus, it has been little emphasized in the spiritual exercises of the Western Church. That is not to say that some form of mantra has not been and, indeed, is used. It is probable that many spiritually minded Catholics, particularly in religious orders, use the Rosary as a form of mantra, a means of keeping the mind in a state of recollection; and in the medieval mystical treatise, *The Cloud of Unknowing*, the use of a definite mantra is recommended. The passage, which is a perfect description of contemplative prayer, reads as follows:

And yet, nevertheless, it behoveth a man or a woman that hath long time been used to these meditations [i.e. on his own unworthiness, on the Passion of Christ, etc.], nevertheless to leave them, and put them and hold them far down under the cloud of forgetting, if ever he shall pierce the cloud of unknowing betwixt him and his God. Therefore what time thou purposest thee to this work, and feelest by grace that thou art called to God, lift then up thine heart into God with a meek stirring of love; and mean God that made thee, and bought thee, and that graciously hath called thee to thy degree, and receive none other thought of God. And yet not all these, but if thou list; for it sufficeth enough, a naked intent direct unto God without any other cause than Himself.

And if thee list have this intent lapped and folden in one word, for thou shouldest have better hold thereupon, take thee but a little word of one syllable; for so it is better than of two, for ever the shorter it is the better it accordeth with the work of the Spirit. And such a word is this word GOD or this word LOVE. Choose thee whether thou wilt, or another; as thee list, which that thee liketh best of one syllable. And fasten this word to thine heart, so that it never go thence for thing that befalleth . . .

With this word, thou shalt beat on this cloud and this darkness above thee. With this word, thou shalt smite down all manner of thought under the cloud of forgetting.

Quaint though this passage may be to modern ears, seldom has the intent and practice of the use of a mantra been brought out more simply, clearly and precisely. The repetition of the syllable, *Om*, in Eastern meditation is exactly the same.

There is, further, a story of someone who wanted to know how St Francis prayed. He was sharing a room with the saint and when St Francis got up in the night to pray listened to what he would say. All he heard was the constant repetition of the single word, 'Jesus'.

But the reader may be asking: What precisely is a mantra? That he may not know is not surprising. The *Concise Oxford Dictionary* gives no definition of the word, 'mantra'. So let me first set out a few of the definitions which I have found:

1. A sacred sentence or a form of creative sound.

2. A microcosm of some eternal reality, or a particular aspect of it which it is desired to contemplate.

3. A peg on which to hang one's most profound inner experience.

4. A means of polarizing the mind in the direction in which one wants it to go and preventing it wandering, so that it remains firmly fixed on an idea in order that the idea may have its fullest revealing effect.

5. A means of awakening dormant forces in the soul, so that it may be enabled to establish contact with the depth-consciousness and so to enter into a wider life and a deeper illumination.

The most famous Eastern mantras are of unknown antiquity. The theory of their efficacy is based on a belief in the effect of particular sounds, the spiritual and psychological effects of which have been subjects of long study. Some spiritual exercises are definitely designed to cultivate increased sensitivity to different sounds.

This theory is not difficult to understand. Most of us are aware from our own experience that a particular musical phrase or a particular grouping of instruments can have a deep emotional effect. Similarly some line or stanza of verse can strike deep chords of feeling, one cannot say exactly why.

Does it reside only in the sound of the words? Or does some hidden association play a part?

There is, for instance, one poem in William Morris' *Early Prose Romances* which has that effect on me. It runs:

> Christ keep the Hollow Land
> All the summertide;
> Still we cannot understand
> Where the waters glide;
> Only dimly seeing them
> Coldly slipping through
> Many green-lipped cavern mouths
> Where the hills are blue.

There seems to be little in it; a pleasant little romantic poem. Yet the lines:

> Christ keep the Hollow Land
> All the summertide;

have haunted me ever since I first read them as far back as 1913. I could quote other examples.

Let us next consider some of the best known Eastern mantras. One, the Great Mantra, *Om mani padme hum* has been discussed earlier. Not only do all mantras begin with *Om*; it is also itself a complete mantra. It is the mantra of the invocation of the Sacred Name of God, the mantra of dedication. It has also been called the mantra of the nature of the True Self, which is found by one who is prepared to look into the depths of himself, 'with a seeing that is himself seeing himself', and realize what he, in his essential nature, is, and not what outwardly he appears to be. It is clear that what the author of *The Cloud of Unknowing* is describing in his own particular way is the *Om* mantra. The repetition of the word, Jesus, by St Francis was a Christo-centric mantra.

One of the best known Hindu mantras is the Gayatri mantra. In Sanscrit it runs as follows: *Om. Bhūr bhuvah swah: Tat savitur varenyam bhargo devasya dhīmahi; Dhiyo yo nah prachodayāt. Om.* Though mantras cannot be adequately translated this has been translated: 'Let us meditate upon the glorious radiance of that Supreme Being who has created the universe. May He enlighten our hearts and direct our understanding.'

Of this mantra Maharishi Devendranath Tagore, father of the better-known Rabindranath Tagore, wrote in his autobiography:

For generations we have been initiated in the Gayatri mantra. It runs in our blood. I continued to worship Him daily by means of the Gayatri mantra, before touching food. . . . And now I obtained this thing beyond all hope that He was not far from me; not only a silent witness, but that He dwells within my soul and inspires all my thoughts.*

In the seventeenth chapter of the *Bhagavad Gita* Krishna, the Hindu Christ, tells his devotees to worship him by means of the *Om Tat Sat* mantra. In the same chapter the significance of the mantra is explained. Each of the three words is a designation of Brahman. The meaning of *Om* has already been explained. *Tat* designates Brahman regarded as the Absolute and is used by those seeking liberation and enlightenment and renouncing all reward for their good deeds. The word *Sat* contains a number of meanings. Its primary meaning is Being and so it may be said to designate God as Being-in-itself. It also, however, contains the idea of goodness, so that all actions carried out in faith and dedicated to God are *sat*.

The next mantra to be considered, *Om namo Nārāyanāya*, is of peculiar interest. It is called the eight-syllable mantra of the Supreme Being. Into these eight syllables is packed a complete religious philosophy. *Om* is God, conceived as the Inexpressible, the Unconditioned, the Unknowable to the intellect. *Namo* expresses the idea of the approach to the inexpressible, attributeless Godhead through aspects of Its activity, self-giving and manifestation in the phenomenal world. This is expressed in the theology of Hinduism in the Trinity, Vishnu, Shiva and Ishwara, regarded as 'lesser gods', or as symbols of the Unknowable One, Brahman. In Christianity a similar doctrine is found, the doctrine of the Blessed Trinity in Unity. *Nara* means 'man', *ayana*, 'the coming';

* Quoted in Tillyard: *Spiritual Exercises.*

thus *Narayana** is 'the coming man', the divine and Universal Self, perfect, Archetypal Man, man as he shall be when he attains perfection. Translated, the mantra would run: 'In the presence of the divine (*Om*) I make devotion to the Archetypal Man.' But the Archetypal Man is also called the Son of Man, the title which Jesus took for Himself, and by some of the early Christian writers He is regarded as the Representative Man, every man in his potentiality. So *Narayana* also contains the idea of the Incarnation of the Supreme Being, in whom the perfect man is revealed. Thus for a Christian using the mantra it would mean: 'In the presence of the God Most High, I adore and invoke the Lord Jesus Christ as True God and True Man; and I place myself within His Risen and Glorified Life, that through inner participation in that life I may be made one with Him.'

This mantra, therefore, is a Christ-mantra of great beauty. Not only that, it is also a mantra of the Perennial Philosophy,† in which the That we call God may be contemplated in three ways, in His non-personal aspect as the ineffable, attributeless Godhead, in His personal, active, self-revealing aspect – in Christianity, as we have seen, this takes the form of the doctrine of the Blessed Trinity – and in the Incarnation of the Divine Being – in Christianity, again, found in the Incarnation of the Divine Logos, the Second Person of the Holy Trinity, in Jesus Christ, who is the Representative, Archetypal Man.

So far we have been discussing mantras as they are found in the Eastern religions. We have already said, however, that in the Prayer of Jesus mantric prayer is practised in the Eastern Orthodox Church. It will be useful, therefore, to consider the practice of the Prayer of Jesus in some detail.

The material for the study of the Prayer of Jesus is easily available in English. All the ascetic writings on it are contained in the five volumes of the *Philokalia*, preserved in the

---

* The change from *Narayana* to *Narayanaya* is to satisfy that rule of euphony which governs the construction of eastern mantras. See Wood: *Yoga* (Penguin Books), pp. 200–201.

† For a full description, see my *Religious Faith and Twentieth-Century Man*, Chapter 11 (Penguin Books).

monasteries of Mount Athos, selections from which have been published in *Writings from the Philokalia* (Faber and Faber). A shorter and more useful account for the general reader is *On the Prayer of Jesus, from the Ascetic Essays of Bishop Ignatius Brianchaninov*,* translated by Father Lazarus (John Watkins). It contains a very clear introduction on the Prayer by Alexander d'Agapeyeff.

The spiritual exercise based on the Jesus Prayer is called *Hesychasm*, and has been developed in Christian monasteries in the East since almost Apostolic times. The important point to note is that its performance is regarded as a method of enlightenment, a technique of passing into a higher spiritual state. The words of the Jesus Prayer are simple: 'Lord Jesus Christ, Son of God, have mercy on me, a sinner.' Thus it is similar to the '*Kyrie eleison, Christe eleison, Kyrie eleison*', the very early Christian prayer which is used in the Eucharistic Liturgy.

It is a way of praying, but, as is made clear, it differs from the ordinary idea of prayer, e.g. of prayer as asking for something. It has a different objective; it is, in d'Agapeyeff's words, 'a scientific attempt to change the one who prays'.

The Jesus Prayer is practised as follows: first of all it is said aloud a specific number of times each day 'in silence and solitude'; then it is repeated silently an increased number of times during the day and night, and, finally, it is taken down into the 'heart'. Thus it has all the characteristics of the mantras developed in the Eastern religions.

The repeating of the prayer aloud is regarded as a conditioning of the body, i.e. the acquiring of a habit. The silent repetition is a conditioning of the mind and a means of acquiring concentration. At this stage the prayer is being 'thought'. When the habit of concentration has been acquired, it is then possible to take the prayer down into the 'heart', where it 'lives ITSELF with every heart beat'. 'When the Jesus Prayer is used in this way,' writes d'Agapeyeff, 'the disciple

* Bishop Brianchaninov was an early nineteenth-century bishop of the Russian Orthodox Church.

changes himself, remakes himself and becomes a totally different person.'

A prayer of the 'mind' becomes a prayer of the 'heart'. What does that mean and how does it happen? I cannot do better than quote d'Agapeyeff again:

Man is a trinity of energies, which may be called spirit, soul and body; of these soul may be regarded as a vehicle for the spirit in the body. By repeating the Jesus Prayer with 'warmth of feeling' and conscientious fervour, man touches that part of himself which is created in the image and likeness of God and learns how he, himself, can become a Son of God.

Here, put in a particular way, is a very clear description of the objective not only of the Jesus Prayer, but also of all mystical prayer and all contemplative meditation.

It is the objective also of a great deal of Hindu and Buddhist meditation. In a description of her experience of a course of meditation in a Thailand monastery one of my English Buddhist friends wrote:

He [her spiritual director] taught the importance of developing the heart position of the mind. This could best be described as the state of mind one adopts when looking at a non-representational painting. A sort of baffled questioning from the heart. I have found the value of this enormous because it stops the incessant chatter of the mind and allows things to appear in their own right.

Before bringing this description of the practice of the Jesus Prayer to an end, let me quote a few illuminating passages from Bishop Brianchaninov's book:

Experience will soon show that in using this method, especially at first, the words should be pronounced with extreme unhurriedness so that the mind may have time to enter the words as into forms. . . . One must train oneself as if one were reading by syllables – with the same unhurriedness.

In order that the true teaching in the elementary stages of this mental prayer should not be lost, they [i.e. the spiritual directors] expound in writing the actual beginning, ways and exercises – how beginners must train themselves to enter with the mind into the land of the heart, and there truly and without delusion perform prayer with the mind.

Try to restore, or more exactly, to enclose your thoughts in the words of the prayer. If on account of its infancy, it wearies and wanders, lead it in again.

It is one thing frequently to look into the heart, and another to entrust the watch of the heart to the mind, that prince and bishop that offers spiritual sacrifices to Christ.

Thus, he who prays by the method proposed by St John of the Ladder will pray with the lips and the mind and the heart. And when he becomes proficient in prayer, he will acquire mental prayer and the prayer of the heart.

It is one thing to pray with attention with the participation of the heart; it is another thing to descend with the mind into the temple of the heart and from there to offer mystical prayer filled with divine grace and power. The second is the result of the first. The attention of the mind during prayer draws the heart into sympathy. With the strengthening of the attention, sympathy of heart and mind is turned into union of heart and mind. Finally when attention makes the prayer its own, the mind descends into the heart for the most profound and sacred service of prayer.

Seldom has the path of contemplative meditation and mystical prayer been so well described.

Before we leave the Jesus Prayer let me make two further points:

1. There are no short cuts either into the depths and completeness of the Jesus Prayer or into any of the higher stages of prayer. The beginner must be content to start at the beginning and not think that everything is easy or quickly accomplished.

2. There are constant warnings on the dangers which beset those who would ascend to the higher reaches of prayer. Some writers on the Jesus Prayer regard a spiritual director as essential. The reason is that the deeper sorts of prayer can have profound psychological effects. One is delving down

into the depths of the psyche, into the dark corners of the soul. One begins to see oneself as one really is, and it may not be pleasant; indeed it may be more than merely unpleasant. As d'Agapeyeff writes: 'As a pool when vigorously stirred becomes muddy before the dirt subsides and the water becomes crystal clear, so the inner psyche of man becomes turbulent and even violent when stirred by such a deeply religious exercise as Hesychasm.'

The Jesus Prayer was, moreover, first designed for monks and only later did it come to be used by the laity. Among monks the practice of the Prayer was a continuous occupation going on day and night. Those of us who lead the active life have neither time nor inclination to live our prayer-life with the same intensity as is possible for members of religious orders. The practice of the higher types of prayer and the use of mantras are, however, not only fully suitable but definitely valuable for those who are not highly endowed spiritually, provided that they know their possible results and do not try to run before they can walk. Unfortunately skilled directors thoroughly versed in spiritual psychology are not easily to be found, particularly in the Anglican and Protestant Churches, especially for those who find themselves compelled to stand at the intersection of Christianity and everything which is not nominally Christian. And, as both St Teresa and St John of the Cross discovered, not all spiritual directors are to be trusted.

As has already been said, the deliberate use of mantras has not been systematically developed in the Western Church nor, though the spontaneous use of what are in effect mantras or of other prayers which have a mantric quality, is probably not uncommon, is their value widely realized, or their practice widely taught.

Not all present-day Christians are likely to find the particular words of the Jesus Prayer congenial, nor will more than a small minority be attracted towards the use of one or more of the ancient Eastern mantras.

As I thought about this there dawned on me that in the

middle of one of St Paul's duller Epistles, the Epistle to the Galatians, there was a perfect Christian mantra. In Greek it runs thus: *Christo sunestaurōmai. Zō de, ouketi ego; zē de en emoi Christos.* Translated it is: 'I am crucified with Christ. Nevertheless I still live; but it is not I any more [not the old phenomenal ego]; it is the Christ who now lives in me.' It can be called the 'transformation into Christ' mantra, the mantra of the transformation of the psychical man into the spiritual man. It may, or may not, have some affinity with the mantra in the Buddhist *Heart Sutra*: *Om. Gatē, Gatē, Paragatē, Parasamgatē, Bodhi Svaha.* (Gone, Gone, Gone beyond, Gone altogether beyond, O what an awakening.)

When repeated in Greek this Christian mantra has something of the sonority of the Eastern mantras. Actually it is two mantras, which may be combined or be used separately. 'I am crucified with Christ', is the renouncement of the lower self. The second part expresses the transformation which results from this renouncement, the inner realization of one's true Self as the Christ who dwells within. In practice, when said in Greek, the mantra may be reduced to seven words: *Christo sunestaurōmai – ouketi ego – Christos en emoi.*

Those who do not wish to repeat a mantra in Greek may use a similar mantra in English: Christ in me and I in Him.

How may mantras be used with effect in contemplative meditation by ordinary people? Eastern spiritual directors speak of being initiated into a mantra. The guru helps the pupil to find the mantra most suitable for himself. All mantras are not suitable for everyone. Since we may have no one to direct us, most of us will have to discover our own mantras. As has already been pointed out, mantras must be used with discretion. They can be 'words of power' and, if used too intensely, can have profound psychological effects, not always safe or beneficial.

One Eastern writer has stated that simply repeated without understanding a mantra is spiritually valuable, i.e. the sound itself does the work; if understood, its value is, however, much increased. For many Westerners, to understand may be necessary for a mantra to work its spiritual effect.

The definitions given earlier show clearly what a mantra is and what its use is designed to effect. The descriptions and interpretations of the Jesus Prayer and of a number of famous Eastern mantras will have assisted some intellectual understanding of them. That is all that is possible here. Real understanding can only come through experience of their use. Let me emphasize again, a mantra is a prayer of the heart. By means of mantras we endeavour to take our prayer down from the head centre into the heart centre of being, to bring about a union of mind and heart, so that what is first understood intellectually is understood intuitively, so that the prayer may 'live itself'. Thus our prayer may become not only an instrument of deeper understanding of the real, but also of transformation of the whole being.

May I conclude this chapter by repeating one of the passages from Brianchaninov's book already quoted, which summarizes his basic teaching:

The attention of the mind during prayer draws the heart into sympathy. With the strengthening of the attention, sympathy of heart and mind is turned into union of heart and mind. Finally when attention [i.e. concentration] makes the prayer its own, the mind descends into the heart for the most profound and sacred service of prayer.

Perhaps before concluding this chapter something ought to be said, even though it be briefly, about *mandalas*. For much fuller information I must refer the reader to the section, 'The Mandala in Contemplation', in my *The Journey Inwards* (pages 80–90), where a number of illustrations are given, and to Tucci: *The Theory and Practice of the Mandala* (Rider).

A mandala is a visual symbol in which some truth (or truths) about spiritual reality is expressed in pictorial or diagrammatic form. A true mandala must be a spontaneous creation which originates at a deep layer of personality, when, like all true symbols, it has an innate revealing power, and so can be used as an object of contemplation. It is used in the same way as a crucifix, picture or ikon can be used. One concentrates one's mind on it, while at the same time trying to keep the analytic intellect as quiet as possible, simply gazes at it, contemplates it, and allows it to work on one. In order that it may work, it is necessary to know, at one level of the mind, even if only dimly, the truth it is intended to show forth. The use of mandalas has been more fully developed in the East than in the West.

14. The Higher Levels of Prayer

THE time has now come to describe the higher ranges of the prayer-life, the path trodden by the contemplative, the so-called Mystic Way.

The Mystic Way is divided by Christian writers into the three stages of *Purgation*, *Illumination* (also called *Contemplation* or *Proficiency*) and *Union*. The Blessed John Ruysbroeck uses a somewhat different schema which is in some ways simpler and more illuminating. In *The Adornment of the Spiritual Marriage* he tells of three stages which he calls (1) the *Active Life*, a life which may become in a real sense illuminated, but is not yet the life of the fully 'inward man'; (2) the *Interior Life*, the life of the truly 'inward man', which, in its advanced stages, seems to be one of almost complete union with God; and (3) the *Super-essential or God-seeing Life*, in which there is complete and permanent attainment.

The Indian philosopher, Radhakrishnan, also divides the Way into three stages, which he calls *Purification*, *Concentration* and *Identification*. He describes the path to full perfection and attainment as lying 'through a gradual increase in impersonality by an ever deeper and more intense unifying of the self with a greater than itself.' 'In this process,' he writes, 'prayer, worship, meditation, philosophy, art and literature all play their part, since all help in purifying the inner being and disposing it more and more for contact with the divine.'*

* Radhakrishnan: *Eastern Religion and Western Thought* (Oxford University Press).

These descriptions of the Mystic Way supplement each other. No plan of the Way should be regarded as more than a general one. A study of the literature of mysticism makes it perfectly clear that the spiritual journeys of the mystics have varied considerably and that the divisions between the different stages are not definite and clear cut; there is a good deal of overlapping. There are, further, confusing variations in the use of descriptive terms.

In an illuminating passage in her Seventh Revelation, Julian of Norwich describes her own experience of passing from one state to another time after time:

> After this He shewed a sovereign ghostly pleasance in my soul. . . . I was in all peace and rest. . . . This lasted but a while and I was left to myself in heaviness and weariness of life. . . . And anon after this our blessed Lord gave me again the comfort and the rest in soul . . . and then the pain showed again to my feeling, and then the joy and the blessing, and now that one, and now that other, divers times – I suppose about twenty times.*

The nature of the full Illuminative Life is vividly described by St John of the Cross in *The Spiritual Canticle*. In full Illumination, he writes, the soul has a vision and a foretaste of the high state to which it will eventually rise. To it is revealed the secret wisdom of God. It possesses a strange sort of knowledge of Him, a knowledge of an intuitive kind, stripped of all accidents and images. Truth is seen in its purity, though not as yet clearly; in St John's words, it is 'dim'; the knowledge is not yet complete. He compares what is seen to a ray or image of that full Beatific Vision, which can only be possessed in heaven.

In this state of the Illuminative Life the mind becomes completely tranquil; it rests in God. It has, moreover, and this is important, a new vision of the phenomenal world, for the whole creation is seen as glorifying God in its own particular way, and possessing Him according to its particular capacity.

* Julian of Norwich, *Revelations of Divine Love*, edited by Grace Warrack (Methuen).

Further, the whole nature of the man is changed. The soul is completely conformed to the divine will; it is at last freed from the violence of the passions. It rests, happy and passive, in its participation in the Divine Essence.* It has passed beyond the stage of words and petitions; it is inarticulate. One medieval mystic described this level of prayer as 'naught else but a yearning of soul', wherein the soul is united to God in its ground without the intervention of imagination or reason or of anything but a simple attention of the mind and a humble, self-forgetting action of the will.

In order that the nature of these higher ranges of prayer may be grasped by the reader as clearly as possible, I shall describe them as they have been formulated not only in the writings of Christian contemplatives but also by the mystics of the East. As may be expected, there is a good deal of variation in description. Not only, as we have already seen, do these prayer-experiences vary according to different temperaments, not only are what are described spiritual states which do not lend themselves to precise description, and which those who have experienced them confess they do not fully understand, but also the descriptions and formulations are expressed in terms of different religious philosophies.

But in spite of these different descriptions and formulations, one cannot escape the conviction that the inner experiences described are contacts with the same Reality. In the next chapters the reader will be able to examine the evidence and reach his own conclusion.

15. The Higher Levels of Prayer in the Christian Tradition

FOR those who wish to explore this spiritual journey the writings of the great contemplatives provide a mass of

---

* In *The Dark Night of the Soul* St John of the Cross gives a somewhat different, though not conflicting, description of what he calls the 'Ten Degrees of the Mystical Ladder of Divine Love'.

various and fascinating material.* Within the Christian tradition some may prefer the poetic and symbolic quality of the Blessed John Ruysbroeck, some the paradoxical intellectuality of Meister Eckhart, some the 'homeliness' of Julian of Norwich, some the scientific precision of St John of the Cross, the 'mystic's mystic' *par excellence*. Many may, however, find St Teresa the most useful guide to start on. She has a particularly vivid charm and a deep modesty. Since she wrote for the sisters of her own community, many of whom were not capable of going very far, she takes immense pains to make herself crystal clear. She is a mistress of the apt simile and, throughout her writings, one is continually conscious of a spirit of frank exploration; she does not mind confessing that in some previous account her description may not have been sufficiently exact. So, since the space at my disposal is limited, I shall base the main part of this chapter on her writings.

THE PRAYER OF QUIET

There is a way of contemplative prayer which any reasonably spiritual individual should be able to follow with benefit. Sincerely and regularly followed it is able to lead, occasionally and perhaps only for a short time at first, into the Prayer of Simplicity and Simple Regard.† In the earlier forms of contemplative prayer the mental faculties are wide awake. One is still moving in a world of forms and images; one is fully aware of one's own individuality. Though one may be conscious of the Divine Reality, one is still also conscious of one's own separateness. In the Prayer of Inward Silence and Simply Looking, one *begins* to move into a new world, on to a new place of silence, where imagination and thought begin to fade out. The self begins to find itself released from the burden of time. The voices of the world begin to die away.

* *Vide* the Anthology of my *Mysticism* (Penguin Books). In the first part of the book the stages of Contemplation and Union are fully described.

† This is the formal name of this form of prayer. It may be called the Prayer of Inward Silence (or Passivity) and Simply Looking and Waiting.

Those who are capable of this Prayer of Inward Silence and Simply Looking and Waiting may, through grace, move into the *Prayer of Quiet*. With the Prayer of Quiet we reach the stage of true mystical prayer. It is something definitely 'given' and cannot be obtained by one's own effort. One can only prepare oneself for its onset. In the *Way of Perfection* St Teresa gives a very clear description of it:

This is a supernatural thing, which we cannot obtain by any effort on our own part. The soul rests in peace ... all [her] powers are at rest. The soul understands with an understanding quite different from that given by the external senses, that she is now quite close to God and that, if she drew a little nearer, she would become one thing with Him by union. ... The soul understands He is here, though not so clearly. She does not know how she understands; she sees only that she is in the Kingdom ...

It is like the suspension of all internal and external powers. ... The faculties are at peace and do not wish to move. ... I think, therefore, that since the soul is so completely happy in this prayer of quiet, the will must be united, during most of the time, with Him who alone can satisfy it.*

Meister Eckhart may have been thinking of something like the Prayer of Quiet when he said:

To achieve the interior act one must assemble all one's powers as it were into the corner of one's soul, where, secreted from images and forms, one is able to work. In this silence, this quiet, the Word is heard.

THE FOUR WATERS

In the little opuscule of the Four Waters, in her autobiography, St Teresa compares the degrees of prayer to four ways of watering a garden. At first the water has, as it were, to be drawn up by hand from a deep well; this involves a lot of hard work. When, as a result of progress in the prayer-life, the senses have been stilled and are not getting too much in the way, the work becomes easier. It is as if the well had been

* St Teresa: *The Way of Perfection*, translated by Alice Alexander (The Mercier Press, Cork).

fitted with a windlass; it becomes possible to get more water by less effort. The third degree is when all voluntary activities of the mind have ceased. Then it is as if a little river flowed through the garden, by means of which the garden is irrigated. Finally, in the last and highest degree, God Himself waters the garden with His rain; no human effort at all is called for.

The Interior Castle: THE SEVEN MANSIONS

The Interior Castle, written later, when St Teresa had become more proficient, is much longer and more detailed. In it the stages of the spiritual life are imaged as a passing from the outer courtyard, through seven mansions, to the innermost mansion of the castle of the soul. Somewhat confusedly, another 'map' of the castle is introduced for a particular purpose. The castle has not only seven main mansions but also many mansions, some above, some below, others at each side, through which the spiritual adventurer may 'roam about'. What St Teresa is intent on making clear is that different people progress towards perfection, not by one but by different paths, and that the experiences are never the same. We need not, however, bother about this secondary map.

The courtyard of this castle is cold and dark, filled with all sorts of obnoxious and poisonous creatures; inside everything is full of light. The keys which open the gates of the castle are vocal prayer and the beginnings of the Prayer of Meditation. The first three mansions correspond approximately to the stages of what is commonly called the Way of Purgation or Purification, the stage of the 'true active life', described by Ruysbroeck in the First Book of *The Adornment of the Spiritual Marriage*.

Up to now the aspirant has only caught glimpses of those ultra-natural realms, in which the true contemplative lives. As he enters the Fourth Mansion he finds that he has entered them, that something is happening, something which is not of his own volition, which is no longer dependent on his own effort. The Fourth Mansion corresponds to the Second Water

of the autobiography and to the Prayer of Quiet. Indeed St
Teresa uses the same simile:

Let us imagine two fountains with two basins which fill with
water. . . . Now these two fountains are supplied with water by
different means. One is obtained from far away, by a number of
aqueducts and much machinery; the other receives it direct from
the spring, and the basin fills without the least sound. When the
spring is plentiful, as this of which we are speaking, from the full
basin there flows a great stream. . . . Very different from this is the
water which comes by aqueducts. This water signifies the satis-
factions derived from meditation. We obtain them by reflections,
by the consideration of created things, and by teasing our minds.
. . . To the other fountain the water comes from the spring itself,
which is God.*

St Teresa's expanding experience of mystical prayer enables
her, in *The Interior Castle*, to describe a type of prayer, which
she calls the Prayer of Recollection, which immediately
precedes the Prayer of Quiet. It seems to have affinities with
what above has been called the Prayer of Simplicity and Simple
Regard, rather than with Recollection, as, up to now, it has
been described.

The eyes may close involuntarily and one may experience a desire
for solitude. Though there is no conscious effort on our part, the
soul seems to be constructing an edifice for the prayer of which I
have spoken, and the senses and exterior things seem to be losing
their hold. . . . Some say that the soul enters into herself, others that
she rises above herself.†

Yet meditation and other activities of the understanding
continue. This Prayer of Recollection seems to be a sort of
ante-room to the Fourth Mansion.

The Fifth Mansion corresponds approximately to the Third
Water and describes what is known as The Prayer of Passive
Union or the Spiritual Betrothal. While this prayer lasts the
soul is completely asleep to the things of the world, completely
abandoned to God, who has for the moment taken complete

* *The Interior Castle*, translated into English by a Discalced Carmelite
(Sands and Co.).
† op. cit.

possession of it. St Teresa states that never in her experience did it last for more than half an hour, but that it was quite unforgettable.

To describe this state St Teresa uses one of her inimitable similes, the simile of the silkworm:

You must already have heard of the marvellous way silk is produced . . . and how seeds resembling small grains of pepper . . . in the warm weather, when the mulberry trees begin to put forth leaf, come to life . . . the silkworms are fed on the leaves of the mulberry, and when they are fully grown, some twigs are placed for them, among which, from their little mouths, they spin silk from within their own bodies, and make very compact cocoons, in which they enclose themselves. And thus end these great ugly worms, and from those same cocoons issue very graceful little white butterflies.*

The Sixth Mansion, the state of incipient union is, in St Teresa's description, one of a mixture of intense joy and deep pain. It may have affinities with the state which St John of the Cross calls the Dark Night of the Spirit. The soul knows and has occasional meetings with the Divine Lover, but the state of full and permanent union has not yet been attained. The betrothed soul restlessly longs for the consummation of the Spiritual Marriage.

In the Seventh Mansion St Teresa tells of this consummation, the most sublime and intimate of all spiritual experiences; so vividly and exactly described by St John of the Cross:

The understanding of the soul is now the understanding of God; and its will is the will of God; and its memory is the memory of God; and its delight is the delight of God; and the substance of the soul, although it is not the substance of God, for into this it cannot be changed, is nevertheless united in Him and absorbed in Him, and is thus God by participation in God.†

The Spiritual Marriage is (as are all the higher levels of the spiritual life), by its very nature, indescribable. St Teresa uses a series of similes. It is 'as if two wax candles were

* *The Interior Castle*, op. cit.
† Allison Pear's translation: *The Living Flame of Love*.

joined together so closely that their light is but one'; yet the candles can be separated one from the other. Or it may be compared to 'water falling from the sky into a river or fountain, where the waters are united, and it would no longer be possible to divide them, or to separate the water of the river from that which has fallen from the heavens'. She also likens it to 'a tiny stream which falls into the sea; there is no possibility of separating them'; or to light entering a room through two windows and making one light.

The Four Degrees of Passionate Love

As I said at the beginning of this chapter, there is no space to tell of all the different ways this ascent to union with God is described by the Christian contemplative saints. I should have liked, for instance, to include the vivid description given of it by the Blessed John Ruysbroeck in *The Adornment of the Spiritual Marriage*. But I shall conclude with a particularly beautiful account from *The Four Degrees of Passionate Love* of Richard of St Victor, which in describing the fourth and highest degree as a descent in compassion into the humility of Christ differs from any other account I know:

In the first degree the soul returns to itself; in the second it ascends to God; in the third it passes into God; in the fourth it descends below itself. In the first and second it is raised; in the third and fourth it is transfigured. In the first it ascends to itself; in the second it transcends itself; in the third it is conformed to the glory of Christ; in the fourth it is conformed to the humility of Christ. Again in the first it is led back; in the second it is transferred; in the third it is transformed; in the fourth it is resurrected.*

Seldom has so much spiritual wisdom and experience been put into so few words.

* Richard of St Victor: *Select Writings on Contemplation*, translated by Clare Kirchberger (Faber).

16. The Higher Levels of Prayer in Hinduism, Buddhism and Islam

THIS same path of mystical prayer from Purgation, through Illumination, to Union, to adopt the classical description of the Mystic Way, is found described in varying ways in the literature of other higher religions.

In the Hindu Vedanta it is called *raja-yoga*, the 'kingly' way to union. The follower of *raja-yoga* aims at the experience of inward illumination beyond all sensation, unaffected by any influence from the outside world of sense, and without resting on any object. A common symbol to describe this way is that of the lotus, which rises in the mud, grows upward through the water and flowers in the air and sunshine, drawn ever upward by the inner impulse of its own being.

THE PASSING THROUGH THE EIGHT *Jhanas*

In the Pali Canon of Theravada Buddhism the Way is described as a passing through eight *jhanas*, four lower and four higher. The equivalent of these eight *jhanas* is also found in Mahayana Buddhism. To translate the word, *jhana*, as rapture or ecstasy, as is sometimes done, is, in view of the normal meaning given to these words in ordinary language and the way they are used in the literature of Christian mysticism, misleading. The *jhanas* are better defined as progressive expansions of consciousness in which both our false ideas of life and matter and the fetters of rational thought are dispersed by the rays of enlightenment.

(1) In the first the ordinary processes of thought are still active. The mind continues to reflect, but without any attachment to such objects of sense as are still present.

(2) In the second *jhana* the mind gradually grows more still and the things of the world become more remote and unreal. While it remains conscious of self, it is much more under complete control, so that its concentration can be intense.

And over all it feels a great joy and peace. This state has been compared to a stillness as of a mountain pool, unruffled by the conflicting winds of desire.

(3) In the third *jhana* the sense of selfhood is still further diminished. All sense-desire has now faded away. There is a feeling of complete and happy tranquillity; only unruffled unconscious bliss remains. 'That unrest which men miscall delight' is at an end.

(4) The fourth *jhana* appears to be a refinement of the third. It is described in the Buddhist Sutras as a state of 'utter purity of mindfulness' in which the consciousness of the polar opposites which condition normal human perception have been transcended; the subject-object relationship no longer exists.

One acquainted with the literature of Christian mysticism cannot but be conscious of the similarities between these psycho-spiritual experiences and those experienced by Christian contemplatives. An essential difference in declared objective must, however, be noted. The Christian objective is union with a God who, though in His aspect as the ineffable, attributeless Godhead is apprehended in non-personal terms, has also a 'personal' aspect; or, to put it into different words, the Christian envisages a communion of 'personalities', a union between God's spirit and man's spirit. For the Buddhist contemplative there is no 'personal' Deity with whom there can be communion and eventual union. He aims at the bliss of Nirvana, a state of 'ceasing to be', when 'the dewdrop slips into the shining sea'.

I would not, however, wish to stress this difference too strongly. Experientially the Christian's 'union with God' and the Buddhist's Nirvana may be the same. It is not possible logically to demonstrate the difference. Moreover, there is a marked 'non-personal' element in the descriptions of the state of 'union with God' in some of the Christian contemplative saints. Consider, for instance, Ruysbroeck's description of the culmination of the Super-essential Life:

And here there is death in fruition, and a melting and dying into the Essential Nudity, where all the Divine names, and all conditions and all the living images which are reflected in the mirror of Divine

Truth lapse in the Onefold and Ineffable, in waylessness and without reason. For in this unfathomable abyss of the Simplicity, all things are wrapped in fruitive bliss; and the abyss itself may not be comprehended, unless by the Essential Unity. To this the Persons, and all that lives in God, must give place; for here there is nought else but an eternal rest in the fruitive embrace of an outpouring Love. And this is that wayless being which all interior spirits have chosen above all other things. This is the dark silence in which all lovers lose themselves.*

This is very close to a description of the state which a Buddhist would call Nirvana.

The 'non-personalism' of Buddhist religious philosophy is particularly evident in the descriptions of the four *arupa* (or *formless*) *jhanas*.

(1) In the first of these the aspirant becomes conscious of 'boundless space', in which all awareness of separate forms is absent.

(2) In the second a condition is reached in which all knowledge is grasped, not by any process of discursive thought, not as a conglomeration of separate parts, but intuitively, as a whole.

(3) As the contemplative arrives at the third *arupa jhana* he passes into a state of 'nothingness', a state in which no-thing exists for him any longer, not even the perception of no-thing-ness.

(4) Finally, in the fourth *arupa jhana*, a point is reached when there is neither consciousness of perception nor of non-perception. Everything, words, concepts, opposites, self, no longer exist.

These advanced states of consciousness and not-consciousness are not easy for the Western mind to grasp. They are states which few attain. They seem to occur, however, at the highest levels of mystical experience in all religions.

For instance, the Sufi mystic, Al-Ghazali, writes of a state known by some Moslem contemplatives thus:

When this state prevails, it is called in relation to him who experiences it, Extinction, nay Extinction of Extinction, for the soul

* *The Adornment of the Spiritual Marriage* (Watkins).

has become extinct to itself, extinct to its own extinction; for it becomes unconscious of itself and unconscious of its own unconsciousness, since were it conscious of its own unconsciousness, it would be conscious of itself.*

THE SEVEN PORTALS

In some fragments of a Buddhist Tibetan Scripture, *The Book of the Golden Precepts*,† the Path is described under the imagery of the seven portals, each of which has a golden key.

The first key is the key of charity and immortal love, the second of harmony in word and act, the third of unruffled patience, the fourth of indifference to pleasure and the passing beyond the illusion of normal awareness.

The last three portals lead to those high realms which are hinted at by the mystics of all religions. The key to the fifth portal is described as that of 'dauntless energy that fights its way to supreme Truth, out of the mire of lies terrestrial'; the sixth opens the gate which leads to a realm of eternal Stillness and to its ceaseless contemplation; and the seventh to that state which 'makes a God of man, creating him a Bodhisattva'.

This passing through the Seven Portals is not an easy path. It is described as 'the dreary Path of Sorrow', fraught with danger and difficulty. Though joy comes at the end, the journey is not for the timid and those who are in quest of spiritual delights.

And it is not a safe one for those who are not spiritually and mentally equipped to tread it. The ascent to the heights of the spiritual life is like climbing a high mountain, the summit of which cannot be reached except by way of steep precipices and dangerous walls, not to be attempted except by expert mountaineers.

Further, before the aspirant is even ready to pass through the first portal he must be already in a comparatively advanced

* Quoted in Smith: *Sufi Path of Love* (Luzac).

† Translated into English: *The Voice of the Silence* (Theosophy Company – India, Bombay). There are some differences among scholars on the authenticity of this fragment.

psycho-spiritual state. The author of this fragment describes this state as follows:

> Before thou canst approach the foremost gate thou hast to learn to part thy body from the mind, to dissipate the shadow, and to live in the eternal. For this thou hast to live and breathe in all, as all thou perceivest breathes in thee; to feel thyself abiding in all things, and all things in SELF.*

THE SEVEN VALLEYS

Finally, let us conclude our survey of the highest degrees of prayer with a particularly interesting description from the Islamic religious tradition. It is contained in the allegory, *The Conference of the Birds*, by the Sufi mystic, Farid al din 'Attar.

The spiritual journey from its start to its final attainment is pictured as one through seven valleys. The first valley is called the Valley of the Quest. It corresponds roughly to the Way of Purgation. In it all encumbrances are stripped away, so that the heavenly light may enter. Next comes the Valley of Love, the beginnings of the mystical life, the first stage of Illumination. In the next valley, the Valley of Knowledge and Enlightenment, the state of Contemplation proper is reached. In the fourth valley, that of Detachment, the soul becomes utterly absorbed in the Divine Love; while in the fifth, the Valley of Unity, the contemplation of the naked Godhead, stripped of all images, is reached.

The vision is, however, as yet transient, the light is too bright; the soul is dazzled and blinded. In the next valley, the Valley of Bewilderment, the vision seems to have disappeared. The aspirant is, however, now ready to enter the seventh and last valley, the Valley of Annihilation, where the soul is completely lost and merged in God.

As I have already written, what is significant in these various descriptions of the higher degrees of prayer in the different religious faiths is not so much the differences, which may be attributed to differing religious philosophies and

---

* I find this passage somewhat puzzling. It reads like a description of a very advanced stage of the mystic Way, yet it is only the beginning.

psycho-spiritual biases as the underlying similarities. Must one conclude on the evidence that all are descriptions of intimate contacts with the same Reality? I leave the reader to arrive at his own conclusion and to ponder on the theological consequences.

17. The Life of Prayer and the Life of Action

WHAT we have been describing in the last chapters has been the way of the true contemplative, the pioneer of the spiritual adventure, the mountaineer of the spirit. It is not the path which the majority of those who are not advanced contemplatives can or are called upon to tread.

The world-view of the *Bhagavad Gita*, the Song of God, is in several ways different from the world-view of the New Testament. Nevertheless, there are striking similarities in the teaching of this beautiful Hindu scripture and the teaching of Jesus on the nature of human action and the living of the active life. Much of what follows is based on the teaching of Krishna in the *Gita* and the teaching of the Lord Jesus.

In the *Bhagavad Gita* Prince Arjuna puts to his charioteer, Krishna, the incarnation of God, the question: 'Tell me by what path I may attain the Supreme?' to which question Krishna replies: 'In this world the path is two-fold, for the contemplative the path of spiritual wisdom, for the man of action the path of dedicated action.'

Not only are the majority not contemplatives, still less are they contemplative saints; neither are they philosophers or theologians. They may have felt the touch of the Most High, but the contacts are faint and intermittent. They may have asked themselves the question: What does it all mean? But to try to penetrate to the mystery of the universe is too difficult. They have neither the inclination nor the ability to be spiritual explorers. The everyday problems of life press too closely. Their chief concern is with the problems of right action in the world.

Action is, however, the expression, even though it may be an unconscious one, of an underlying belief about the nature and meaning of the world. Life is like sailing a boat. If one is to reach port one must have some idea of where the port is. If one is to arrive there safely, one must not only know how to sail the boat without disaster, one must also know the direction in which to go. One must know, too, the laws of wind and tide and current; one must have a compass and a map.

One cannot avoid having a philosophy, a creed. To say 'I could not care less' is in essence a credal statement, an expression of belief about the nature of things. Action has its origin in what one believes. If one's belief (or faith) is false, then one is steering with a defective compass and will inevitably land on the rocks. It is, therefore, necessary to find a philosophy of action, to understand the nature of human action.

The ultimate end of every man is 'union' with God. How shall he attain it? The *Gita* gives the answer:

> All mankind
> Is born for perfection
> And each will attain it
> Will he but follow
> His nature's duty *

For those called to the life of action, the right leading of the active life is their road to God. For them prayer is primarily a means of becoming the sort of person who is able to lead the active life most effectively. Prayer is for them the fertilizer of action.

So long as we live in this world few of us can avoid living the life of action; it is the proper life for the ordinary man. Human action, viewed *sub specie aeternitatis* is, however, ephemeral, insignificant and meaningless, a voyage

> in a drifting boat with a slow leakage,
> The silent listening to the undeniable
> Clamour of the bell of the last annunciation.†

* *Bhagavad Gita, The Song of God* translated by Prabhavananda and Isherwood (Phoenix House).

† T. S. Eliot: *The Dry Salvages.*

It only takes on meaning when it is related to something higher than itself, when it is not performed for itself alone.

'The world is imprisoned in its own activity,' said Krishna to Prince Arjuna, 'except when actions are placed in something higher than themselves and become worship of God. Therefore you must perform every action sacramentally and be free from all attachment to results.'

Except in so far as their actions are performed as worship of God, when they take on the character of sacraments, outward expressions of what is in its essence spiritual, men are imprisoned in their activity. They are shut up in the prison of a closed universe; they are so absorbed in the phenomenal world that they can see nothing else; action is their god; they are bound to time; the true end of action is hidden from them; so they cannot know how to act in the best way. Only in so far as the true nature and pattern of things are realized, only in so far as one has become the sort of person who is capable of acting in accordance with that realized faith, is it possible to act rightly.

There is a further point. There is a tragic quality in human action. The results of any action are incalculable and unknowable; they are outside the control of the doer. An action may be done with what appears to the doer to be the purest motive, yet the result may turn out to be evil.

How can this tragedy, inherent in human action, be avoided, or, at least, mitigated? Only in so far as every action is, as it were, put sacramentally into God. For when work, whether it be mental or physical, is done in this way it becomes work done in God and so belongs to God and not to the doer. Something happens to it; it is changed. The doer must not, however meritorious the action, claim any reward. He cannot both have his cake and eat it. He must ever strive for complete non-attachment to results.* 'You have the right to work,' said Krishna, 'but for the work's sake only. You have no right to the fruits of work. Desire for the fruits of work must never be your motive in working.'

Moreover, action seldom offers a free choice. This is as

* See the meditation 'On Detachment' in The Prayer Book.

true of communities as of individuals. The possible courses of action are limited by what at that moment men are in themselves and by the field of action in which they are forced to act, a field which is the result of choices which have already been made and of events which have already occurred. The possible choice is rarely between a clear and obvious right and a clear and obvious wrong. One is forced to act within a particular human situation from which there is no escape. Idealism can be very dangerous unless it is wedded to an appreciation of possibilities and practical commonsense.

There is a pattern, a law, of the universe, from which there is no escape. The moral teaching of all religions is an attempt to explain this law, this pattern, so that men may be impelled to act in accordance with it. 'Thy law is a lamp unto my feet,' say the Jewish scriptures. 'Well proclaimed by the Blessed One is the Law [the Dharma], perfectly visible, timeless, bidding all come and see, giving guidance, to be understood by the intelligent each for himself,' says the Buddhist. 'To unite the heart with God and then to act: that is the secret of unattached work,' says the *Gita*. 'Seek ye first the Kingdom of God and his righteousness* [or, in the old sixteenth-century translation, 'and its rightwiseness'] and all these things shall be added unto you.' So spake Jesus in the collection of sayings known as the Sermon on the Mount.

This collection of sayings may appear at first sight as mere impractical idealism, a collection of moral precepts far beyond the ability of ordinary men to follow. True, they are difficult to follow, so difficult that few have ever tried. Yet they are a superb piece of analysis of right and successful action within the pattern of things as they really are and not as they may appear to be on the surface. It is as if Jesus were saying: 'There is a law of the universe, a texture or pattern of things. It was not invented by man; it is simply there; what I am telling you is how you may act in harmony with it. It has its origin in That which you call God. If you frame your actions in

* The word 'righteousness' conveys a wrong impression of what Jesus meant. The meaning is better conveyed by phrases such as 'what is appropriate to it', 'what is in accordance with it'.

accordance with it, you are identifying yourself with God and with the action of God. Therefore you cannot fail, for you have the backing of the law inherent in the very texture of things behind you. The stars in their courses will work for you. Make your choice – and take the consequences of that choice; they are inevitable. If you follow my teaching you will be like a man who builds his house on solid rock; if you do not, you are like one who builds on sand. The house may look all right; but when the storms come, down it will fall. How wonderful have seemed some of the social and political structures which have been built in our age. How many of them have collapsed or are collapsing. They have been built on sand.*'

The life of the active man, the majority of mankind, is the life of action in the world. That is his destiny. Though he may, indeed must, strive to enter deeper and deeper into that ground of his being which is the dwelling place of the Inner Light, prayer for him is primarily a means of enabling him to lead the active life in accordance with the inherent pattern of the universe, to accomplish in himself that transformation which will enable him to lead rightly the sort of life which it is his destiny to lead, to integrate in himself the 'contemplative' and 'active' lives. That is his pathway to union with God.

Now you shall hear how a man may become perfect, if he devotes himself to the work which is natural to him. A man will reach perfection if he does his duty as an act of worship to the Lord, who is the source of the universe, prompting all action, everywhere present.†

To glimpse the vision of a new and living relationship between the temporal and the eternal, between activity and spirituality, in which they are seen, not as separate, but united one with the other, is, for many in our age, in which the old foundations are shaken, the old images shattered, and

* See the meditation 'On the Dharma of the Lord Jesus' in The Prayer Book.

† Bhagavad Gita, The Song of God translated by Prabhavananda and Isherwood (Phoenix House).

there is no widely accepted philosophy of life, not easy. It calls for a high adventure of mind and spirit. To realize this relationship is to find the superb truth which is enshrined at the very heart of the Christian revelation and has its supreme expression in time in the God-man, Jesus Christ, who 'by His Incarnation gathered into one things earthly and heavenly'. In this vision man may live and work in hope, for they will have grown, or at least they are growing, each within the limitations of his nature, towards the state of that 'most inward man' who, in the words of the Blessed John Ruysbroeck,

lives his life in these two ways: namely in work and in rest. And in each he is whole and undivided; for he is wholly in God because he rests in fruition, and he is wholly in himself because he lives in activity; and he is perpetually called and urged by God to renew both the rest and the work.*

No one in our time has realized and expressed this coinherence between the temporal and the eternal more fully than Pierre Teilhard de Chardin. In him the mystic, the priest of the Society of Jesus and the palaeontologist and scientist are joined together in perfect harmony and balance. The marriage in him of religious faith and scientific knowledge resulted in an illumination which enabled him to express a mystical vision which could not have been grasped with the same clarity and intensity until our own scientific age.

The sense of the co-inherence of matter and spirit is evident in everything that Father Teilhard wrote, and nowhere more appealingly than in *The Mass on the World*,† that lovely mystical prose-poem of which we have already written.

'For me, my God,' he there wrote,

all joy and all achievement, the very purpose of my being and all my love of life, all depend on this one basic vision of the union between Yourself and the universe. Let others, fulfilling a function more august than mine, proclaim your splendours as pure spirit; as for me, dominated as I am by a vocation which springs from the

* *The Adornment of the Spiritual Marriage* (Watkins).
† Included in *Hymn of the Universe* (Collins).

inmost fibres of my being, I have no desire, I have no ability, to proclaim anything except the innumerable prolongations of your incarnate Being in the world of matter; I preach only the mystery of your flesh, you the Soul shining forth through all that surrounds us.

'He who sees not God everywhere sees Him truly no-where.' Faith, prayer, work, as Father Teilhard knew, are all one in the Divine Heart; to work is to pray. The prayer-life and the work-life need not be, nor should they be, regarded as separate activities; each must be integrated in the other. There are some who are called to the life of pure contemplation; for most of us the good life is one of a right balance of work and prayer.

Prayer must not, however, be thought of as a means of avoiding making decisions, which can only be reached by precise thinking and common sense. One cannot, and must not, use God as a stop gap, either as a means of explaining as yet unexplained physical phenomena, nor as an agent to do that which one is called upon to do oneself. Nevertheless, prayer is the hygiene of the active life. To pray sincerely and persistently is continuously to sink one's roots into something deeper than oneself. It is a means of becoming more sensitive and more aware, of gaining release from the domination of the phenomenal ego, of realizing one's true Self, and so attaining a state of inner freedom in which one is enabled to live equally in the eternal and the temporal in perfect balance and harmony.

There is a life-pattern of the prayer-life. Different objectives and different sorts of prayer are appropriate for different people at different times of their lives. In adolescence and early manhood there are sometimes spiritual experiences, which can be of great intensity. Later, they may become dim. The growing man becomes absorbed in his work and in the bringing up of a family. The world is very much with him. It is at this stage that the main objective of prayer becomes a means of fertilizing the life of action. Then the time of retirement comes, one's family has gone out into the world, one's active life is finished, life is drawing to its close.

There is much to be said for the Hindu attitude. For most the proper life is regarded as the life of the 'householder', the life of action. When the duties of that stage are fulfilled, however, the wise man may properly put aside the life of action and pass more and more into the life of contemplation, separating himself increasingly from the workaday world in order that he may seek the eternal things.

The trilogy, which I started to write on my retirement from the headmastership of Bishop Wordsworth's, Salisbury, in 1960, is at last almost finished. In each of the first two volumes I wrote an Epilogue, in *Mysticism*, 'The Mystic's Universe'; in *Religious Faith and Twentieth-Century Man*, 'He who sees not God everywhere sees Him truly nowhere'. This Study of the Nature and Practice of Prayer has no formal Epilogue; its Epilogue is the final paragraphs of this chapter on the life of prayer and the life of action. It is the story of a great man of action, who I am proud to call a friend.

He is the same age as myself; though we never met there, he was my contemporary at Cambridge during the years immediately preceding the 1914–18 War; and, like myself, was a soldier in that war. He was wounded and captured and spent several years in a prisoner of war camp. His career has been a very distinguished one; when he retired he was Governor-General of a vast African Province.

He started the practice of meditation while a prisoner of war and has continued it throughout his active career and into his retirement. He can now get up in the morning, pass without effort into a state of contemplation for a couple of hours while at the same time carrying on with his normal duties.

Of the nature of the profound spiritual experience on that Macedonian hilltop, which changed his life, I may not speak. I am one of the very few to whom he has told it. Of it he wrote to me: 'Even after fifty years I have not yet fathomed all the implications of my Macedonian experience. Almost daily some new revelation comes rolling in like a wave, bringing intimations of Power and Glory.'

Here, however, is what this man of action, who has led a life of prayer and meditation throughout the whole of his active life, now, at the age of seventy-six says about prayer:

As I have told you before, everything is a prayer, every act, thought and emotion. This by virtue of my Macedonian hill-top, my Damascus road, wherein I was and am literally rooted and grounded in the risen Christ, the Spirit. I have only recently begun to see the implications; all St Paul's experience, repeated in myself; there are innumerable proofs, my marvellous health, my journey from a Midlands industrial slum to rule over ten million of the toughest tribesmen in Africa. I could go on for ever, but if you want *my* sailing directions they are simply: 'Be still and know that I am God', with its corollary of absolute control of body, mind and heart, leading to union, illumination, pure love.

Finis coronat opus. The rest is silence.

THE PRAYER BOOK

Offices, Prayers and Meditations

Introduction

THE first part of this book, a Study of prayer in general, is in itself an introduction to this manual of devotion, intended for the use of those who, in ways appropriate to each, desire to lead the life of prayer in its fullness. It will, however, be helpful to add a less general and more practical introduction to this second part of the book.

Its title, 'Offices, Prayers and Meditations', describes its character, at least in general. Now that it is completed, however, I feel that this title may not be sufficiently exact; it is more than that. It could just as well be called 'A Manual of Devotion'. I think it has a unique flavour, for it includes a great deal of original material, much of it in verse, never before published. Perhaps the title does not, however, matter very much; what is important is the contents. At the end I have written a number of notes, giving the sources of the material used and describing how the different parts, particularly the meditations, may be used in practice.

The special meaning of the word, *office*, was explained in the chapter on Christian Prayer. It is here used as a general term for an act of worship of a definite pattern. Many of the *offices* included were originally drawn up for use at the morning service with which each day opened in the Chapel of Bishop Wordsworth's, Salisbury, during my headmastership of that school. They are suitable for use as individual or corporate devotions.

How should one pray? The answer is a simple one: In whatever way one finds most helpful and congenial for oneself, in order to enable one to lead a dedicated, recollected life, a life lived in the presence of God, so that every thought, word and deed, every feeling, every emotion, becomes a prayer. George Herbert expresses this ideal in one of his hymns, which begins:

Teach me, my God and King,
In all things Thee to see;
And what I do in anything
To do it as for Thee

Father Thomas Merton, in *No Man is an Island* (Hollis and Carter), gives the best description of Recollection I know:

Recollection makes me present to myself by bringing together two aspects, or activities, of my being as if they were two lenses of a telescope. One lens is the basic semblance of my spiritual being, the inward soul, the deep will, the spiritual intelligence. The other is my outward soul, the practical intelligence, the will engaged in the activities of life.

The leading of the dedicated, recollected life, if it is to become spontaneous, calls for training through prayer.

This prayer book is made up of a mass of varied material, drawn from many sources, designed for the use of different types of people, in training themselves in the spontaneous habit of prayer and recollection. The value of the regular recitation of some sort of office, combined, if one wishes, with meditation, is that it is an effective instrument in this training.

The monastic offices were recited by the monks at intervals throughout the day and night; for those leading the active life the normal times will be in the morning and evening. It is, however, a good thing to say some sort of set office, for instance the little Act of Dedication printed below, or to make some definite act of Recollection in the course of one's daily duties. My friends have written for me a number of short prayers for this purpose, which are printed in this Prayer Book.

How should this Prayer Book be used? Again the answer is: 'In whatever way you find most useful.' If you find the morning and evening offices, litanies and other patterns of devotion suited to your particular need and temperament, then use them as they are set out here. If not, choose what you wish, for instance, such prayers as appeal to you, and use them in any way you like. If you find it more helpful to concentrate primarily on some form of meditation, concentrate on that. The Golden Rule of prayer is that there is no rule.

The Prayer Book is divided into three parts:

1. The first opens with a collection of Adorations, Invocations etc. Then follow a number of offices and devotions of different sorts for use at different times for a variety of different purposes. I have also in this section included 'A Solemn Liturgy' which was composed for and sung as part of a magnificent service in Salisbury Cathedral on a special occasion in October, 1959, and a simple *Credo*. This part ends with an 'Anthology of Prayers', gathered together from many sources, ancient and modern, and of many different types, and a section on the Practice of the Presence of God.

2. The second part is devoted to the Holy Eucharist, the central act of worship of the Christian Church. It consists of prayers intended to be used either as preparation for the service or during the service itself, a hymn for use during the Offertory or Oblation, i.e. the offering of the bread and wine by the people, with which the Eucharistic Action opens, a collection of Eucharistic hymns, and a number of meditations on the Eucharist. In this section I have also included my own experimental Eucharistic Liturgy, which was originally published as a Prism Pamphlet (No. 25), under the title, *A Cosmic Liturgy*. It is now out of print. In this version of it I have made a few changes.

3. The third part is entitled 'The Prayer of Meditation and Contemplation'. Though in the study much has been written in general terms about this type of prayer, it will be useful to write more fully here about its actual practice.

I have entitled this section 'The Prayer of Meditation and Contemplation' since I think one could with advantage abandon the word, 'meditation', for any sort of meditation except the primarily reflective type and use the word, 'contemplation', instead. Meditation, as has already been said, is not a very precise term and conveys different meanings to different people. In common speech 'to meditate' is simply 'to think about'. The word is, however, used to describe a number of different sorts of prayer-activity. It is conducive to clarity if one tries, difficult though it is, to be as precise as possible. I have not, however, been able, in this Introduction, to be as precise as I should like. I have at times been compelled to use the word, 'meditation', as a general term, to include both 'reflective meditation' and 'contemplation'. I trust, however, that my meaning is clear.

In The Study I divided the Prayer of Meditation into two main types, *reflective* meditation and *contemplative* meditation. The first I call the 'Prayer of the Head', the second the 'Prayer of the Heart'. While it is necessary, for purposes of description and discussion, to treat these two types separately, as I have done in The Study, in practice they are often combined, the two interlocking, merging into and cross-fertilizing each other.

The most spiritually valuable part of the practice of meditation is when one passes into what has been very vividly described as 'the womb of silence', the time when one is doing nothing, when the analytic mind is still and one simply 'waits on God'. It is then that *reflective* meditation becomes *contemplative* meditation or contemplation; the Prayer of the Head becomes the Prayer of the Heart. Those proficient in the art of meditation may during the Silence pass into the state of the Prayer of Simplicity and Simple Regard, of Simply Looking and Waiting. St Teresa gave this advice to her nuns: 'I do not require of you to form great and curious considerations in your understanding, I require of you no more than to look.'

The words, to know, to see, knowledge and seeing, have more than one meaning. The normal meaning of the word knowledge, is rational knowledge, i.e. knowledge through the rational mind. Similarly the word, seeing, is normally used with reference to the sense perception of sight. There is, however, another sort of *knowledge*,* intuitive or spiritual

* Except that its use may be misunderstood owing to its association with Gnosticism, a heresy which the early Christian Church, I believe rightly, rejected, this spiritual knowledge may be called *gnosis*, in the sense that St Paul uses the word in I Corinthians XIII 2: 'If I have the gift of prophecy and know all the mysteries and all *gnosis* . . .'

knowledge. There is also another sort of *seeing* than that through the eyes of the body; it is a *seeing* through the eyes of the soul. Through this intuitive, spiritual *knowing* and *seeing* it is possible for man to apprehend aspects of reality which cannot be apprehended through the faculty of reason alone. One of the objects of the contemplative levels of the Prayer of Meditation is to attain to this more profound state of *knowing* and *seeing*.

It is not easy to write about the practice of the Prayer of Meditation and Contemplation. Perhaps it is not possible really to understand what it is except through experience. In the first place, one cannot know whether the terms one is compelled to use will be intelligible to the ordinary reader, terms such as mystical, contemplation and contemplative, intuitive, contemplative insight, etc. Secondly, there are so many different methods, one appropriate for one temperament, another for another. The desire and inner urge of different people vary.

One type of person may have an urge to see more deeply into the real nature of things by developing a greater capacity of intuitive *seeing* and *knowing*. Another may have an urge to enrich and deepen his inner life, so that he may draw closer and closer to God in the ground of his being. Another, absorbed in worldly affairs, may have an inner urge to make his active life more fertile and useful to others by living it more in the Presence of God, in a more profound state of Recollection. Yet another, unhappy, lost and disillusioned, may seek in the practice of Meditation illumination and consolation, yet another, healing and alleviation of bodily sickness.*

While it is not easy to describe the practice of meditation at all clearly, it is useful for one inclined towards its practice to know something of the various forms it may take. One

* In her recent book, *Studies in Spiritual Healing* (World Fellowship Press), Miss A. Graham Ikin gives some fascinating, detailed descriptions of how Dorothy Kerin, Brother Mandus and others were prepared by very profound inner illuminations for their widespread, effective work in this field.

method, which has proved effective in group meditations, I described in *The Journey Inwards*. In it various 'spiritual exercises' are used. Each meditation session falls into three parts, 'going into' the Silence, the Silence itself, which is the most important part, and the 'coming out' into the active life. I have called it the 'theme' method, since both the 'going in' and the 'coming out' are built around a particular 'theme'. In that book the 'themes' were arranged in a particular order; in this book, which has a wider intent, the various meditations are arranged differently.

The Prayer of Meditation and Contemplation may take a variety of forms, which I shall try to tabulate below. This tabulation must not, however, be regarded in any way as rigid or exclusive.

1. *Reflective Meditation* in the sense of *Mental Prayer* as usually understood. This is primarily a Prayer of the Head.

2. *Reflective/Contemplative Meditation* or *Mixed Meditation*, in which rational/reflective and intuitive/contemplative both play a part. It is a combination, sometimes but not necessarily, with the aid of spiritual exercises, of the Prayer of the Head and the Prayer of the Heart. This is the most congenial method of meditation for many people.

3. *Prayer/Meditation*. There was a time when I regarded ordinary praying as of little value in the enrichment of the spiritual life. I now think that I was wrong. The mechanical repetition of prayers may be of little value, but once one's prayers become an activity of the heart it is different. Why should one not talk to God as to a Friend? Such praying is a form of 'colloquy' or of 'affective' prayer. Some very beautiful examples are found in the writings of Teilhard de Chardin. Such verbal prayer can be a very effective form of devotion, particularly when combined with periods of silence.

Prayers in verse form are especially potent on account of their rhythmic character. Indeed any suitable poetry can be used. I have myself used the whole of Francis Thompson's *The Hound of Heaven* with my little meditation group. I have included a great deal of verse of various sorts in this Prayer Book. This leads us to:

4. *Mantric Meditation*. In the pure type of mantric* meditation some mantra is used as the sole aid to lead into the Silence. It is continuously repeated until eventually, having fulfilled its purpose, it fades away. This form of the Prayer of Meditation is extensively used in the East, and also in the *Prayer of Jesus*. One of my friends has told me that he has found the continuous repetition of the mantra, 'Be still and know', the most congenial and helpful form of prayer for him; indeed he uses little else. Mantras are, however, useful in any form of contemplative meditation, for instance, in order to prevent the mind wandering during the Silence.

In Chapter 13 of The Study five definitions of the word, mantra, are given. Among them are: 'a microcosm of some eternal reality, or a particular aspect of it, which it is desired to contemplate' and 'a means of awakening dormant forces in the soul, so that it may be enabled to establish contact with the depth-consciousness and so to enter into a wider life and a deeper illumination'.

If we accept these definitions, which are not my own, there is, thus, a form of mantric meditation other than the continuous repetition of a particular mantra. It is to take some idea, which may be expressed in verbal form, and, after suitable preparation, concentrate one's mind on it, 'contemplating' it until it sinks deep into the subconsciousness and, there, as it were 'lives itself' at that deeper level of perception and thus becomes luminous and transforming.

5. *Meditation with the aid of music*. For those who love music this is one of the most effective ways. In his book, *The Renaissance*, Walter Pater made the illuminating remark that all great art endeavours to attain the state of music. Music is the most universal, since the most undifferentiated, of all the arts. In itself it is absent of all intellectual concepts. It speaks by means of a language of sound symbols, which, like all symbols, have an innate quality, conveying different meanings

---

* I think that it is possible that I myself may have invented the term, 'mantric'. I have never found the word anywhere else, though others who know my writings are now using it. It may be noted here that the Tibetan form of the word, mantra, is *mantrum*.

to different people. The greatest poetry, the greatest painting, the greatest sculpture have this quality; they say something to the receptive mind which is not on the surface.

Music can thus be a potent aid in the practice of contemplative meditation. There are two possible ways of using it. The first is to take some musical composition, with which one is thoroughly familiar, sit back in a chair, make the analytical mind as quiet as possible and simply listen. Or rather, do not listen in the usual sense at all but let the music work on you so that, as it were, you 'become the music while the music lasts'. As I have recorded in *The Journey Inwards* one of the most profound illuminations I have ever known, an experience of the sort which, in the Introduction to The Study, I have called *the mystical in the second degree*, happened when, with a friend, I was listening to a performance of Beethoven's Emperor Concerto.

In the East much attention has been given to the study of the potency of particular sounds.* Music can be used in the same way as the repetition of a mantra. A particular phrase, or group of phrases, is recorded on a tape, so that it goes on repeating itself for as long as it is needed.

6. *Meditation with the aid of symbolic objects.* By meditation with the aid of symbolic objects is meant meditation through the contemplation of a picture or ikon, a mandala, a crucifix, a light or flower, or indeed any object of this sort which has a symbolic significance for the one using it. This form of meditation is of great value to certain types; it can be used in association with other forms which have been described above.

7. *The Meditation of Pure Silence.* Here no words, or any other aid except perhaps rhythmic breathing are used. In those sufficiently advanced the mind becomes immediately stilled and there is nothing but a simple waiting in profound inner silence for 'the still voice of God'.

While it is valuable for one inclined towards the practice of the Prayer of Meditation and Contemplation to know

* See Wood's *Yoga*, Chapter 11, 'The Use of Sounds in Yoga Practice' (Penguin Books).

something of the forms prayer can take, it is only by its practice that anyone can discover what it really is and the effect it has on the development and enlargement of personality. Some, as the result of an inherent spiritual urge or of some deep spiritual experience, are led spontaneously into the practice of some sort of meditation and gradually discover the way most appropriate to themselves. The beginning is not seldom a mixture of the type of prayer known to them, combined with a good deal of reflection, which results in occasional flashes of contemplative insight. In course of time their prayer-life becomes more profound, less and less an activity of the rational, analytical mind, more and more intuitive and contemplative. All the time the Spirit is carrying out the work which It alone can do.

Possibly the best way for most to learn the art of effective meditation is through regular group meditation under a skilled director, capable of using a variety of techniques. He should be able to assess the psycho-spiritual state and needs of his group and be willing to abandon one method and use another if he feels that it is likely to be more helpful. One virtue of group meditation is that every member of the group is helping the rest. A spiritual atmosphere is generated which all feel. Group meditation does not, however, make private individual meditation unnecessary; the most intimate and profound illuminations usually occur in solitude.

As I have been writing these pages, particularly when I was dealing with reflective/contemplative meditation, some sentences which I had read in the treatise on the Prayer of Jesus by the early nineteenth-century Bishop Ignatius Brianchaninov, which I have quoted earlier, have been running through my mind:

It is one thing to pray with attention with the participation of the heart; it is another *to descend with the mind into the temple of the heart* and from there to offer mystical prayer filled with divine grace and power. The second is the result of the first. The attention of the mind during prayer draws the heart into sympathy; with the strengthening of attention, *sympathy of heart and mind is turned into union of heart and mind.* Finally *when attention makes the prayer its own,* the mind descends into the heart for the most profound and sacred service of prayer.

Earlier in the same book the Bishop wrote:

He who prays by the method proposed by St John of the Ladder [one of the contemplative saints of the Eastern Orthodox Church] will *pray with the lips and the mind and the heart*.

[The italics are my own. 'Attention' has the same meaning as 'concentration' or 'mindfulness', which is so stressed in Buddhist meditational practice.]

Let, therefore, one who would make progress in the Prayer of Meditation and Contemplation, or, indeed, in prayer in general, acquaint himself with the different ways of prayer and then decide the method which he finds most helpful and congenial to him. Let him not worry himself too much about the distinctions between petitionary, reflective and contemplative prayer, nor examine too closely which type he is using at any particular time; but remembering always that his objective is to enter, if only occasionally and for a short time, that place of silence when he ceases to do anything on his own initiative and, completely passive,* is open to the impact of the Spirit, that abyss of inner consciousness when, in the words of one writer, 'the psychology of man mingles with the psychology of God'.

In leading the life of prayer let there be as little strain as possible – sometimes it cannot be avoided – and let barren speculation as to whether one is making progress or not be pushed on one side; sometimes one feels that one is making no progress at all, rather that one is going back. It is impossible to know. The real happenings are taking place in a part of the soul into which the speculative mind cannot penetrate.

The leading of the spiritual life is like climbing a high mountain; it is an ascent of the Holy Mount of God. Sometimes the ascent is easy and progress is swift. At other times it is arduous and slow. There are steep precipices which must be climbed. The route is not clear and one may find that one

* This passivity is not inertia or dreaming. At one level of personality, an intense activity is taking place. It is difficult to explain this.

has to retrace one's steps and try another route; there are false summits; one thinks that over the next rise one will have reached the mountain top, only to find that it looks as distant as ever. And the summit is wrapped in mist; only occasionally do the mists open and it is seen in its sunlit glory; then they close again.

It was one of the greatest mountaineers of our time, Tensing, who, with Hillary, was the first man to reach the summit of Mount Everest who, in his autobiography wrote: 'It is with God as it is with a high mountain. The important thing is to come to Him not with fear but with love.'

So let no one be afraid or lose heart. The leading of the spiritual life through the practice of prayer is not a journey along a smooth road lit by neon lighting. It is a journey along a rough and often dark track. There are times of aridity, of 'the dark night of the soul'. One may even have to endure the awful and terrifying inner experience of 'the death of God', when, quite literally, God dies in the soul and one has to fight furiously to preserve any faith at all. If it should happen to one, there is no need to be afraid. The Lord Jesus knew it as He hung on the Cross; He had to go through it in order that He might become the Redeemer of mankind. It wrung from Him the bitter cry of despair, 'My God, my God, why hast Thou forsaken me?' That, however, was not the end of the story. The clouds began to open, the light became brighter and brighter. 'I am very thirsty', He whispered; and a soldier in pity soaked a sponge in the harsh wine the Roman soldiers drank, put it on the haft of his spear and held it to his lips. The full light of realization broke forth, and there came the triumphant cry: '*Consummatum est*. It is accomplished. The work for which the Father sent me into the world to do is done.' Then, hardly heard, the last serene words: 'Father, into Thy hands I commend my spirit.'

'And on the third day He rose again.' The sad way of the Cross was the necessary condition of the Resurrection. And so it may be for those who would follow the way of the Lord Jesus.

Let another mountaineer speak:

Man overcomes himself, affirms himself, and realizes himself in the struggle towards the summit, towards the absolute. In the extreme tension of the struggle, on the frontier of death, the universe disappears and drops away beneath us. Space, time, fear, suffering no longer exist. As on the crest of a wave, or in the heart of a cyclone, we are strangely calm – not the calm of emptiness, but the heart of action itself. Then we know with absolute certainty that there is something indestructible in us, against which nothing shall prevail. A flame is kindled that can never be extinguished. When we have lost everything we find ourselves most rich . . . *

The summit is at our feet. Above the sea of golden clouds other summits pierce the blue and the horizon stretches to infinity. The summit we have reached is no longer the Summit.

What I am trying to say cannot really be expressed in words. Our language has evolved to speak of the things of normal, mundane experience. There is no commonsense language in which to speak of the things of the Spirit. One is compelled to use a language of symbols, which convey different meanings to different people, a language more akin to the language of poetry and music than to that of prose. I cannot do what the greatest have failed to do.

I have stressed the importance of prayer as a means of enabling one to lead the life of action more effectively. There are aspects of prayer other than the fertilization of the active life, for instance, prayer as the way of union with God. Of these I have written in The Study.

I have tried to compile a Prayer Book for the use of many different temperaments and at different stages in the development of the spiritual life. Let it be regarded as a larder, stocked with a variety of foods, from which you may select according to your individual taste and need. Everyone must work out his own pattern of prayer for himself. All that an author such as myself can do is to describe, to offer such advice, based on his knowledge and experience, as he can, and to provide as sufficient a variety of material as will meet the needs of as many as possible.

* Lucien Davies in the Preface to Herzog: *Annapurna* (Jonathan Cape).

At the heart of the universe there is a Someone or Something, an Ultimate Reality, which is both without and within, with whom, or with which, man can have communion, participation and union. If one has realized that, even if one is able to accept it only as an act of faith, one is able to pray, and to pray with effect. All that is necessary is a sincere, selfless desire to find and know in the ground of one's being that transcendent and immanent Reality which simply IS.

PART I

Short Offices, Devotions and Prayers

1. Adorations and Invocations

THE DIVINE PRAISES

Blessed be the ineffable Godhead.
Blessed be God, holy and most glorious Trinity.
Blessed be God in the depth and in the height.
Blessed be God, within and without.
Blessed be Jesus Christ, true God and true man.
Blessed be God, holy and life-giving Spirit.
Blessed be God in His Angels and in His saints.

Praise be to God; He is God. All are his servants and all are standing by his command. (1)

THE SONG OF THE THREE CHILDREN

Blessed art Thou, O Lord of our fathers:
Worthy to be praised and glorious for ever.
And blessed is the name of Thy majesty:
Yea, holy is Thy name and worthy to be praised and glorious
    for ever.

Blessed art Thou on the throne of Thy kingdom:
Worthy to be praised and glorious for ever.
Blessed art Thou in the seat of Thy Godhead:
Worthy to be praised and glorious for ever.
O let all Thine angels and saints bless Thee:
Who art worthy to be praised and glorious for ever.
O let the heavens and the earth bless Thee:
For Thou art worthy to be praised and glorious for ever.

O ye works of the Lord, bless ye the Lord:
Praise Him and magnify Him for ever.
O ye heavens bless ye the Lord:
O ye suns and stars, bless ye the Lord:

O ye nights and days, bless ye the Lord:
O ye winds and rain, snow and tempests, bless ye the Lord:
Praise Him and magnify Him for ever.

Let the earth also bless the Lord:
Yea let it praise Him and magnify Him for ever.
O ye mountains and hills, rivers and seas, bless ye the Lord:
O ye green things upon the earth, bless ye the Lord:
O ye creatures of earth, air and water, bless ye the Lord:
Praise Him and magnify Him for ever.

O ye children of men, bless ye the Lord:
O ye seekers after truth, bless ye the Lord:
O ye philosophers and scientists, bless ye the Lord:
O ye poets, artists and musicians, bless ye the Lord:
O ye architects, engineers and craftsmen, bless ye the Lord:
O ye holy and humble men of heart, bless ye the Lord:
O ye spirits and souls of the righteous, bless ye the Lord:
Praise Him and magnify Him for ever.

O give thanks unto the Lord, for He is gracious:
And His mercy endureth for ever.   (2)

THE HALLOWING OF THE SACRED NAME

God is Spirit: and they who would come to Him must come in spirit and in truth.

God is Love: he that loveth is born of God and God is in him.

God is Light; and His light lighteneth our darkness.

God is Truth: and whosoever shall know the truth shall enter into eternal life.

God is Power: they that wait upon the Lord shall renew their strength; they shall mount up with wings as eagles; they shall run and not be weary; they shall walk and not faint.

Thou art the Eternal One, Creator and Sustainer of all life, unchanging, unfathomable, beyond human thought and conceiving. Yet we may call Thee Father and Thy Spirit speaks to our spirits. The pure in heart shall see Thee and Thou revealest Thyself to those who seek Thee with humility.

May Thy Name be hallowed throughout all ages, worlds without end. Amen.

GLORIA IN EXCELSIS

Glory be to God on high, and in earth peace, good will towards men. We praise Thee, we bless Thee, we worship Thee, we glorify Thee, we give thanks to Thee for Thy great glory, O Lord God, heavenly King, God the Father Almighty.

O Lord, the only-begotten Son Jesus Christ; O Lord God, Lamb of God, Son of the Father, that takest away the sins of the world, have mercy upon us.

Thou that takest away the sins of the world, have mercy upon us.

Thou that takest away the sins of the world, receive our prayer.

Thou that sittest at the right hand of God the Father, have mercy upon us.

For Thou only art holy; Thou only art the Lord; Thou only, O Christ, with the Holy Ghost, art most high in the glory of God the Father. Amen.

HYMN TO WISDOM

Thou, Wisdom, art the breath of the power of God: a pure influence flowing from the glory of the Almighty.

Thou art the brightness of the everlasting light: the unspotted mirror of the splendour of God.

Through thee are all things accomplished: thou makest all things new.

In all ages thou enterest into holy souls: thou makest them friends and prophets of God.

God loveth them that dwell in thee: for thou art more beautiful than the sun and above the order of the stars.

Thou reachest from one end to another mightily: and sweetly
   dost thou order all things.
Teach me, O Wisdom, breath of God: give me an understanding spirit, lively, clear and undefiled.   (3)

ADORATION OF THE TRINITY IN UNITY

Adoration be to Thee, O most high God, who in creating
human nature didst so marvellously ennoble it, and hast still
more marvellously restored it, and hast implanted in us Thy
Spirit to lighten our darkness and guide us into the fullness
of truth, so illuminate our minds that we may attain to that
mount of vision whereon we may know the perpetual intersection of the timeless with time.

Adoration be to Thee, O Lord of Life and Light, in
and through whom the redemption of creation shall be
accomplished, when there shall be no darkness nor dazzling
but one pure light, no sound nor silence but one perfect
harmony, no hopes nor fears but one full possession, no
discords nor opposites but one single truth, no beginning nor
ending but one eternity, in the splendour of Thy Glory and
the fruition of Thy Love.

Adoration be to Thee, holy, blessed and most glorious
Trinity, ever enthroned in the unity of the one Godhead,
before Thee creation bows in awe and wonder and with angels
and archangels and all the company of heaven cries:

> Holy, holy, holy, Lord God of Hosts,
> heaven and earth are full of thy glory.
> Glory be to Thee, O Lord most high.

ST FRANCIS' HYMN OF THE CREATURES

O most high, almighty, good Lord God, to Thee belongeth
   praise, glory, honour and all blessing.
Praised be my Lord God, with all His creatures, and especially

our brother the sun, who brings us the day and who brings
us the light.

Fair is he, and shining with a very great splendour.

O Lord, he signifies to us Thee.

Praised be my Lord for our sister the moon, and for the
stars, the which He has set dear and lovely in heaven.

Praised be my Lord for our brother the wind, and for air and
cloud, calms and all weather, by which Thou upholdest in
life all creatures.

Praised be my Lord for our sister water, who is very service-
able unto us, and humble and precious and clear.

Praised be my Lord for our brother fire, through whom Thou
givest us light in the darkness; and he is bright and pleasant
and very mighty and strong.

Praised be my Lord for our mother the earth, the which doth
sustain us and keep us, and bringeth forth divers fruits, and
flowers of many colours, and grass.

Praise ye and bless ye the Lord and give thanks unto Him,
and serve Him with great humility.

2. The Radiation of Love

DIVINE LOVE [*or* Love of Jesus]* so fill me with Yourself that I may be all love; and in the power of Your love dwelling in me, may I now radiate love and compassion over all mankind in benediction, peace and joy.

May we, who [in this holy mystery]* have entered into the all-pervading Love and Compassion of God, emptied of all self-love, diffuse boundless love over all beings. May the Love of God be radiated over the entire world in benediction, peace and joy.

Adoration be to Thee, Divine Love shining in the ground of my being, so possess me that in the strength of thy presence within me I may be enabled to suffuse all mankind with love, compassion, joy and peace.

May all be happy; may all enter into thy peace.

* When used at the celebration of the Holy Eucharist, the words in brackets may be added.

3. New Every Morning

MORNING MEDITATIONS

Awake, my soul, and with the sun
Thy daily course of duty run;
Shake off dull sloth and joyful rise
To pay thy morning sacrifice.

By influence of the Light Divine
Let thine own light in good works shine;
Reflect all heaven's propitious ways
In ardent love and cheerful praise.

Heaven is, dear Lord, where'er Thou art,
O never then from me depart;
For to my soul 'tis hell to be
But for one moment void of Thee.

Lord, I my vows to Thee renew;
Scatter my sins as morning dew;
Guard my first springs of thought and will,
And with Thyself my spirit fill.

Direct, control, suggest, this day
All I design, or do, or say;
That all my powers, with all their might,
In Thy sole glory may unite.   (1)

New every morning is the love
Our wakening and uprising prove;
Through sleep and darkness safely brought
Restored to life, and power, and thought.

If on our daily course our mind
Be set to hallow all we find,

New treasures still, of countless price,
God will provide for sacrifice.

Old friends, old scenes, will lovelier be,
As more of heaven in each we see;
Some softening gleam of love and prayer
Will dawn on every cross and care.

The trivial round, the common task,
Will furnish all we ought to ask,
Room to deny ourselves, a road
To bring us daily nearer God.

Only, O Lord, of Thy dear love
Fit us for perfect rest above;
And help us this and every day
To live more nearly as we pray.   (2)

Teach me, my God and King,
In all things Thee to see;
And what I do in anything
To do it as for Thee.

All may of Thee partake;
Nothing can be too mean,
Which with this tincture 'for Thy sake',
Will not grow bright and clean.

A servant with this clause
Makes drudgery divine;
Who sweeps a room, as for Thy laws,
Makes that and the action fine.

This is the famous stone
That turneth all to gold;
For that which God doth touch and own
Cannot for less be told.   (3)

A BUSY MAN'S MORNING DEVOTION

In the morning will I praise Thee, O God.
And at eventide will I make my prayer unto Thee.

I thank Thee, my Lord, that Thou hast kept me during the
past night and brought me in safety to this morn. May Thy
Presence be with me during this coming day to guide, sustain
and sanctify me; and when the evening comes, may I with a
pure heart and a quiet conscience make my prayer and praise
to Thee.

> Christ be with me, Christ within me,
> Christ behind me, Christ before me,
> Christ beside me, Christ to hold me,
> Christ to comfort and restore me.
> Christ beneath me, Christ above me,
> Christ in quiet, Christ in danger,
> Christ in heart of all that love me,
> Christ alike in friend and stranger.   (1)

> Christ, as a light,
> Illumine and guide me!
> Christ as a shield o'ershadow and cover me!
> Christ be beside me
> On left hand and right!
> Christ be before me, behind me, about me!
> Christ this day be within and without me!

> Christ, the lowly and meek,
> Christ, the All-powerful, be
> In the heart of each to whom I speak,
> In the mouth of each who speaks to me!
> In all who draw near me,
> Or see me or hear me!   (1a)

Grant unto us, O Lord, the royalty of inward happiness, and the serenity which comes from being close to Thee. Daily renew in us the sense of joy, and may Thy spirit dwell in our hearts, that we may bear about with us the infection of a good courage, and may meet all life's ills and accidents with a gallant and high-hearted happiness, giving Thee thanks always for all things. (2)

My God, I dedicate this day to Thee, the thoughts I think, the words I speak, the work I do. Take it all into Thyself and make it Thine.

God be in my head and in my understanding;
God be in mine eyes and in my looking;
God be in my mouth and in my speaking;
God be in my heart and in my thinking [*or* knowing];
God be at mine end and my departing. (3)

Be with me through this long and busy day; and though I may forget thee, do not, my Master, be far from me. Amen.

A MORNING THANKSGIVING

Almighty God, our Heavenly Father, who hast brought us safely to the beginning of another day, with thankful hearts we would raise our voices in Thy praise, offering unto Thee sincere adoration and dedicating ourselves once more to Thy service.

For our creation and preservation and for all the blessings of
    this life,
For health and strength and for the vigour of our youth,
For the work through which our minds are trained and the
    play whereby our bodies are made supple and strong,
For the joys of friendship, for laughter and mirth, and for all
    the pleasant things about us,
For hard tasks to attempt, for battles to fight and evil to

conquer, and for the hope that in Thy strength we may rise victorious over all difficulties and overcome all temptations.

After each clause of the Act of Praise 'Thanks be to Thee, O God' is said or sung.

Wherefore, O blessed Trinity, we raise our morning hymn to Thee and, though we are unworthy to offer Thee anything, do Thou of Thy great goodness accept our duty and service, for Jesus Christ's sake.

> Now thank we all our God,
> With heart and hands and voices,
> Who wondrous things have done,
> In whom the world rejoices;
> Who from our mother's arms,
> Have blessed us on our way
> With countless gifts of love
> And still is ours today.
>
> All praise and thanks to God,
> The Father now be given,
> The Son and Him who reigns
> With them in highest heaven,
> The one eternal God,
> Whom heaven and earth adore;
> For thus it was, is now
> And shall be evermore.   Amen.

ANOTHER MORNING THANKSGIVING

> Praise the Lord! Ye heavens adore Him;
> Praise Him, angels, in the height;
> Sun and moon, rejoice before Him;
> Praise Him, all ye stars and light:

Praise the Lord, for He hath spoken;
Worlds His mighty voice obeyed;
Laws which never shall be broken,
For their guidance hath He made.

Worship, honour, glory, blessing,
Lord, we offer to Thy name;
Young and old, Thy praise expressing,
Join their Saviour to proclaim.
As the saints in heaven adore Him,
We would bow before Thy throne;
As Thine angels serve before Thee
So on earth Thy will be done.

Praise be to Thee, O Divine Spirit, for the wonder of the world, for the brightness and warmth of the sun, for the silver moon, for the everchanging sky, the shifting clouds and the glory of sunrise and sunset.

Praise be to Thee for the earth, the sustainer of all that lives, for the beauty of hills, plains and valleys, for meadows and fields, flowers and trees, animals and birds and for all the myriad forms of life.

Praise be to Thee for water, for the rain that refreshes the earth, for rushing torrents and slow-moving streams, for the sea, beautiful in its stillness and terrible in its storm.

Praise be to Thee for the gifts of science and invention, for singers and musicians, for poets and craftsmen, and for all those who work in form and colour to increase the beauty of life.

Praise be to Thee for the courage of heroes, the example of thy saints and the splendour of all noble deeds; for the memory of our dead and for the hope of the life everlasting.

When used by a group 'Praise be to Thee, O God' may be said or sung after each clause.

Spirit of life, who fillest all things, open our eyes that we may love the beauty of this world and grant that through this temporal beauty we may be brought at length to the heavenly beauty which is eternal.   Amen.

To Him from whom all splendour springs,
The source of all creation;
Inspirer of all lovely things
In every age and nation;
Begetter of each noble deed,
Of every perfect work the seed,
Be praise and adoration.   Amen.

ADDITIONAL MORNING PRAYERS

Into Thy hands, O God, we commend ourselves this day. Let Thy presence be with us to its close; enable us to feel that in doing our work we are doing Thy will, and in helping others we are serving Thee.

O God, I thank Thee for Thy goodness: for Thy protection, and for the refreshment of the past night, and for bringing me in health and happiness to the light of another day. I thank Thee also, O Lord, for all my opportunities of serving Thee. Grant that I may be worthier of Thy blessings.

Lord, I beseech Thee to be present with me throughout this day. Strengthen me, that I may think and speak and act as a true follower of Jesus Christ, and that I may, in however small a way, be doing something for the advancement of Thy kingdom. Help me to remember Thy presence and to live worthy of Thy calling.   (1)

Lord, be Thou this day within me to purify me, above me to draw me up, beneath me to sustain me, before me to lead me, behind me to restrain me, round me to protect me. (2)

O God, the true light of the faithful, the everlasting glory of the just, whose light goeth not out, whose splendour knoweth no end, grant that we may live in Thy glory and enter into the light of Thy eternity; so that as Thou hast made light to dawn upon us after the night, by Thee we may attain to that blessed and eternal day.   (3)

At the beginning of this new day I dedicate myself once more to Your service, resolving to be Your faithful servant and to try to do your will. Preserve me both in soul and body;

give me health and wisdom; uphold me in temptation; keep me from sin; and assist me in all things to please You.

Spirit of life, who fillest all the world, I worship and adore Thee; in the morning I raise my voice in praise to Thee. Dwell in my heart, O Spirit of God, that I may be full of light and that, knowing the will of the Father, I may follow the path which leads to eternal life; through the power of the Christ.

O Lord, help me to remember that Your divine strength is in me always and that it is in my power to make my life what You would have it be.

FOR BOYS AND GIRLS

O Lord our God, who art everywhere present, teach us in home and school to serve one another and to conquer self; help us to make our bodies strong and healthy and our minds alert and keen, that both may be used worthily in Your service; and give us thankful hearts that we may love and praise You always.

A MORNING RECESSIONAL HYMN

Lord of our life, in whom alone we live,
Without whose touch all action fades to nought,
Now as our worship ends, Thy blessing give
And strength to each to serve Thee as he ought.

Our morning praise is sung, our prayers are said,
Now forth we go our duties to fulfil.
May all we do by Thee be hallowed,
Each thought and deed conforming to Thy will.

Not in this sacred place alone be prayer,
But in the humdrum labours of our days
Grant we may find Thy presence everywhere
And make each task a sacrament of praise.

Glory and adoration be to Thee,
The God most high, whom heaven and earth adores
Glorious and blessed, holy Trinity
Which was and is and shall be evermore.

A MORNING RECESSIONAL HYMN

Schubert   John Milne

This hymn was written for use at the conclusion of a corporate act of worship. The version printed below is designed to be said by an individual either as part of his morning prayer or on setting out for work.

Lord of our life, in whom alone we live,
Without whose touch all action fades to nought,
Now as I start this day Thy blessing give,
And strength and will to serve Thee as I ought.

My morning vows I've made, my prayers I've said,
Now forth I go my duties to fulfil.
May all I do by Thee be hallowed,
Each thought and deed conforming to Thy will.

Not in some place apart alone be prayer,
But in the humdrum labours of my days
Grant I may find Thy presence everywhere
And make each task a sacrament of praise.

Glory and adoration *etc.*

4. At Eventide there shall be Light

A NIGHT MEDITATION

Dear night! this world's defeat;
The stop to busy fools; care's check and curb;
The day of spirits; my soul's calm retreat
        Which none disturb!
Christ's progress and His praying time;
The hours to which high Heaven doth chime.

God's silent, searching flight;
When my Lord's head is filled with dew, and all
His locks are wet with the clear drops of night
        His still, soft call;
His knocking time, the soul's dumb watch,
When spirits their fair kindred catch.

There is in God – some say –
A deep but dazzling darkness; as men here
Say it is late and dusky, because they
        See not all clear.
O for that night! where I in Him
Might live invisible and dim!

AN EVENING OFFICE

Adoration and thanksgiving be to Thee, my Lord this night. I praise Thee, I bless Thee, I glorify Thee.

O joyful light of the holy glory of the immortal Father, who is heavenly, holy, blessed, O Jesu Christ: having come to the going-down of the sun, and beholding the light of evening, we sing praise to God, Father, Son and Holy Spirit. Worthy art Thou at all times to be praised with thankful voices, O

Son of God, Giver of life; therefore the world doth glorify
Thee.   (1)

or, in this translation:

> Hail, gladdening Light, of His pure glory poured,
> Who is the immortal Father, heavenly blest,
> Holiest of Holies, Jesus Christ, our Lord.
>
> Now we are come to the sun's hour of rest,
> The lights of evening round us shine,
> We hymn the Father, Son, and Holy Spirit divine.
>
> Worthiest art Thou at all times to be sung
> With undefiled tongue,
> Son of our God, Giver of Life, Alone!
> Therefore for ever doth the world Thy glories own. (1)

Here, if you wish, say the Radiation of Divine Love and Compassion.
Several forms are given above. Then continue as follows:

> Within this Radiation of Love I place (*or* I pray for)

– my relations, friends and acquaintances;
– those in trouble, sorrow, need, sickness or any other
  adversity;
– those to whom are entrusted power, decision and influence;
– all departed souls;
– all mankind;
– all creation.
To each and all grant Thy benediction and peace.

O God and Father of all, whom the heavens adore, may
the whole earth also worship Thee, all kingdoms obey Thee,
all tongues confess Thee, and the sons of men love and serve
in unity, security and peace.

I pray also for myself,
– for forgiveness of all my sins,
– for renewal of bodily vigour,
– for illumination of mind,

- for the hallowing of every thought and word and deed.
May I love You more truly, see You more clearly, and serve
  You more faithfully.

*The prayer from Compline, 'Be present, O merciful God', may be
said here.*

Into Thy hands I commit myself and all who are dear to
me. Watch over us with Thy loving care while we sleep and
bring us safely to another day, refreshed and ready for Thy
service.

Support us, O Lord, all the days of this earthly life, till the
shades lengthen, the evening comes, the busy world is
hushed, the fever of life is over, and our work is done. Then,
in thy mercy, grant us a safe lodging, a holy rest and peace
at the last.   (2)

Now unto God, holy, blessed and most glorious Trinity,
ever enthroned in the Unity of the One Godhead, be adoration throughout all ages, worlds without end.   Amen.

Father, into Thy hands I commend my spirit this night and
for ever.

Deo gratias, or Thanks be to God for everything.

Preserve us, O Lord, while waking and guard us as we
sleep; that awake we may watch with Christ, and may rest in
peace.

May the Lord Jesus Christ, who is the splendour of the
eternal light, remove from our hearts all darkness, this night
and evermore.   Amen.

BEFORE FALLING ASLEEP

Lord of my dreaming, let me dream in You,
Cradled within Your arms the whole night through,
Serene and quiet in Your love's embrace.
Then, Lord of my waking, let me wake in You.

or

> Be Thou, Lord, in my sleeping;
> Be Thou, Lord, in my dreaming;
> Be Thou, Lord, in my awakening to a new day.

Evening Prayers

(a) PRAYERS AND HYMNS FROM THE OFFICE OF COMPLINE

Visit, we beseech Thee, O Lord, this place [*or* house] and drive from it all the snares of the enemy [*or* all evil]. May Thy holy angels [*or* Thy spirit] dwell herein to preserve it in harmony and peace; and may Thy blessing rest upon it always.

Lighten our darkness, we beseech Thee, O Lord; and by Thy great mercy defend us from all perils and dangers of this night; for the love of Thine only Son, our Saviour, Jesus Christ.

O Lord Jesus Christ, Son of the living God, who at this evening hour didst rest in the sepulchre, and didst thereby sanctify the grave to be a bed of hope to Thy people; make us so to abound in sorrow for our sins, which were the cause of Thy Passion, that when our bodies lie in the dust, our souls may live with Thee.

Look down, O Lord, from Thy heavenly throne; illuminate the darkness of this light with Thy celestial brightness; and from the sons of light banish the deeds of darkness.

Be present, O merciful God, and protect us through the silent hours of this night, so that we who are wearied by the changes and chances of this fleeting world, may repose upon Thine eternal changelessness.

> To Thee before the close of day,
> Creator of the world, we pray
> That with Thy wonted favour Thou
> Wouldst be our guard and keeper now.

From all ill dreams defend our eyes,
From nightly fears and fantasies;
Tread under foot our ghostly foe,
That no pollution we may know.

O Father, that we ask be done,
Through Jesus Christ, Thine only Son,
Who with the Holy Ghost and Thee,
Doth live and reign eternally.

O Christ, who art the Light and Day,
Thou drivest darksome night away;
We know Thee as the Light of light,
Illuminating mortal sight.

All-holy Lord, we pray to Thee,
Keep us tonight from danger free;
Grant us, dear Lord, in Thee to rest,
So be our sleep in quiet blest.

And while the eyes soft slumber take,
Still be the heart to Thee awake;
Be Thy right hand upheld above
Thy servants resting in Thy love.

Remember us, dear Lord, we pray,
While in this mortal flesh we stay:
'Tis Thou who dost the soul defend –
Be present with us to the end.

(b) OTHER EVENING PRAYERS

AN ISLAMIC EVENING PRAYER

My Lord and my God, eyes are at rest, stars are setting,
hushed are the movements of birds in their nests. And Thou
art the Just who knowest no change, the Equity that swerveth
not, the Everlasting that passeth not away. The doors of men
are locked; but Thy door is open to him who calls on Thee.

My Lord, each lover is now alone with his beloved, and Thou
art for me the Beloved.   (1)

EVENING PRAYER OF A JEWISH CHILD

Blessed art Thou, O Lord our God, King of the universe,
who makest the bands of sleep to fall upon mine eyes, and
slumber upon mine eyelids.

May it be Thy will, O Lord my God and God of my
fathers, to suffer me to lie down in peace, and let me rise up
again in peace . . .

Blessed be the Lord by day; blessed be the Lord by night.
Blessed be the Lord when we lie down; blessed be the Lord
when we rise up.

Behold He that guardeth Israel will neither slumber nor
sleep.

Into Thy hands I commend my spirit; Thou hast redeemed
me, O Lord God of truth.   (2)

FROM THE JEWISH SABBATH EVENING SERVICE

Blessed art Thou, O Lord our God, King of the universe,
who at Thy word bringest on the evening twilight . . . Thou
createst day and night; Thou rollest away the light before
the darkness, and the darkness before the light; Thou makest
the day to pass and the night to approach, and dividest the day
from the night . . . Blessed art Thou, O Lord, who bringest
on the evening twilight.   (2)

A LITTLE EVENING PRAYER FOR EVERYONE

Watch Thou, dear Lord, with those who wake, or watch,
or weep tonight, and give Thine angels charge over those who
sleep. Tend Thy sick ones, O Lord Christ. Rest Thy weary
ones. Bless Thy dying ones. Soothe Thy suffering ones. Pity
Thine afflicted ones. Shield Thy joyous ones. And all for
Thy Love's sake.

5. Forms of Confession

We confess to God Almighty, the Father, the Son and the Holy Ghost, that we have sinned in thought, word and deed, through our own grievous fault. Wherefore we pray God to have mercy upon us.

May the Almighty and merciful Lord grant us pardon and remission of all our sins, time for amendment of life, and the grace and comfort of the Holy Spirit.

O merciful Lord, forgive my feebleness in following You; pardon all that has been unworthy in my life; forgive my neglect of Your will and my forgetfulness of Your presence. Teach me Your way, O Lord, and draw me nearer to Yourself.

O God, the Father of mercies, I Your unworthy child, who have erred and strayed from Your ways, return to You with contrite heart, beseeching You to forgive me and to deliver me from evil. Remembering my weakness, I ask You to help me to lay aside all evil thoughts, words and deeds. May the power of evil be broken in me, and may the power of good be strengthened; through Jesus Christ, my Lord.

O Lord Jesus, who for my sake didst undergo the shame of the Cross, forgive me for all the sins I have committed this day. Grant me knowledge to see my faults, strength to resist temptation and willingness to endure hardness in Your service.

Almighty God, Father of our Lord Jesus Christ, we have sinned exceedingly in thought, word and deed against Thee, against our neighbour and against ourselves. For Thy Son, our Lord Jesus Christ's sake forgive us all that is past; and grant that we may serve Thee in newness of life, to the glory of Thy Name.

6. Matins and Evensong

Abbreviated from the Book of Common Prayer

℣ O Lord, open Thou our lips;

℟ And our mouths shall show forth Thy praise.

℣ O God, make speed to save us;

℟ O Lord, make haste to help us.

℣ Glory be to the Father, and to the Son, and to the Holy Ghost;

℟ As it was in the beginning, is now, and ever shall be, world without end.   Amen.

℣ Praise ye the Lord;

℟ The Lord's name be praised.

Venite, exultemus Domino

O come, let us sing unto the Lord: let us heartily rejoice in the strength of our salvation.

Let us come before His presence with thanksgiving: and show ourselves glad in Him with psalms.

For the Lord is a great God: and a great King above all gods.

In His hand are all the corners of the earth: and the strength of the hills is His also.

The sea is His and He made it: and His hands prepared the dry land.

O come, let us worship and fall down: and kneel before the Lord our maker.

For He is the Lord our God: and we are the people of His pasture, and the sheep of His hand.

Glory be to the Father and to the Son: and to the Holy Ghost:

As it was in the beginning, is now, and ever shall be: world without end.   Amen.

A psalm may follow; at Evensong the Venite *is omitted; only a psalm is said or sung. A Lesson or suitable reading follows.*

Then at Matins

TE DEUM LAUDAMUS

PRAISE TO THE BLESSED TRINITY

We praise Thee who art God:
We confess Thee who art the Lord.
All the earth doth worship Thee:
Who art the Father everlasting.
To Thee all angels cry aloud:
The heavens and all the powers therein.
To Thee Cherubim and Seraphim continually do cry
Holy holy holy Lord God of hosts:
The heavens and the earth are full of the majesty of Thy
    glory.
The glorious band of the Apostles praiseth Thee:
The noble company of the Prophets praiseth Thee:
The white-robed army of the Martyrs praiseth Thee:
The holy Church throughout all the world confesseth Thee,
The Father of an endless majesty:
Thy worshipful true and only Son, also the Comforter the
    Holy Ghost.

PRAISE AND PRAYER TO CHRIST THE SON

Thou O Christ art King of Glory:
Thou art the Father's everlasting Son.
When Thou tookest our nature upon Thee to deliver man-
    kind:
Thou didst not shrink from the Virgin's womb.
When Thou hadst vanquished the sting of death:
Thou didst open the kingdom of heaven to all that believe in
    Thee.

Thou sittest at the right hand of God:
In the glory of the Father;
And we believe that Thou art the Judge that is to come.
Therefore we pray Thee help Thy servants:
Whom Thou hast redeemed with Thy precious blood;
Make them to be numbered with Thy saints:
In glory everlasting.   (1)

At Evensong

MAGNIFICAT

My soul doth magnify the Lord: and my spirit hath rejoiced in God my Saviour.

For he hath regarded the lowliness of His handmaiden.

For behold, from henceforth: all generations shall call me blessed.

For He that is mighty hath magnified me: and holy is His name.

And His mercy is on them that fear Him: throughout all generations.

He hath showed strength with His arm: He hath scattered the proud in the imagination of their hearts.

He hath put down the mighty from their seat: and hath exalted the humble and meek.

He hath filled the hungry with good things: and the rich He hath sent empty away.

He remembering His mercy hath holpen His servant Israel: as He promised to our forefathers, Abraham and His seed for ever.

and/or

NUNC DIMITTIS

Lord, now lettest Thou Thy servant depart in peace: according to Thy word.

For mine eyes have seen: Thy salvation.

Which Thou hast prepared: before the face of all people.

To be a light to lighten the Gentiles: and to be the glory of
Thy people Israel.

The Apostles' Creed may be said here.

℣ The Lord be with you;
℟ And with Thy spirit.

Let us pray.

Lord, have mercy upon us.
Christ, have mercy upon us.
Lord, have mercy upon us.

Our Father

℣ O Lord, shew Thy mercy upon us;
℟ And grant us Thy salvation.
℣ O Lord, save the Queen;
℟ And mercifully hear us when we call upon Thee.
℣ Endue Thy ministers with righteousness;
℟ And make Thy chosen people joyful.
℣ O Lord, save Thy people;
℟ And bless Thine inheritance.
℣ Give peace in our time, O Lord;
℟ Because there is none other that ruleth the world, but only
Thou, O God.
℣ O God, make clean our hearts within us;
℟ And take not Thy Holy Spirit from us.

Here follow the Collect or Collects for the Day.

Then at Matins:

O God, who art the author of peace and lover of concord,
in knowledge of whom standeth our eternal life, whose service
is perfect freedom: defend us Thy humble servants from all
assaults of our enemies; that we, surely trusting in Thy

defence, may not fear the power of any adversaries; through the might of Jesus Christ our Lord.

O Lord our heavenly Father, almighty and everlasting God, who hast safely brought us to the beginning of this day, defend us in the same by Thy mighty power; and grant that this day we fall into no sin, neither run into any kind of danger; but that all our doings may be ordered by Thy governance, to do always that which is righteous in Thy sight; through Jesus Christ our Lord.

At Evensong:

O God, from whom all holy desires, all good counsels, and all just works do proceed, give unto Thy servants that peace which the world cannot give; that both our hearts may be set to obey Thy commandments, and also that by Thee we, being defended from the fear of our enemies, may pass our time in rest and quietness; through the merits of Jesus Christ our Saviour.

Lighten our darkness, we beseech Thee, O Lord; and by Thy great mercy defend us from all the perils of this night; for the love of Thy only Son, our Saviour, Jesus Christ.

At both Matins and Evensong:

Almighty God, who hast given us grace at this time with one accord to make our common supplications unto Thee; and dost promise that when two or three are gathered together in Thy Name Thou art in the midst of them: Fulfil now, O Lord, the desires and petitions of Thy servants, as may be most expedient for them, granting us in this world knowledge of Thy truth, and in the world to come life everlasting.   (2)

The grace of our Lord Jesus Christ, and the love of God, and the fellowship of the Holy Ghost, be with us all evermore.   Amen.

A GENERAL THANKSGIVING

Almighty God, Father of all mercies, we Thine unworthy servants do give Thee most humble and hearty thanks for all Thy goodness and loving-kindness to us, and to all men. We bless Thee for our creation, preservation, and all the blessings of this life; but above all, for Thine inestimable love in the redemption of the world by our Lord Jesus Christ, for the means of grace, and for the hope of glory. And we beseech Thee, give us that due sense of all Thy mercies, that our hearts may be unfeignedly thankful, and that we shew forth Thy praise, not only with our lips, but in our lives, by giving up ourselves to Thy service, and by walking before Thee in holiness and righteousness all our days; through Jesus Christ our Lord, to whom with Thee and the Holy Ghost be all honour and glory, world without end.   Amen.

7. Litanies

I.

A LITANY

Based on the Litany in the Book of Common Prayer

O God the Father of heaven: have mercy upon us when we call upon Thee;

O God the Son, Redeemer of the world: have mercy upon us when we call upon Thee;

O God the Holy Ghost, proceeding from the Father and the Son: have mercy upon us when we call upon Thee;

O holy, blessed and glorious Trinity, three Persons and one God: have mercy upon us when we call upon Thee.

Jesus, by the mystery of Thy holy Incarnation: by Thy holy Nativity and Circumcision: by Thy Baptism, Fasting and Temptation: good Lord, deliver us.

By Thine Agony and bloody Sweat: by Thy Cross and Passion: by Thy precious Death and Burial: by Thy glorious Resurrection and Ascension: and by the coming of the Holy Ghost: good Lord, deliver us.

Then follow these petitions, all replying 'We beseech Thee to hear us, good Lord'.

We beseech Thee to hear us, O Lord God: and that it may please Thee to show Thy mercy upon all men:

That it may please Thee to keep and strengthen Thy servant, Elizabeth, our most gracious Queen and Governor:

That it may please Thee to further the work of Thy Church in all the world, and to bring all men to the knowledge of Thy truth:

That it may please Thee to endue the High Court of Parliament, and all the ministers of the Crown, with grace, wisdom and understanding:

That it may please Thee to bless our native land, and ever to preserve it in order, liberty and justice:

That it may please Thee to inspire with Thy Holy Spirit those who take counsel for the nations of the world, so that they may bring to all peoples unity, peace and concord:

That it may please Thee to fill our homes with mutual affection and trust, to bless our parents, relations and friends, and to protect them in all dangers:

[That it may please Thee to bless this school (university, college), with virtue, diligence and piety, so that in all we do we may worthily serve Thee:

That it may please Thee to incline unto the true serving of Thee all who have gone forth from this school (university, college), and to keep them under Thy gracious care and protection:]*

That it may please Thee to succour, help and comfort all that are in danger, necessity and tribulation:

That it may please Thee to give and preserve to our use the kindly fruits of the earth, so as in due time we may enjoy them:

That it may please Thee to bring into the way of truth all such as have erred and are deceived:

That it may please Thee to give us true repentance; to forgive us all our sins, negligences and ignorances; and to endue us with the grace of the Holy Spirit:

Son of God, we beseech Thee to hear us.

O Lamb of God, that takest away the sins of the world:
grant us Thy peace.

O Lamb of God, that takest away the sins of the world:
have mercy upon us.

O Christ, hear us.

Lord have mercy upon us.

Christ have mercy upon us.

* When used in the Chapel of a school, university or college.

Lord have mercy upon us.
Our Father. . .

Almighty God, who hast given us grace at this time with
one accord to make our common supplications unto Thee;
and dost promise that when two or three are gathered together in Thy Name Thou art in the midst of them: Fulfil
now, O Lord, the desires and petitions of Thy servants, as
may be most expedient for them, granting us in this world
knowledge of Thy truth, and in the world to come life
everlasting.

The grace of our Lord Jesus Christ, and the love of God,
and the fellowship of the Holy Ghost, be with us all evermore.   Amen.

2.

A LITANY OF THE GOOD LIFE

Let us make our petitions to God, our heavenly Father.

Most holy and most merciful God, the strength of the
weak, the Saviour of the sinful, the refuge of Thy children
in every time of need, hear us, O Father, as we make our
prayer to Thee.

> Father, whose very name is Love,
> Through whom all creatures live,
> Creator Spirit, who dost move
> In all things, hear, forgive.
> We need not leave our earthly state
> Nor climb the heavenly stair
> To find Thee, for the golden gate
> In here, is everywhere.

When our faith grows weak and our love cold; when we
lose our vision of Thee and the spiritual world seems far
away:

Gracious Father, help us.

When we are tempted to mean and wicked ways and sin grows less sinful in our sight; when duty is difficult and Thy service is hard:

> Gracious Father, help us.

When the unknown future troubles us and in our fears and anxieties we forget Thine eternal love and care:

> Gracious Father, help us.

> Father, on bended knees I pray
> To Thee, my Lord, my God,
> That I may know the Christlike way
> And tread the path He trod.
> Thy Holy Spirit now impart
> And through my being shine,
> That I may hold within my heart
> The Radiance Divine.

Deliver us, O Father, from all sin and enlighten us by the indwelling of Thy Holy Spirit, that, loving Thee perfectly, we may serve Thee with steadfast hearts.

From irresolute purpose, from uncontrolled desires and from a weak and wavering will:

After each petition is said 'Loving Father, deliver us'.

From slackness and indolence, from indifference to knowledge and truth and from refusal to use the gifts with which Thou hast endowed us:

From low ideals and false ambitions, from pride and vanity, from envy and hypocrisy, from self-assertion and self-seeking and from blindness to the common good:

From dislike of criticism and desire for popularity, from cowardice and love of ease and from unreadiness to do our duty at all times:

From dishonesty and unfaithfulness, from cruelty and injustice and from indifference to the sufferings of others:

From fear and suspicion, from intolerance and hatred, from
harshness of judgement and from unwillingness to forgive:

Almighty God, in whom is no darkness, give us Thy light
to guide us and Thy strength to sustain us; that, in all our
ways being guided and guarded by Thee, we may be kept
from falling and come at length to full and happy communion
with Thyself; through Thy mercy in Jesus Christ our Lord.
Amen.

3.

A LITANY FOR ALL MEN

Almighty God, who hast taught us to make prayer and
intercession for all men, we pray:

For all who guide and direct the thoughts and lives of the
people, for ministers of religion, for statesmen, administra-
tors and journalists, for artists, authors and musicians, that
our common life may be crowned with truth and beauty;

After each petition is said 'O Christ, hear us'.

For all who heal the mind and body and tend the sick and
afflicted, that they may follow in the footsteps of Christ,
the great physician;

For all on whose work we depend for the necessities of life,
that we may respect their labours and that they may seek
no private profit which would hinder the good of all;

For parents and children, that purity, love and honour may
dwell in our homes, and duty and affection may be the
bond of our family life;

For all who are afflicted in mind, body or estate; for those in
pain and trouble; for the blind, the deaf, the dumb and the
maimed; for those whose livelihood is insecure or who are
hungry, homeless or destitute; for those who are depressed,
anxious or afraid; that they may be comforted and sustained
by Thy love and care.

FOR OUR OWN LAND

O heavenly Father, who holdest all things in the hollow of
Thy hand, guard our country, we pray Thee, in these difficult
times. Endow its rulers with wisdom and strength, its people
with understanding and patience, that both working for the
common good, this land may be brought safely through all
its troubles.

FOR THE WHOLE WORLD

And while we pray for our own land, we pray to Thee
also for the whole world. Shed Thy benediction upon all
men. Look down in pity on our striving world, still its
conflicts and hatreds, infuse it with Thy spirit of understanding love, that nation and nation, class and class may learn to
dwell together in unity, peace and concord; and give us, in
the midst of earthly tumult and strife, hearts so stayed on
Thee that we may know the peace that passeth understanding,
which no outward thing can destroy.

Almighty God, from whom all thoughts of truth and peace
proceed, kindle, we pray Thee, in the hearts of all men the
true love of peace, and guide with Thy pure and peaceable
wisdom those who take counsel for the nations of the earth;
that in tranquillity Thy kingdom may go forward, till the
whole world is filled with the knowledge of Thy love.

O God, the physician of men and nations, the restorer of
the years that have been destroyed, draw all men unto Thee
and one to another by the bands of Thy love, that the world
may be united in a sacred brotherhood, wherein justice and
mercy, truth, faith and freedom may flourish, and Thou
mayest ever be glorified.

FOR THE CHURCH

O God of unchanging power and eternal light, look favour-
ably on Thy whole Church, that wonderful and sacred

mystery, and, by the tranquil operation of Thy perpetual providence, carry out the work of man's salvation.

Peace I leave with you; my peace I give unto you. Not as the world giveth give I unto you. Let not your heart be troubled neither let it be afraid.

8. Memorials of Our Lord Jesus Christ

HIS INCARNATION

Let us rejoice in the coming of the Holy Child, Jesus, who, being the very Word of God, took upon himself our manhood that He might redeem mankind.

> His robes of light he laid aside,
> Which did His majesty adorn,
> And the frail state of mortals tried,
> In human flesh and figure born.
>
> The Son of God thus man became,
> That men the sons of God might be,
> And by their second birth regain
> A likeness to His deity.   (1)

THE GOSPEL

And it came to pass in those days that there went out a decree from Caesar Augustus that all the world should be enrolled. And all went to be enrolled, every one into his own city. And Joseph also went up from Galilee, out of the city of Nazareth, into Judaea, unto the city of David which is called Bethlehem; because he was of the house and lineage of David; to be enrolled with Mary, his espoused wife, being great with child. And so it was, that, while they were there, the days were accomplished that she should be delivered. And she brought forth her first-born son, and wrapped him in swaddling clothes, and laid him in a manger; because there was no room for them in the inn.

O God, who in creating human nature didst marvellously ennoble it, and hast still more marvellously restored it, grant

that by the mystery of the Holy Incarnation of Thy Son we
may be made partakers of His divinity, who vouchsafed to
become partaker of our humanity, even Jesus Christ, our
Lord, who with Thee in the unity of the Holy Ghost liveth
and reigneth world without end.   (2)

℣ In the beginning was the Word, and the Word was with
    God, and the Word was God.
℟ All things were made by Him and without Him was not
    anything made that was made.
℣ And the Word was made flesh.
℟ Alleluya.
℣ And the Word was made flesh and dwelt among us; and
    we beheld His glory.
℟ And we beheld His glory, the glory as of the only-
    begotten of the Father, full of grace and truth. Alleluya.

By the mystery of the Incarnate Word the new light of Thy
brightness hath shone upon the eyes of our mind; that we,
knowing God seen of the eyes, by Him may be snatched up
into the love of that which eye hath not seen.   (3)

Wherefore to Thee, O Christ, who by Thine Incarnation
hast gathered into one things earthly and heavenly, we raise
our hearts and voices in praise and adoration:

> O come, all ye faithful,
> Joyful and triumphant,
> O come ye, O come ye to Bethlehem;
> Come and behold Him
> Born the King of Angels;
> O come, let us adore Him,
> O come, let us adore Him,
> O come, let us adore Him, Christ the Lord.
>
> God of God,
> Light of Light,
> Lo, He abhors not the Virgin's womb;
> Very God,

Begotten not created:
O come, *etc.*

Sing, choirs of angels,
Sing in exultation,
Sing, all ye citizens of heaven above;
Glory to God
In the highest:
O come, *etc.*

or, alternatively:

O come, O come, thou Lord of Light,
And dawn upon our darkened sight;
Open our eyes, that we may know
In Thee God manifest below.

Rejoice, rejoice, a Child is born,
Who comes to save a world forlorn.

O come, O come, Thou Perfect One,
The Father's co-eternal Son,
That man in mortal flesh may see
The image of the Deity.

Rejoice, *etc.*

O come, O come, eternal Word,
Which was before creation stirred,
Incarnate now with man to dwell,
The Christ, the Lord Emmanuel.

Rejoice, *etc.*

O come, O come, thou Prince of Peace.
From earthly warfare bring release,
Rest to our souls, and, after strife,
The gift of everlasting life.

Rejoice, *etc.*

O come, O come, Thou Love unknown,
Descending from Thy heavenly throne;
O come, the world's Redeemer, come,
And guide us to our destined home.

Rejoice, rejoice, a Child is born,
Who comes to save a world forlorn.   (4)

Jesus, Son of God, bless and keep us; and to the fellowship
of the citizens above may the King of Angels bring us all.
                                                    Amen.

2.

HIS PASSION

Let us remember with reverence the Passion of our Lord
Jesus Christ.

Greater love hath no man than this, that a man lay down
his life for his friends.

Pange lingua gloriosi proelium certaminis

Sing, my tongue, the glorious battle,
Sing the ending of the fray;
Now above, the Cross, the trophy,
Sound the loud triumphant lay:
Tell how Christ, the world's redeemer,
As a victim won the day.

How, the thirty years accomplished,
Went He forth from Nazareth,
Destined, dedicate and willing,
Wrought His work, and met His death;
Like a lamb he humbly yielded
On the Cross His dying breath.   (1)

THE GOSPEL

And when they were come to the place which is called Calvary, there they crucified Him, and the malefactors, one on the right hand, and the other on the left. Then said Jesus: 'Father, forgive them, for they know not what they do.'

And they parted His raiment, and cast lots. And the people stood beholding. Then the rulers also with them derided Him, saying: 'He saved others; let Him save Himself, if He be the Christ, the chosen of God.' And the soldiers also mocked Him.

And when the sixth hour was come, there was darkness over the whole land until the ninth hour. And at the ninth hour Jesus cried with a loud voice, saying: '*Eloi, Eloi, lama sabachthani*?' which is, being interpreted, My God, my God, why hast thou forsaken me?

After this, Jesus knowing that all things were now accomplished, that the scripture might be fulfilled, saith, 'I thirst.' Now there was set a vessel full of vinegar; and they filled a sponge with vinegar, and put it upon hyssop, and put it to His mouth.

When Jesus therefore had received the vinegar, He said: 'It is finished'; and he bowed His head, and gave up the ghost.

> O sacred head, sore wounded,
> Defiled and put to scorn;
> O kingly head, surrounded
> With mocking crown of thorn;
> What sorrow mars Thy grandeur?
> Can death Thy bloom deflower?
> O countenance whose splendour
> The hosts of heaven adore!   (2)

Hear us, O Christ, have mercy upon us; for we have sinned against Thee.

O Victor-Victim, who from Thy Cross dost look down with pity on human sorrow and sin, hear us, Thy children, as we make our supplication to Thee.

Hear us, O Christ, etc.

For all the cruelty and oppression, the hatred and injustice, with which the world is marred, fill us, O Lord, with shame and contrition.

Hear us, O Christ, etc.

For the sins by which we crucify Thee afresh, for our weakness and cowardice and failure to follow Thine example, grant us, O loving Saviour, Thy forgiveness.

Hear us, O Christ, etc.

By the great love which Thou hast shown for us, draw us, O Jesus, closer to Thyself; strengthen us that we may conquer the sin within us.   (3)

Hear us, O Christ, etc.

Lord Jesus Christ, who by the yielding of Thyself unto death hast redeemed mankind, grant that we may crucify our lower natures and serve Thee in lowliness of heart, seeking not our own glory but ever striving to follow the pattern of Thy humility.

> My song is love unknown,
> My Saviour's love to me,
> Love to the loveless shown
> That they might lovelier be.
> O who am I,
> That for my sake
> My Lord should take
> Frail flesh and die?
>
> He came from His blest throne,
> Salvation to bestow;
> But men made strange, and none
> The longed-for Christ would know.

But O, my Friend,
My Friend indeed,
Who at my need
His life did spend!

Sometimes they strew His way,
And His sweet praises sing;
Resounding all the day
Hosannas to their King.
Then 'Crucify!'
Is all their breath,
And for His death
They thirst and cry.

Here might I stay and sing,
No story so divine;
Never was love, dear King,
Never was grief like Thine.
This is my Friend
In whose sweet praise
I all my days
Could gladly spend.   (4)

Behold the salvation of mankind is set upon the Tree of
the Cross, so that whence came death, thence also life might
rise again; so that He who by the Tree was vanquisher might
also by the Tree be vanquished.   (5)

℣ O Saviour of the world, who by Thy Cross and precious
    Blood hast redeemed us;
℟ Save us and help us we humbly beseech Thee, O Lord.

Faithful Cross! above all other,
One and only noble tree!
None in foliage, none in blossom,
None in fruit thy peer may be;
Sweetest wood and sweetest iron!
Sweetest weight is hung on thee.

Bend thy boughs, O Tree of Glory!
Thy relaxing sinews bend;
For awhile the ancient rigour
That thy birth bestowed, suspend,
And the King of heavenly beauty
On thy bosom gently tend!   Amen.   (6)

3.

HIS RESURRECTION

Now is Christ risen from the dead and hath become the
first fruits of them that slept. For as by man came death, by
man came also the resurrection from the dead.

Alleluya.

The strife is o'er, the battle done;
Now is the Victor's triumph won,
O let the song of praise be sung: Alleluya!

Death's mightiest powers have done their worst,
And Jesus hath His foes dispersed:
Let shouts of praise and joy outburst: Alleluya!

On the third morn He rose again,
Glorious in majesty to reign;
O let us swell the joyful strain: Alleluya!

THE GOSPEL

And when the Sabbath was past, Mary Magdalene, and
Mary the mother of James and Salome had brought sweet
spices, that they might come and anoint Him. And very early
in the morning the first day of the week, they came unto the
sepulchre at the rising of the sun. And they said among
themselves, Who shall roll us away the stone from the door
of the sepulchre? And when they looked they saw that the
stone was rolled away.

And entering the sepulchre, they saw a young man sitting on the right side, clothed in a long white garment; and they were afraid. And he saith unto them, Be not afraid: ye seek Jesus of Nazareth, which was crucified: He is risen: He is not here: behold the place where they laid Him. But go your way, tell His disciples and Peter that He goeth before you into Galilee: there shall you see Him, as He said unto you. And they went quickly, and fled from the sepulchre; for they trembled and were amazed.

Then the eleven disciples went away into Galilee, into a mountain where Jesus had appointed them. And when they saw Him, they worshipped Him: but some doubted. And Jesus came and spake unto them, saying, All power is given unto me in heaven and in earth. Go ye therefore, and teach all nations, teaching them to observe all things whatsoever I have commanded you: and, lo, I am with you alway, even unto the end of the world.

> Sing ye together, morning stars,
> And shout for joy, ye sons of God;
> A glory flames along the path
> The Crucified has trod.
>
> A new creation now is born,
> A lovelier shape, a fairer birth
> Than that which seraph choirs proclaimed
> When God first made the earth.
>
> The winter of the world is past;
> The rain is gone. A song undreamed
> Wells up within the heart of man,
> The song of man redeemed.   (1)

I am Alpha and Omega, the Beginning and the End, saith the Lord. I will give unto him that is athirst of the fountain of the water of life freely. He that overcometh shall inherit all things; and I will be his God and he shall be my son.

℣ The first Adam was made a living soul; the last Adam was made a quickening spirit.

℟ Alleluya.

℣ The first man is of the earth earthy; the second man is the
Lord of heaven.

℟ Alleluya, alleluya.

℣ As in Adam all die, even so in Christ shall all be made
alive.

℟ Alleluya, alleluya, alleluya.

℣ For this corruptible must put on incorruption; and this
mortal must put on immortality. So when this corruptible shall have put on incorruption and this mortal shall
have put on immortality, then shall be brought to pass
the saying that is written:

℟ Death is swallowed up in victory. O death, where is thy
sting? O grave, where is thy victory?

Alleluya, alleluya.   (2)

O Lord Jesus, who by the giving up of Thyself unto death
hast conquered death and brought unto mankind the hope of
the life eternal, knit us with Thee in Thy risen and glorified
life; and grant that we may enter into that heavenly city in
which there is no darkness but the inhabitants thereof walk
in the brightness of Thy celestial light; for Thy Name's sake.

Hail the Lord of earth and heaven!
Praise to Thee by both be given:
Thee we greet triumphant now,
Hail, the Resurrection, Thou!   Amen.   (3)

9. Office of the Holy Spirit

℣ Dwell in our hearts, O Spirit of the living God.
℞ And depart from us never.
℣ Illumine our souls by Thy presence.
℞ And lead us in the way of truth.

Holy Spirit of God, who alone art the source of all beauty, all goodness, all truth; without whose inspiration nothing is permanent, nothing worthy; so work in us, we pray Thee, that we may follow after that which is beautiful and good and true, and by Thine aid may finally attain to that divine wisdom which is the life eternal.

THE GOSPEL

On the eve of His Passion Jesus said to His disciples: It is expedient for you that I go away; for if I do not go away the Comforter would not come to you. But if I depart, I will send Him unto you. And when He comes He will overthrow this world's idea of sin and will reveal to it the nature of true righteousness and of judgement; of sin in that it had no faith in me, of true righteousness because I go to the Father and you see me no more, of judgement because the Prince of this world is judged.

I have many more things to say to you, but you are not ready to receive them now. But when the One about whom I am telling you comes, even the Spirit of Truth, He will guide you into all truth.

Veni, sancte Spiritus

Come thou Holy Paraclete
And from Thy celestial seat

Send Thy light and brilliancy.
Father of the poor draw near;
Giver of all gifts, be here;
Come, the soul's true radiancy.

What is soiled, make Thou pure;
What is wounded, work its cure;
What is parched, fructify;
What is rigid, gently bend;
What is frozen, warmly tend;
Strengthen what goes erringly.

Fill Thy faithful, who confide
In Thy power to guard and guide,
With Thy sevenfold mystery.
Here Thy grace and virtue send,
Grant salvation to the end.
And in heaven felicity.   (1)

We pray Thee, Spirit of God, that Thou wilt lead us into
all truth, revealing and interpreting to us the words of
Christ.

Hear us, Holy Spirit

That Thou wilt enable us to walk in the way of Christ and
to offer Him faithful and acceptable service.

Hear us, Holy Spirit

That Thou wilt bring us to that liberty which Christ has
promised to those who truly follow him.

Hear us, Holy Spirit

And that Thou wilt drive from our hearts all hatred and
fear and enable us to have a right judgement in all things.

Hear us, Holy Spirit

Abide with us always, O Holy Ghost, the Comforter, and
daily increase in us Thy manifold gifts of grace: the spirit of
wisdom and understanding: the spirit of counsel and ghostly

strength; the spirit of knowledge and true godliness; that, inspired by Thine indwelling Presence, we may come at last to the life eternal; who livest and reignest with the Father and the Son, one God, now and ever.

10. Commemorations

I.

COMMEMORATION OF THE FAITHFUL ONES

℣ Blessed are the faithful ones.
℟ Their names are written in the Book of Life.

The souls of the righteous are in the hand of God: there shall no torment touch them.

In the eyes of the foolish they seemed to die, and their departure was accounted to be misery; but they are at peace.

Even if in the sight of men they were punished: yet is their hope full of immortality.

For having been a little chastened, they shall receive great good: God proved them and found them worthy of Himself.

As gold in the furnace He tried them: and as a sacrifice He received them.

They shall judge nations and have dominion over peoples: and God Himself shall reign over them for ever more.   (1)

After each of the following thanksgivings 'Thanks be to God' is said or sung.

For all who have courageously and humbly sought after truth:

For all who have added to the sum of human knowledge and understanding:

For all who have created beauty in word or form or sound:

For all who have relieved human suffering and given their lives to the service of their fellow men:

For all who have been faithful to the voice within them even through pain and death:

For all who have served Thee in their generation and whose lives were modelled on the pattern of the Lord Jesus:

Finally for Him whose wisdom was higher than the wisdom of men, whose pity was deeper than the pity of men, whose courage was greater than the courage of men, the Captain of our salvation, Jesus Christ:

We give Thee most high praise and hearty thanks for all Thy Saints, especially . . . , who have been the chosen vessels of Thy grace, and lights of the world in their several generations; and we pray that, rejoicing in their fellowship, and following their good examples, we may be partakers with them of Thy heavenly kingdom.

or

O God, who art the inspirer of all fine thoughts and noble actions, we give Thee thanks for those who have served Thee faithfully here upon earth; and we pray that we too may, according to our several abilities, render unto Thee the loyal service which Thou dost demand of us, through the power of Him who by His death conquered death, our risen and glorified Lord, Jesus Christ.

> To Him from whom all splendour springs,
> The source of all creation;
> Inspirer of all lovely things
> In every age and nation;
> Begetter of each noble deed,
> Of every perfect work the seed,
> Be praise and adoration.   Amen.

2.

COMMEMORATION OF THE DEPARTED

Kyrie eleison
Christe eleison
Kyrie eleison

O gracious and loving Shepherd of the sheep, we remember before Thee at this time Thy servant. . . . Unto Thee, who holdest in Thine hands the souls of the living and the dead,

we commend him, beseeching Thee that Thou wilt grant
unto him a quiet resting place and full and happy communion
with Thyself, who by Thy death hast conquered death and
given unto men the hope of eternal life.

Pass on [or Go forth upon] your journey, Christian soul, in
peace:
In the name of God the Father who created you;
In the Name of Jesus Christ who redeemed you;
In the Name of the Holy Spirit who sanctified you;
In the name of Angels and Archangels, in the name of
Cherubim and Seraphim, in the name of Thrones and Domin-
ions, in the name of Principalities and Powers, in the name of
the saints and heroes of the living God, pass on [or go forth],
O Christian soul.

O Father of all, hear us as we pray to Thee for him whom
we knew [or we loved] but see no longer: Grant him Thy
peace; let light perpetual shine upon him; and in Thy loving
wisdom and almighty power work in him the good purpose
of Thy perfect will; through Jesus Christ our Lord.

Rest eternal grant to him, O Lord, and may light perpetual
shine upon him.
O God, the light of faithful souls, grant unto Thy servant,
whose body rests in Christ, a place of refreshment, a blessed
tranquillity and the splendour of light.
O Lamb of God, that takest away the sins of the world,
grant him rest.
O Lamb of God, that takest away the sins of the world,
grant him eternal rest.

O eternal Lord God, who holdest all souls in life, we
beseech Thee to shed forth upon Thy whole Church in
Paradise and on earth the bright beams of Thy light and
heavenly comfort; and grant that we, following the good
examples of those who have loved and served Thee here,
and are at rest, for whose blessed memory we continually give
thanks unto Thee, may with them at length enter into Thine
unending joy; through Jesus Christ our Lord.   (1)

And I heard a voice from heaven, saying: Blessed are the dead which die in the Lord; they rest from their labours and their works live after them.

and/or

Thou didst support him all the long, hot day,
To the lengthening of the shadows and the setting sun;
Now is the fever of life over; the busy world is hushed;
             And his work done.

Grant him, Lord, at the ending of his quest,
             All journeyings past,
A safe lodging and a holy rest
             And peace at the last.   (2)

A prayer for those who are bereaved

Almighty God, Father of all mercies and giver of all comfort: deal graciously, we pray Thee, with those that mourn, that, casting every care upon Thee, they may know the consolation of Thy love; through Jesus Christ our Lord.

11. Dedication

I.

AN OFFICE OF DEDICATION

They that wait upon the Lord shall renew their strength; they shall mount up with wings as eagles; they shall run and not be weary; they shall walk and not faint.

Jesus, knowing that the Father had given all things into His hands, and that He came forth from God, and goeth unto God, riseth from supper, and layeth aside His garments; and He took a towel, and girded himself. Then He poured water into the basin and began to wash the disciples' feet and to wipe them with the towel wherewith He was girded.

So when He had washed their feet, and taken His garments, and sat down again, He said unto them, 'Know ye what I have done to you? Ye call me Master and Lord; and ye say well; for so I am. If I then, the Lord and the Master, have washed your feet, ye also ought to wash one another's feet. For I have given you an example, that you also should do as I have done to you.

Whosoever would become great among you shall be your minister; and whosoever would be first among you shall be servant of all. For verily the Son of Man came not to be ministered unto, but to minister, and to give His life as ransom for many.'

Have this mind in you, which was also in Christ Jesus; who being in the form of God, counted it not a prize to be on an equality with God, but emptied Himself, taking the form of a servant, being made in the likeness of men; and being found in fashion as a man, He humbled himself, becoming obedient even unto death, yea, the death of the cross.

Therefore let us remember the high service to which we are called.

We are called to make our minds alert and keen and our bodies supple and strong that we may use them in the service of our fellow men.

We are called to the complete surrender of ourselves, to give all and to ask nothing in return.

We are called to the perpetual search for truth, to the pursuit of knowledge, to humility, and to perfect charity.

We are called to the following of the Christ, which is the life of selfless dedication and sacrifice.

So let us dedicate ourselves anew to the high service of the King of Heaven, trusting not in our own strength, but in the strength of Christ, our Leader, who put off His celestial glory that He might become the Redeemer of all.

THE DEDICATION HYMN

O God, of earth and heaven the King,
Lord of all life and joy and love,
From whom grace, truth and beauty spring,
In whom all creatures live and move;
Not in the feebleness of age
But while my limbs are strong and free,
Thy work to do, Thy war to wage,
My body, Lord, I offer Thee.

My brain make nimble, keen and clear,
Fit instrument of mental fight;
Purge it alike of hate and fear;
Illumine with Thine own pure light.
Wisdom of God, O make me wise,
To follow truth where'er it be;
Give me, Lord, understanding eyes,
And knowledge, with humility.

To Thee I consecrate my soul;
Keep it, O Master, clean of sin;
Each impulse of my will control;
Shine, O celestial Light, within.
Spirit of Christ, direct my ways
And seal me with Thy love's impress,
That I may serve Thee all my days
And walk with Thee in holiness.

Thou art in all things. Energy,
Wisdom and Holiness Thou art.
Dwell Thou in every part of me,
Possess my head, my hands, my heart.
In me set up Thy secret shrine,
Wherein Thy voice alone is heard,
Lit by the radiance divine,
The temple of the Incarnate Word.

THE DEDICATION HYMN

Dedication   *J. Carol Case*

Andante

Organ

vv. 1, 2, 3.

O God of earth and heav'n the King, Lord of all

life — and joy and love, from whom grace, truth and

beau - ty spring, in whom all crea - tures live and

move; Not in the fee - ble - ness of age but

cresc.

while my limbs are strong and free, Thy work — to

do, Thy war — to wage, my bo - dy, Lord, I

of - fer Thee.

Descant:

Thou art   in   all — things. En - er - gy,

Thou art   in   all — things. En - ergy,

me, pos - sess___ my hands, my heart.

- sess___ my head, my hands, my heart.

In me set up Thy___ sec - ret shrine, where-

In me set up___ Thy sec - ret shrine, where-

- in＿ Thy voice＿ a - lone is heard. Lit＿

- in Thy voice a - lone is heard. Lit

by the ra - di - ance di - vine,＿ the

by＿ the ra - di - ance＿ di - vine, the

tem - ple of th'In - car - nate word.

tem - ple of th'In - car - nate word.

fff

Lord Jesus, who by Thy life on earth and by the sacrifice of Thyself on the Cross of Calvary, hast given to us a pattern of selfless devotion, enable us to follow to the uttermost the example which Thou hast set us; and let not any weaknesses of our nature hinder us from giving to Thee the loyal service which is Thy due; for Thy Name's sake.

Make us, O Lord, the instruments of Thy will. Where there is hatred let us bring understanding; where there is despair let us bring hope; where there is suffering let us bring relief; where there is discord let us bring harmony; where there is ignorance let us bring knowledge; and may our souls, our minds and our bodies be dedicated entirely and absolutely to Thy service.

Finally let us sum up our petitions in the prayer which Christ himself has taught us:

The Lord's Prayer.

THE DISMISSAL
(When the Office is used by a group)

Go forth in the strength of Christ Victorious; have faith and fear not; do justly; love mercy and walk humbly with God; and may the spirit of the Lord Jesus be in your hearts.

Amen.

2.

A SIMPLE ACT OF DEDICATION

Let me rededicate myself to You, O Lord of all good life.

In the work of my hands may I glorify You.
In the words of my lips may I praise You.
In the thoughts of my mind may I adore You.
In the longing of my spirit may I reach out to You.

Most high eternal and ineffable Wisdom, enlighten me.
Most high and eternal Strength, support me.
Most high and incomprehensible Light, illuminate me.
Most high and infinite Mercy, have mercy upon me.

Deathless One, the Strong, the Holy,
Wisdom of the God most high,

Light of Light, the Word incarnate,
Whom the ages glorify,
Jesus, Brother, Friend, Redeemer,
Hear me, bless and sanctify.   Amen.

12. A Solemn Liturgy

Showing forth the wondrous mystery of the co-inherence of the temporal and eternal, of matter and spirit, revealed and given its perfect expression in the Incarnation of the Divine Logos in our Lord Jesus Christ.

Cantor: In the beginning God created the heaven and the earth. And the earth was waste and void: and darkness was upon the face of the deep.

Choir: And the Spirit of God moved upon the face of the waters.

Cantor: And God said: Let there be light;

Choir: And there was light.

Cantor: And God created man in His own image; in the image of God created He him.

Praise be to Thee, Giver of life and light, Creator and Sustainer of all that is; Thou who art the everlasting essence of things, beyond space and time, and yet within them; Thou who transcendest yet pervadest all things. Thou hast made man in Thine own image and our hearts are restless till they rest in Thee. Manifest Thyself to us, the creatures of Thy love, seeking Thee in the shades of ignorance. Stretch forth Thy hand to help us who cannot without Thee come to Thee and reveal Thyself to us who seek nothing beside Thee.

The Choir sings:

℣ In the beginning was the Word, and the Word was with God, and the Word was God.

℟ All things were made by Him and without Him was not anything made that was made.

℣ And the Word was made flesh.

℟ Alleluya.

℣ And the Word was made flesh and dwelt among us; and
   we beheld His glory.

℞ And we beheld His glory, the glory as of the Only-
   Begotten of the Father, full of grace and truth. Alleluya.

Brightness of the glory of the everlasting Father and express
image of Him who begat Thee before all worlds, God of God,
Light of Light, Wisdom of the Most High, who wast revealed
in the body of our manhood and in Thine Incarnation didst
gather into one, things earthly and heavenly, showing forth
in Thyself the wondrous co-inherence of the temporal and
eternal, enlighten our understanding, we beseech Thee, by
the inbreathing of the Spirit of Truth, that, by Thy grace, we
may enter into the fullness of truth.

The Choir sings this hymn to the Divine Wisdom:

Thou, Wisdom, art the breath of the power of God: a pure
   influence flowing from the glory of the Almighty.

Thou art the brightness of the everlasting light: the unspotted
   mirror of the splendour of God.

Through Thee are all things accomplished: Thou makest all
   things new.

In all ages Thou enterest into holy souls: thou makest them
   friends and prophets of God.

God loveth them that dwell in Thee: for Thou art more
   beautiful than the sun and above the order of the stars.

Thou reachest from one end to another mightily: and sweetly
   dost Thou order all things.

Teach me, O Wisdom, breath of God: give me an understanding spirit, lively, clean and undefiled.

Cantor: The sufferings of this present time are not worthy to
           be compared with the glory that shall be revealed
           in us. For the earnest expectation of the creation
           waiteth for the revealing of the sons of God. For
           the creation was subject to frustration, not for
           some deliberate fault of its own, but by reason of

Him who so subjected it in the hope that the creation itself also shall be delivered from the bondage of corruption into the liberty of the glory of the sons of God.

The Choir sings:

℣ The first Adam was made a living soul; the last Adam was made a quickening spirit.

℟ Alleluya.

℣ The first man is of the earth earthy; the second man is the Lord of heaven.

℟ Alleluya, alleluya.

℣ As in Adam all die, even so in Christ shall all be made alive.

℟ Alleluya, alleluya, alleluya.

℣ For this corruptible must put on incorruption; and this mortal must put on immortality. So when this corruptible shall have put on incorruption and this mortal shall have put on immortality, then shall be brought to pass the saying that is written:

℟ Death is swallowed up in victory. O death, where is thy sting? O grave, where is thy victory? Alleluya, alleluya.

THE PRAYER OF COMPLETION

Adoration be to Thee, O God, who in creating human nature didst so marvellously ennoble it, and hast still more marvellously restored it, and hast implanted in us Thy Spirit to lighten our darkness and guide us into the fullness of truth, so illumine our minds, we beseech Thee, that we may attain to that mount of vision whereon we may know the mystery of the perpetual intersection of the timeless with time.

And bring us, O King of Love, at the last to that timeless waking when the redemption of all creation shall be revealed, when there shall be no darkness nor dazzling but one pure light, no sound nor silence but one perfect harmony, no hopes nor fears but one full possession, no discords nor opposites but one single truth, no beginning nor ending but one eternity, in the splendour of Thy glory and the majesty of Thy dominion.

Adoration be to Thee, holy, blessed and most glorious Trinity, ever enthroned in the unity of the one Godhead, before Thee creation bows in awe and wonder and with angels and archangels and all the company of heaven cries:

Choir: Holy, holy, holy, Lord God of Hosts, heaven and earth are full of Thy glory. Glory be to Thee, O Lord most high. Amen.

13. Credo

I believe that the Dweller in the innermost spiritual sanctum of a human being, which is his real Self, is of the same essence as that spiritual Reality which men call God, which is within, behind and beyond the universe.

I believe that the nature of this ultimate spiritual Reality, unknowable to the intellect, but knowable to the heart, is Love.

I believe that God was in Jesus the Christ, reconciling the world to Himself.

After this nothing more need be said. Everything else, every creed, every dogma, is a variation or elaboration of this basic expression of faith.

14. An Anthology of Prayers in Prose and Verse

PRAYERS FROM THE ANCIENT LITURGIES

Thee, O brightness of the glory of the Eternal Father, who wast revealed in the body of our manhood, and didst enlighten our darkness by Thy light, we confess and worship and glorify at all times.

Glory be to the eternal mercy which sent Thee unto us, O Christ, Light of the world. (1)

O Wisdom that camest out of the mouth of the Most High, reaching from one end to another mightily and sweetly ordering all things, come and teach us the way of understanding.

O Dayspring, splendour of the eternal Light and Sun of Righteousness, come and enlighten those who sit in darkness and the shadow of death. (2)

Lord Jesus Christ, who for the redemption of the world didst ascend the wood of the Cross, that Thou mightest enlighten the whole world which lay in darkness; pour that light, we pray Thee, into our souls and bodies, whereby we may be enabled to attain to the light eternal; who, with the Father and the Holy Ghost, livest and reignest One God, world without end. (3)

We beseech Thee, O Lord, let our hearts be graciously enlightened by the holy radiance of Thy Son's incarnation; that so we may escape the darkness of this world, and by His guidance attain to the country of eternal brightness. (4)

O God, who in Thine eternal wisdom, didst make man when as yet he was not, and in Thy mercy didst restore him when he was lost; grant, we beseech Thee, to these souls of ours, so made and so restored, that, by Thine inspiration, we

may love Thee with all our minds, and run unto Thee with
all our hearts.   (5)

Grant to us, O Lord, not to mind earthly things, but rather
to love heavenly things; and whilst all things around us pass
away, we may ever now hold fast those things which abide
for evermore.   (6)

PRAYERS OF SOME CHRISTIAN SAINTS

O God, light of the minds that know Thee, life of the souls
that love Thee, and strength of the thoughts that seek Thee,
enlarge our minds and raise the vision of our hearts, that with
swift wings of thought, our spirits may reach Thee, the Eternal Wisdom, who art from everlasting to everlasting.   (7)

O God, true and highest Life, in whom all things live which
live truly and blessedly, who biddest us to seek Thee, and
grantest that we find Thee; O God, from whom to turn away
is to fall, to whom to turn is to rise, and in whom to abide is
to stand fast for ever, whom to know is to live, whom to serve
is to reign, whom to praise is the joy of the spirit, to Thee I
call, O blessed Trinity, that Thou mayest come to me, and
make me a temple worthy of Thy glory. Guard us, we pray
Thee, now and always, here and everywhere, within and
without, above, beneath, and on every side.   (8)

O most merciful God, we pray that Thou wouldst enter
into our souls, which Thou preparest for Thy reception by
the desire which Thou Thyself inspirest. For before we called
upon Thee, Thou hadst called us, and hadst sought us, that
we might seek Thee. Give us then thyself, O our God.   (9)

Vouchsafe, O gracious and holy Father, to bestow upon
me intellect to understand Thee, perception to perceive Thee,
reason to discern Thee, diligence to seek Thee, wisdom to
find Thee, a spirit to know Thee, a heart to meditate upon
Thee, ears to hear Thee, eyes to behold Thee, a tongue to
proclaim Thee, a conversation pleasing to Thee, patience to

wait for Thee, and perseverance to look for Thee. Grant me a perfect end, Thy holy presence, a blessed resurrection, and Thy recompense, everlasting life. (10)

O God, if only our wills be right towards Thine, do to us whatever it may please Thee. If it be Thy will that we should be in light, be thou blessed; if it be Thy will that we should be in darkness, be Thou also blessed; if Thou vouchsafe to comfort us, be Thou blessed; if Thou afflictest us, be Thou also blessed. We cheerfully receive whatsoever Thou dost appoint, and for all that befalleth us we give thanks. (11)

O Thou who art the everlasting essence of things, beyond space and time, and yet within them; Thou who transcendest yet pervadest all things; manifest Thyself to us, feeling after Thee, and seeking Thee in the shades of ignorance. Stretch forth Thy hand to help us, who cannot without Thee come to Thee and reveal Thyself to us who seek nothing beside Thee. (12)

Teach us, good Lord, to serve Thee as Thou deservest; to give and not to count the cost; to fight and not to heed the wounds; to toil and not to seek for rest; to labour and not to ask for any reward, save that of knowing that we do Thy will. (13)

My Lord and my God, take from me all that blocks my way to Thee;

My Lord and my God, give me all that speeds my way to Thee;

My Lord and my God, take this myself from me and give me as Thine own to Thee. (14)

Make me, O Lord, an instrument of thy peace. Where there is hatred, let me sow love; where there is injury, pardon; where there is doubt, faith; where there is despair, hope; where there is sadness, joy; where there is darkness, light.

O Divine Master, grant that I may not so much seek to be consoled as to console; not so much to be understood as to understand; not so much to be loved as to love. For it is in giving that we receive; it is in pardoning that we are pardoned; it is in dying that we are born again to eternal life.   (15)

PRAYERS FROM VARIOUS SOURCES

O God and Father of all, whom the heavens adore, let the whole earth also worship Thee, all kingdoms obey Thee, all tongues confess Thee, and the sons of men love and serve Thee in security and peace.

O Eternal God, who hast taught us by Thy Holy Word that our bodies are temples of Thy Spirit, keep us, we humbly beseech Thee, temperate and holy in thought and word and deed; that, with all the pure in heart, we may see Thee; and be made like unto Thee in Thy heavenly kingdom.

O God, the Holy Ghost, who dost give to each of us a measure of all Thy gifts and some gifts to each in a special measure, vouchsafe to us Thy wisdom for our foolishness, Thine understanding for our dullness, Thy counsel for our rashness, Thy courage for our cowardice, Thy knowledge for our ignorance, Thy godliness for our hardness of heart: and against all presumption and pride, seal with the spirit of holy fear these Thy gifts, who dost live and reign with the Father and the Son in one blessed Sovereignty.

O Lord Jesus, who alone art the true light of men, illuminate us with Thy divine light that we may know the path we ought to tread; and because we cannot of our own strength follow Thee worthily, fill us with the power of Thy Risen Life, that knowing Thee we may follow Thee and following Thee we may attain our heart's desire.

O God, help me to remember that Thy divine strength is in me always and it is in my power to make my life what Thou wouldst have it be.

O God, who art the light of the minds that know Thee, the life of the souls that love Thee, and the strength of the thoughts that seek Thee, help us so to know Thee that we may truly love Thee, so to love Thee that we may fully serve Thee, whose service is perfect freedom.

Lord, open my ears that my ears may hear You;
Lord, open my eyes that my eyes may see You;
Lord, open my heart that hearing You and seeing You, You may be heard and seen in me.

O God, let me not seek out of Thee what I can only find in Thee. Lift up my soul above the weary round of harassing thoughts to Thine Eternal Presence, that there I may breathe freely, there repose in Thy love, there be at rest from myself and from all things which weary me; and thence return, arrayed with Thy peace, to do and bear whatever shall please Thee. Let nothing disturb my soul, fixed in Thee; nothing draw it down, upheld by Thee, nothing turn it aside, directed by Thee. With my whole heart may I serve Thee, until in the end, by Thy grace, I may arrive at Thee. Let me not be discouraged, O God, my hope. Give me perseverance unto the end, that living or dying I may be Thine.

> We remember this church,
> A place where love is,
> And thank You
> That wherever Love is,
> There is Your Church,
> At that moment
> And for as long as the love lasts.

Lord, I dedicate my life to Thy service. Help Thou my lack of dedication.

To meet life one day at a time, one step at a time;
To have the strength and the will to keep on keeping on,
To have the wisdom to handle the affairs of my life;
To have the ability to make right and good decisions;
To have the courage to let the past go, to forge ahead resolutely;

To have the grace to meet each experience, expectantly,
  happily;
To have the faith to know there is no loss or separation in
  God,
That in Him I am for ever with those I love;
To have the vision to see the good in all things, the Christ in
  all persons;
To have an awareness of God's presence, close, abiding;
To know that 'underneath are the everlasting arms',
That God will never fail me nor forsake me;
This is my Prayer.

Grant, Eternal Spirit, to us who kneel before Thy Darkness
that it may become Light by Thy grace; for we have but a
sickly spark within us.
  Blow upon us with Thy breath though we feel it not;
  Lead us though we follow not;
  Receive us though our pride rejects Thy consolation; for
save by Thee we cannot come to Thee; and unless Thou
showest us the way we can never reach Thee.

O God, we would worship Thee, who art from everlasting
to everlasting, the same God who changeth not; perfect in
holiness, infinite in wisdom, of boundless love and compassion: we in our feebleness cast ourselves upon Thine almighty
strength; in our helplessness upon Thy fatherly care; in our
weariness we stay our souls on Thee. For Thy completeness
flows round our incompleteness; round our restlessness, Thy
rest.

O Thou high and lofty one that inhabitest eternity, whose
Name is Holy: Thou hast graciously promised to dwell with
those that are of a contrite and humble spirit. We, therefore,
pray Thee to cleanse our hearts from every stain of pride
and vain glory, that though the heaven of heavens cannot
contain Thee, Thou wouldst deign to abide with us for ever.

AT A HARVEST THANKSGIVING SERVICE

Gracious Lord, Creator of all things, Father and Lover of men, who makest the sun to shine and the rain to fall upon the earth, who dost bless the toil of the worker and bringest the grain to harvest, accept our prayers and praises as, with joyful hearts, we make our offering to Thee.

MASONIC PRAYER AT LODGE CLOSING

O Sovereign and Most Worshipful of all Masters, who, in Thine infinite love and wisdom, hast devised our Order as a means to draw Thy children nearer Thee, and hast so ordained its Officers that they are emblems of Thy seven-fold power,

Be Thou unto us an Outer Guard, and defend us from the perils that beset us when we turn from that which is without to that which is within;

Be Thou unto us an Inner Guard, and preserve our souls that desire to pass within the portal of these Thy holy mysteries;

Be unto us the Younger Deacon, and teach our wayward feet the true and certain steps upon the path that leads to Thee: Be Thou also the Elder Deacon, and guide us up the steep and winding stairway to Thy throne;

Be unto us the Lesser Warden, and in the meridian sunlight of our understanding speak to us in sacraments that shall declare the splendours of Thine unmanifested light;

Be Thou also unto us the Greater Warden, and in the awful hour of disappearing light, when vision fails and thought has no more strength, be with us still, revealing to us, as we may bear them, the hidden mysteries of Thy shadow;

And so through light and darkness, raise us, Great Master, till we are made one with Thee, in the unspeakable glory of Thy presence in the East.

So mote it be.   (1)

TWO PRAYERS FOR ANIMALS

Lord God, have mercy upon the animals, innocents who are so busy doing the tasks You have set them that it never occurs to them to wonder whether You exist.   (2)

Hear our humble prayer, O God, for our friends the animals; especially for animals that are suffering; for all that are overworked, underfed or cruelly treated; for all unhappy creatures in captivity; for any that are hunted or lost or deserted or frightened or hungry; and for all that must be put to death. May we be true friends to all living things and so share the blessing of the merciful.

A PRAYER OF THE INDIAN POET, RABINDRANATH TAGORE

Life of my life, I shall ever try to keep my body pure, knowing that Thy living touch is upon all my limbs.

I shall ever try to keep all untruths out from my thoughts, knowing that Thou art that truth which has kindled the light of reason in my mind.

I shall ever try to drive all evils away from my heart and keep my love in flower, knowing that Thou hast Thy seat in the inmost shrine of my heart.

And it shall be my endeavour to reveal Thee in my actions, knowing that it is Thy power which gives me strength to act.

PRAYERS IN VERSE FORM

Dear Lord and Father of mankind,
    Forgive our foolish ways!
Reclothe us in our rightful mind,
In purer lives Thy service find,
    In deeper reverence praise.

Drop Thy still dews of quietness,
    Till all our strivings cease;
Take from our souls the strain and stress,
And let our ordered lives confess
    The beauty of Thy peace.

Breathe through the heats of our desire
    Thy coolness and Thy balm;
Let sense be dumb, let flesh retire;
Speak through the earthquake, wind, and fire,
    O still small voice of calm!   (1)

Lord of all being, throned afar,
    Thy glory flames from sun and star;
Centre and soul of every sphere,
    Yet to each loving heart how near!

Sun of our life, Thy quickening ray
Sheds on our path the glow of day;
Star of our hope, Thy softened light
Cheers the long watches of the night.

Our midnight is Thy smile withdrawn,
Our noontide is Thy gracious dawn,
Our rainbow arch Thy mercy's sign;
All, save the clouds of sin, are Thine.

Lord of all life, below, above,
Whose light is truth, whose warmth is love,
Before Thy ever-blazing throne
We ask no lustre of our own.

Grant us Thy truth to make us free
And kindling hearts that burn for Thee,
Till all Thy living altars claim
One holy light, one heavenly flame.   (2)

        O Jesus, I have promised
            To serve Thee to the end;
        Be Thou for ever near me,
            My Master and my Friend;

I shall not fear the battle
  If Thou art by my side,
Nor wander from the pathway
  If Thou wilt be my Guide.

O let me hear Thee speaking
  In accents clear and still,
Above the storms of passion,
  The murmurs of self-will;
O speak to reassure me,
  To hasten or control;
O speak, and make me listen,
  Thou Guardian of my Soul.

O let me see Thy footmarks,
  And in them plant mine own;
My hope to follow duly
  Is in Thy strength alone;
O guide me, call me, draw me,
  Uphold me to the end;
And then in heaven receive me,
  My Saviour and my Friend.   (3)

Breathe on me, Breath of God,
  Fill me with life anew,
That I may love what Thou dost love,
  And do what Thou wouldst do.

Breathe on me, Breath of God,
  Until my heart is pure,
Until with Thee I will one will,
  To do and to endure.

Breathe on me, Breath of God,
  Blend all my soul with Thine,
Until this earthly part of me
  Glows with Thy fire divine.

Breathe on me, Breath of God,
  So I shall never die,

But live with Thee the perfect life
   Of Thine eternity.   (4)

Most ancient of all mysteries,
   Before Thy throne we lie;
Have mercy now, most merciful,
   Most holy Trinity.

When heaven and earth were yet unmade,
   When time was yet unknown,
Thou in Thy bliss and majesty
   Didst live and love alone.

Thou wert not born; there was no fount
   From which Thy being flowed;
There is no end which Thou canst reach
   But Thou art simply God.

How wonderful creation is,
   The work which Thou didst bless,
And O what then must Thou be like,
   Eternal loveliness!

O listen then, most pitiful,
   To Thy poor creature's heart:
It blesses Thee that Thou art God,
   That Thou art what Thou art.

Most ancient of all mysteries,
   Still at Thy throne we lie:
Have mercy now, most merciful,
   Most holy Trinity.   (5)

Lord of our life, and God of our salvation,
Star of our night, and Hope of every nation,
Hear and receive Thy children's supplication
   Lord God Almighty.

Lord, Thou canst help when earthly armour faileth,
Lord, Thou canst save when deadly sin assaileth;
Christ, o'er Thy Rock nor death nor hell prevaileth;
   Grant us Thy peace, Lord.

Peace in our hearts, our evil thoughts assuaging;
Peace in Thy Church, where brothers are engaging;
Peace when the world its busy war is waging:
  Calm Thy foes' raging.

Grant us Thy help till backward they are driven,
Grant us Thy truth, that we may be forgiven;
Grant peace on earth, and, after we have striven,
  Peace in Thy heaven.   (6)

        Jesu, the very thought of Thee
          With sweetness fills my breast;
        But sweeter far Thy face to see,
          And in Thy presence rest.

        Nor voice can sing, nor heart can frame,
          Nor can the memory find,
        A sweeter sound than Thy blest name,
          O Saviour of mankind!

        O hope of every contrite heart,
          O joy of all the meek,
        To those who fall, how kind Thou art!
          How good to those who seek!

        But what to those who find? Ah! this
          Nor tongue nor pen can show;
        The love of Jesus! what it is
          None but His loved ones know.

        Jesus, our only joy be Thou,
          As Thou our prize wilt be;
        Jesu, be Thou our glory now,
          And through eternity.   (7)

        Come, O Thou Traveller unknown,
          Whom still I hold, but cannot see,
        My company before is gone,
          And I am left alone with Thee;
        With Thee all night I mean to stay,
        And wrestle till the break of day.

I need not tell Thee who I am,
   My misery or sin declare;
Thyself hast called me by my name;
   Look on Thy hands, and read it there!
But who, I ask Thee, who art Thou?
Tell me Thy name, and tell me now.

Yield to me now, for I am weak,
   But confident in self-despair;
Speak to my heart, in blessings speak,
   Be conquered by my instant prayer!
Speak, or Thou never hence shalt move,
And tell me if Thy name is Love.   (8)

    God, who created me
      Nimble and light of limb,
   In three elements free,
      To run, to ride, to swim;
   Not when the sense is dim,
      But now from the heart of joy,
   I would remember Him:
      Take the thanks of a boy.   (9)

O loving Father, merciful and tender,
With humble hearts we pray before Thy throne
That Thou wilt be this child's most sure defender;
Bless him, O Lord, and seal him as Thine own.

Grant him Thy strength to stand 'gainst all temptation,
Courage to act and will to persevere,
Glad eyes which see and love Thy whole creation,
Insight and faith to know Thee ever near.

Not ease we ask for him, nor race unheated,
Praise of the world nor victory easily won,
But at the last, a gracious life completed,
He may receive his Captain's proud: Well done.   (10)

There is a place, the certain ground of peace,
The land of heart's desire, secure and lone,
Where stormy souls shall find at last release,
And walk with God, knowing as they are known.

Lord, in that secret place, where ever flow
The quiet waters of the timeless sea,
Grant I may know the truth I longed to know,
And be at last the one I wished to be.   (11)

15. The Practice of the Presence of God

Prayers of Recollection in Daily Life

ON STARTING OUT FOR WORK IN THE MORNING

Dear Lord, I am about to drive to my work. The traffic may be heavy and some of my fellow motorists impatient and in a great hurry. Drive with me Lord, drive with me all the way, that I may go in safety and with love, especially for those who appear to have little thought for others. And if possible Lord, help me to drive so that Your infinite patience and love be shown in me, and that that same patience and love be passed on to others like a good leaven in the daily bread of our journeying.

ON BATHING MY BABY

Dear Lord, here I am again, soaping my baby on my knee, ready to let her kick in the water, and as I see her joy I feel an extra burst of love. You are Love, God, and as I care for my child in love I work with You.

BEFORE MAKING A CAKE

Here am I, with kitchen, stove, pots and pans,
The wish to cook, and a pair of hands,
Cupboards with all I want to take
When busily making a home-made cake.
Dear God, how kind you are.
With thoughts of friends who will come to tea
To eat the cakes which You made for me.
So much to thank You for.

ON TALKING WITH AN ACQUAINTANCE WHO IS AT LOGGERHEADS WITH THE WORLD

His resentment is hurting him, his anger stabs; may I be strong enough to keep loving him, to resist the impulse to catch his mood and hurt myself and him.

May compassion and sympathy link us so that we each know each other in ourselves, and cause disharmony to melt away in love.

A SCHOOLMASTER'S PRAYER ON STARTING THE DAY'S WORK

Lord, help me to remain conscious of Thy Presence in school today. Grant that Thy Holy Spirit may think through my mind, that Thy Holy Spirit may speak through my mouth, that Thy Holy Spirit may act and heal through my body.

A PRAYER OF A SUPERINTENDENT OF A SCHOOL FOR MENTALLY HANDICAPPED CHILDREN

Heavenly Father, help us to realize Your presence with us today. Give us grace to see through the chaotic, unformed behaviour of our children; give us a sense of the unique individuality of each one of them. May their great need arouse in us an answering spark of love, and may our love and our lives together reveal Your Holy Will.

A PRAYER ON PHYSICAL UNION OF MAN AND WIFE

O Lord of all good life, who in Thine Incarnation didst gather into one, things earthly and heavenly, grant that the coming together of our bodies tonight may be a true sacrament of love; and may we through these physical unions grow in mutual love, understanding and trust, unto our lives' end.

A PHYSIOTHERAPIST'S PRAYER

Please help me, Lord, to help others to help themselves, to recover from the damage of injury and disease. And where complete recovery does not come, let me teach them to accept their disability and to use their ability to live a full and happy life.

A DOCTOR'S PRAYER

I shall see many patients today, and each will need help to bear the harder things in life. May I give to each that which he needs, to the sick, health; to the anxious, reassurance; to the frightened, comfort. May my own feelings, in pride in skill, delight in the power to influence, desire to be wanted by others, play only such part in my work as will enable me to fulfil my patients' needs; and may I have such compassion for their frailties and such pity for their pain that my own will be forgotten.

THE PRAYER OF A PARISH PRIEST WHILE CELEBRATING THE EUCHARIST

Every day I meet You in the Bread and Wine of the Blessed Sacrament. Every day You take my hands, my voice, my mind, that through me You may perform your miracle of meeting. Every day, every moment, You would give Your broken body to us, separated and incomplete as we are, that You may make us one and whole.

Go forth with me, my Lord, as I go out to take You to, and to meet You in, others, so many of whom live without the wonder that You daily show to me.

May they see You in my eyes, hear You in my voice, glimpse You in my actions. Break down the spiked fence of our separateness from each other and from You. Reveal to us the knowledge that You are in us and we in You. May we not break that which You have joined or wound that which You would heal.

Take us and make Your miracle of meeting complete.

THE PRAYER OF A BISHOP

O God, You watch over me; You oversee all that I do; You are my Bishop. And like a good Bishop You let me get on with my job without my knowing how You are helping me. But You know all about my mistakes and often put them right. If I have any success, I owe it all to You. Lord, I should like to be a Bishop like that. So help me to watch over the Diocese without fuss and interference; to put mistakes right and to help people to succeed without anybody knowing. Above all, save me from forgetting Him, whose ministry of suffering and self-sacrifice I am called to carry on. Give me courage to take up the cross You put in my path today, for Jesus Christ's sake, Amen.

PART II

The Holy Eucharist

1. Prayers for Use in the Holy Eucharist

Lord, come to us that Thou mayest cleanse us; Lord, come to us that Thou mayest heal us; Lord, come to us that Thou mayest strengthen us; and grant that, having received Thee, we may never be separated from Thee, but may continue Thine for ever and ever; for Jesus Christ's sake.

Let all mortal flesh keep silent, and with fear and trembling stand;
Ponder nothing earthly-minded, for with blessing in His hand,
Christ our God to earth descendeth, our full homage to demand.

King of Kings, yet born of Mary, as of old on earth He stood,
Lord of Lords, in human vesture – in the Body and the Blood –
He will give to all the faithful His own Self for heavenly food.

Rank on rank the host of heaven spreads its vanguard in the way,
As the Light of light descendeth from the realms of endless day,
That the powers of hell may vanish as the darkness clears away.

At His feet the six-winged Seraph: Cherubim with sleepless eye,
Veil their faces to the Presence, as with ceaseless voice they cry,
Alleluya, Alleluya, Alleluya, Lord most high.

Behold us, Lord Jesus, Thy servants assembled here at Thy holy Feast, and come and hallow us; Thou that sittest on high with the Father and yet art here invisibly present, grant to us and to all Thy people that we may be worthy partakers of

Thine undefiled Body and Thy precious Blood; for Thy Love's sake.

Grant, O Father, that we, receiving this Sacrament worth-ily, may have Christ dwelling in our hearts and may be temples of Thy Holy Spirit; and that with all Thy faithful ones, who from the beginning have served Thee, we may become inheritors of those good things that are eternal, which Thou hast prepared for them that love Thee; through Jesus Christ our Lord.

Cleanse our consciences, we beseech Thee, O Lord, by Thy visitation; that our Lord Jesus Christ, when he cometh, may find in us a mansion prepared for Himself.

Blessed Lord, who in Thy forgiving love didst pray for those who nailed Thee to Thy Cross, and hast taught us to forgive one another as Thou hast forgiven us, take from us all bitterness and resentment towards our fellow men, and give us the spirit of mutual forgiveness and brotherly love; that so we may, in perfect charity, be partakers of Thy Feast of Love; for Thy Name and mercy's sake.

Most merciful God incline Thy loving ears to our prayers, and enlighten our hearts with the grace of Thy Holy Spirit, that we may be enabled worthily to approach these holy Mysteries and to love Thee with an unfading love.

Deliver me, O Lord, from all wandering thoughts and distractions that with a quiet and serene mind I may enter into the Holy of Holies.

We praise Thee, O uncreated God, who art unsearchable, ineffable, incomprehensible by any created substance. O Lover of men, O Lover of the poor, who reconcilest Thyself to all and drawest all to Thyself through the advent of Thy beloved son, make us, we beseech Thee, living men!

SIMPLE PRAYERS AT THE CONSECRATION AND COMMUNION

Jesus, my King, I believe that You are here, and with all my heart I worship and adore You.

Jesus, my life, I You adore;
O make me love You more and more.

O loving Jesus, present in these holy Mysteries, I offer to
You my body, my mind and my spirit, to be a holy sacrifice.
Take me and make me the instrument of Your will.

O my God,
I give myself to You
For joy and for sorrow, for sickness and for health, for
success or for failure, in time and in eternity.
Take and keep me for Your own,
For the sake of Jesus Christ.

Come to me now to cleanse me.
Come to me now to heal me.
Come to me now to strengthen me.
O come to my heart, Lord Jesus;
There is room in my heart for Thee.

Heart of Jesus, think on me.
Eyes of Jesus, look on me.
Face of Jesus, shine on me.
Hands of Jesus, bless me.
Feet of Jesus, guide me.
Arms of Jesus, hold me.
Body of Jesus, feed me.
Blood of Jesus, cleanse me.
Make me, Jesus, Your own, here and in the world to come.

A PRAYER OF THANKSGIVING

We give thanks to Thee, O God, the Saviour of all, for
all the good gifts which Thou hast bestowed upon us, and
for the communion of the holy Body and Blood of Thy
Christ: and we beseech Thee, O thou Lover of mankind, keep
us ever under the shadow of Thy wings and grant us all our
lives faithfully to serve Thee in charity and humility.

THE HYMN OF THE OBLATIONS

For the offering of the bread and wine by the people.

Lord of all life, behold, we offer Thee
This bread and wine which first by Thee were given,
That, consecrated, they may truly be
For us the Bread of life, the Wine of Heaven.
Now, when these pure oblations we uplift,
Reveal Thyself the Giver and the Gift.

And with these fruits of earth we humbly bring
Ourselves, our souls and bodies, for Thy use,
A poor, unworthy, sin-stained offering,
But one which Thy dear love cannot refuse.
Look not on what we are but long to be,
And give us back ourselves restored in Thee.

This is the hour of sacramental grace,
Here is the prize which love alone can win.
Roll back concealing doors of time and space
And let the King of Glory enter in.
Let all be still, for now, to ease our dearth,
God stoops to man and heaven touches earth.

A COLLECTION OF EUCHARISTIC HYMNS

Adoro te devote

Thee we adore, O hidden Saviour, Thee,
Who in Thy Sacrament art pleased to be;
Both flesh and spirit in Thy presence fail,
Yet here Thy Presence we devoutly hail.

O blest Memorial of our dying Lord,
Who living Bread to men doth here afford!
O may our souls for ever feed on Thee,
And Thou, O Christ, for ever precious be.   (1)

THE HYMN OF THE OBLATIONS

Bishop Wordsworth's   John Milne

Descant: v. 3. This is the hour of grace ___ here is the prize which love a-lone can win.

Roll back ___ con-ceal-ing doors, and

let the King of Glo-ry en-ter in.

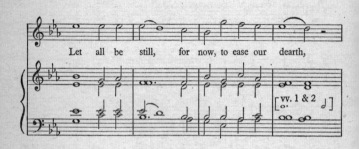

Let all be still, for now, to ease our dearth,

[vv. 1 & 2]

God stoops and hea-ven touch-es earth.

O salutaris hostia

O saving victim! opening wide
The gates of heaven to man below.
Our foes press hard on every side –
Thine aid supply, Thy strength bestow.

All praise and thanks to Thee ascend
For evermore, blest One in Three;
O grant us life which shall not end
In our true native land with Thee.   (2)

Tantum ergo

Therefore we, before Thee bending,
This great Sacrament revere;
Types and shadows have their ending
But the newer rite is here;
Faith, our outward sense befriending,
Makes the inward vision clear.

Glory let us give and blessing
To the Father and the Son;
Honour, might and praise addressing,
While eternal ages run;
Ever too His love confessing,
Who, from both, with both is one.   (3)

Here, O my Lord, I see Thee face to face;
Here faith would touch and handle things unseen;
Here grasp with firmer hand the eternal grace,
And all my weariness upon Thee lean.

Here would I feed upon the Bread of God;
Here drink with Thee the royal Wine of heaven;
Here would I lay aside each earthly load;
Here taste afresh the calm of sin forgiven.

I have no help but Thine; nor do I need
Another arm save Thine to lean upon:
It is enough, my Lord, enough indeed;
My strength is in Thy might, Thy might alone.

Mine is the sin, but Thine the righteousness;
Mine is the guilt, but Thine the cleansing Blood;
Here is my robe, my refuge and my peace –
Thy Blood, Thy righteousness, O Lord my God.   (4)

O Thou, who at Thy Eucharist didst pray
That all Thy Church should be for ever one,
Grant us at every Eucharist to say
With longing heart and soul, 'Thy will be done'.
O may we all one Bread, one Body be,
One through this Sacrament of unity.

For all mankind, O Lord, we intercede;
Make Thou our sad divisions soon to cease;
Draw us the nearer each to each, we plead
By drawing all to Thee, O Prince of Peace:
Thus may we all one Bread, one Body be,
One through this Sacrament of unity.   (5)

Wherefore, O Father, we Thy humble servants,
Here bring before Thee Christ Thy well-beloved,
All-perfect Offering, Sacrifice immortal,
        Spotless Oblation.

See us, Thy children, making intercession
Through Him, our Saviour, Son of God incarnate,
For all Thy people, living and departed,
        Pleading before Thee.   (6)

2. The Eucharistic Action

O Heavenly King, the Comforter, the Spirit of Truth, who art in all places and fillest all things, descend upon us and sanctify us, that with pure and ardent hearts we may make this offering.

Then is said or sung the Thrice Holy Hymn:

O Holy God, holy and mighty, holy, immortal, have mercy upon us;

O Holy God, holy and mighty, holy, immortal, have mercy upon us;

O Holy God, holy and mighty, holy, immortal, have mercy upon us.

The bread and wine, which at the beginning of the service have been placed on a table at the west end of the Nave or in some other convenient place, are carried in procession to the altar, either by the servers or by some other members of the congregation, who may be varied from Sunday to Sunday, while an appropriate hymn is sung. On certain occasions as, for instance, a Harvest Festival, other offerings, additional to the bread and wine, may be made at this stage of the service. The hymn used should make articulate the nature of the action and should be a prayer of the congregation. A Hymn of the Oblations, written for this purpose and used for many years in the Chapel of Bishop Wordsworth's, Salisbury, is printed earlier in Part II.

The bread and wine having been brought up and placed on the altar, the celebrant says the Prayer of Oblation:

O God, who didst send Jesus Christ, our Saviour, to be the bread from heaven and the food of the whole world, receive and bless that which we now offer to Thee. Remember, O gracious Lover of mankind, those by whom, and for whom, they are brought, and sanctify us that without stain we may celebrate these divine mysteries.

Within this our oblation of bread and wine we place ourselves, together with the whole of mankind and all the labour, sorrow, needs and sin of the world, that all may, in and through the Christ, be taken into the Divine Radiance and there, with Him, presented a living and acceptable sacrifice at Thine eternal altar.   Amen.

THE CONSECRATION OF THE OFFERING

The consecration may open with the singing of the Benedictus qui venit, *or may start immediately with the* Sursum corda.

℣ Lift up your hearts.
℟ We lift them up unto the Lord.
℣ Let us give thanks to our Lord God.
℟ It is meet and right so to do.

It is very meet, right and our bounden duty that we should at all times and in all places exalt, glorify and give thanks unto Thee, Giver of life and light, Creator and Sustainer of all that is; Thou who art the everlasting essence of things, beyond space and time and yet within them; Thou who transcendest yet pervadest all things:

Blessed be Thou, ineffable Godhead.
Blessed be Thou, holy, blessed and most glorious Trinity.
Blessed be Thou in thy creative power.
Blessed be Thou in thy sustaining love.

Each blessing is repeated by the congregation.

Glory be to Thee, O Christ, brightness of the everlasting Father and express image of Him who begat Thee before all worlds, God from God, Light from Light, who wast revealed in the body of our manhood and didst gather into Thyself things earthly and heavenly:

Blessed be Thy wondrous Incarnation.
Blessed be Thy life-giving teaching.
Blessed be Thy redeeming Passion.
Blessed be Thy Triumph over death and Exaltation into the
    Glory.

These blessings are also repeated by the congregation.

Wherefore we, Thy servants, now present and offer unto
Thee, O Father of Light and Love, this bread of eternal life
and this cup of everlasting salvation, through and in the Lord
Jesus Christ, who being in the form of God, counted it not a
prize to be on an equality with God, but emptied Himself,
taking the form of a servant, being made in the likeness of
men; and being found in fashion as a man, He humbled
Himself, becoming obedient even unto death, yea, the death
of the cross; who in the same night that He was betrayed, took
bread, and when He had given thanks to Thee, He brake it,
and gave it to His disciples, saying: Take, eat: this is my Body
which is given for you. Do this in remembrance of me.
Likewise after supper He took the cup and when He had
given thanks to Thee, he gave it to them saying: Drink ye
all of this: for this is my Blood of the New Covenant which is
shed for you and for many for the remission of sins. Do this,
as oft as ye shall drink it, in remembrance of me.

And we pray that Thy Holy Spirit may descend upon us
and upon the oblation which we set before Thee, that it may
be for us the Body and Blood of Thy Beloved Son, and that
we and all the world, being gathered into Christ, may with,
in and through Him be offered up, a holy and living sacrifice
unto Thee, that all may be vivified, restored and sanctified
unto that Day of the redemption of creation, when this
corruptible shall put on incorruption, and this mortal shall
put on immortality, and the whole earth shall be delivered up
to the Father in the Christ, the All-in-everything.

*There is silence for a space. Then the celebrant in the name of the
assembled congregation makes the Communion of the World.*

In humility and charity I, Thy unworthy servant, take the sacred Body and the precious Blood for myself, for those assembled in this place to celebrate this mystery and for all men everywhere.

While the celebrant makes the Communion of the World the Agnus Dei *or some other suitable prayer is said or sung; this is a participation, with the celebrant who speaks the actual words and makes the Communion, of the congregation in an action which draws the whole universe into a mystery being celebrated by a particular group in a particular place at a particular time.*

Then follow the Great Adorations and the anticipation of the Pleroma:

Adoration be to Thee, O most high God, who hast implanted in us Thy Spirit to lighten our darkness and guide us into the fullness of truth, so illumine our minds, we beseech Thee, that we may attain to that mount of vision whereon we may see Thee unveiled in Thy divine beauty.

And bring us, O King of Love, at the last to that timeless waking when the redemption of creation shall be revealed, when there shall be no darkness nor dazzling but one pure light, no sound nor silence but one perfect harmony, no hopes nor fears but one full possession, no discords nor opposites but one single truth, no beginning nor ending but one eternity, in the splendour of Thy glory and the majesty of Thy dominion.

Adoration be to Thee, holy, blessed and most glorious Trinity, ever enthroned in the unity of the one Godhead, before Thee creation bows in awe and wonder and with angels and archangels and all the company of heaven cries:

Holy, holy, holy, Lord God of Hosts, heaven and earth are full of Thy glory. Glory be to Thee, O Lord most high.

Amen.

In the splendour of the Sanctus *the Eucharistic Action reaches its culminating point. It is followed by a silence and what may be called an earthward movement, as all, very quietly, join in saying the Lord's Prayer. This is followed by a corporate Act of Love:*

May we, who in this holy mystery have entered into the all pervading Love and Compassion of God, freed from all self-love, diffuse boundless love towards all beings. May the Love of God be radiated over the entire world in benediction, peace and joy.

THE INDIVIDUAL COMMUNION

In the Communion of the World all have made a real Communion and the Eucharistic Action could end here. It may, however, be followed by a more personal and intimate Communion in which those who so desire receive the sacred Body and the precious Blood individually into themselves.

3. Meditations on the Holy Eucharist

THE PATTERN OF THE EUCHARISTIC ACTION

I.

PROLOGUE

The movement of the Eucharist represents under symbols the very movement and meaning of all life. Its ritual actions provide, as it were, an impersonal frame in which the most secret responses of the spirit to God can find shelter and support. So, without ever losing touch with the homely accidents of our physical existence – and indeed by acts and tokens deliberately drawn from that physical existence – the soul is led into the very recesses of the Godhead, and 'by love made visible is snatched up to the Invisible Love'.

2.

OBLATION

After the long preparation of the heart and mind of the worshippers, (through the *Synaxis*, with its introduction, Ministry of the Word, etc., which makes up the first part of the Eucharistic Liturgy), comes the first great moment in the drama of the Eucharist; the Offertory or oblation. Here, in the offering of the Bread and Wine upon the altar, and in and with these tokens the self-offering of every worshipper, the true Eucharist begins. Here is the starting point of that sacrificial movement which shall carry the Church, and each soul with it, to closest communion with God. Here, the human creature presents his little offering, the raw material of his concrete and yet symbolic sacrifice; and with this small gesture of generosity he moves out towards the Supernatural and

goes up to the Altar of God. It is an act of the people, singly
as individual souls and collectively as the Church, offering to
the Eternal their small and perishable gifts. It is the willing
gift which brings man into the Holy Presence; the first faint
movement of charity, earnest of an entire self-offering, lifting
up the things that are seen towards the Unseen Love.

The true offertory is the offering of all, in and for all, the
entire surrender of the creature to the transforming purposes
of the Creative Will. Though as yet there has been no consecrating act, no invocation of the Spirit, man has made his
oblation; and through and in it the Supernatural is already
present. Christ, the Eternal Wisdom, enters our world, but
enters it only in order to go up to the altar; to 'offer and be
offered, receive and be received'.

Thus the Offertory, whether it be surrounded by ritual,
splendour, or reduced to its simplest aspect, the setting forth
of the elements for the sacramental meal, is still a sacred and
essential action. It means the self-offering of Christ in His
human nature; the giving of the whole material of that earthly
life which, through the obedience of Mary, He accepted from
the race, to the painful transformation of the Cross, for the
supernatural purposes of God. For Christians, as members of
His Mystical Body, it must mean this too. 'It is you who lie
upon the altar; it is you, your very life within the cup,' said
St Augustine to the faithful. And moreover, the Church in
her action is here the figure and type of the total action of
human society, in so far as it achieves its true life; and each
worshipper is the figure and type of every human soul that
reaches the level of true life and is eucharisticized. Here each
is self-given for the interests of God and of the world; and
so given, achieves in this act full personality and freedom.
'Take, Lord, and receive all my liberty . . . all that I have and
possess,' must be the Christian communicant's offertory-
prayer.

The theme of sacrifice will receive in each soul a separate
and distinct interpretation; conditioned by its possessions, its
vision, its temper, courage and limitations. It is within the
circumstances of our life that we shall find the stuff of our

oblation. 'We are His sacrifice, and the offering is only the symbol of what we really are,' says St Augustine again. Character in all its manifestations; our habitual thoughts and actions, our interests and our work, our aims and our relationships, our everyday routine, are here to be unselfed and orientated towards eternity; made part of the eternal sacrifice which the created order offers in Christ to God, and thus given a new worth and a new significance.

Perhaps the most costly sacrifice the self is here required to make is its own cherished idea of the creature that it wished to be and to offer, and secretly hoped that perhaps it might be and offer. The strong, devoted beast of burden; used to the utmost, and always able for its task. The faithful dog, whose affection and obedience never flicker. The lamb of unblemished purity, whose coat has somehow escaped the grimy contact of the world. The intrepid and sure-footed chamois, at home upon the Alpine levels of the supernatural life. Or – hardest of all perhaps to relinquish – the meek, devotional little mouse, with fur in excellent condition; secure in a humble and not unattractive mousiness, which makes few demands on real humility but must surely be pleasing to God. Whichever it is, sooner or later that attractive picture of our spiritual situation goes to the altar. Then the soul, stripped of all the garments and disguises which ministered to its secret self-love, sees itself in its shabbiness and emptiness, its mere human second-rateness. Clad only in that self-knowledge it stands alone before the Holy, to offer the one thing that matters; the oblation of a free heart, cleansed of delusions, images and attachments, truly poor, truly chaste, truly obedient, and therefore ready for the invasion of love. Only when the worshipper has thus drawn near and given himself to God under costly tokens, become a living sacrifice, does he begin to be sensitive to the delicate action, the deep transforming power, of the Divine love and will.

3.

CONSECRATION

The Eucharistic Mystery asks first of the Praying Church and the praying soul a double movement of generosity: an entire self-offering in oblation to God, and an unstinted self-spending with and for the purposes of God, by intercessory prayer. Disinterested love is tested in both directions. The great contemplations which the Liturgy puts before us must be translated into action. Now, as the contemplation deepens in awe and intensity, human action falls away. Given to God, confidently offered in their imperfection and their weakness, Church and soul alike await His transforming act. They are to be taken by Him, as the token-gifts which lie upon the altar are taken; submitted to His great, supernatural movement of creation. Here all that truly happens, happens beyond the rampart of the world.

Already God, since He both transcends and indwells His creature, is present with the oblation. He informs, incites, accompanies it, and then takes, crowns and hallows it: welding in the fire of His charity the natural and the supernatural sacrifice that they may become one Thing – 'the holy Bread of Eternal Life and the Chalice of everlasting Salvation'. So the gifts of bread and wine, originating in the practical needs of the situation, become in their passage to the altar charged with high spiritual significance. They are now the token-sacrifice by and in which Christ accepts, and adds to His eternal offering, the oblation of men.

Consecration is a creative act. It does not merely mean taking something that is already complete in itself, and applying it unchanged to a new purpose: but making it that which indeed it should be, and has not yet become. So the consecration of the Eucharist takes the gifts of bread and wine and lifts them up into a new sphere of reality; makes them something which they were not before. For the mystery of consecration is the mystery of the achievement of God's purpose in His creature; not by way of the operation of law, but by way of the free action of grace. It brings home to us the plastic, half-real, half-finished character of the physical world; the fact that it points beyond itself and awaits at every level transformation in God, in order to achieve completeness through the quickening action of His supernatural life.

Once we have entered the supernatural region it is God alone who is the mover, the doer of all that is done. He alone uplifts, renews, transforms, converts, consecrates by the independent action of His grace; and this His consecrating action is mostly unperceived by us. His invisible rays beat upon, penetrate, and transform the soul. Sometimes their action quietens and steadies us; sometimes it burns and convicts us, induces a profound religious discomfort which we do not understand. But the full power of those transforming rays could not be endured by us at all, if it rose to the level of consciousness and was felt by sensitive nature. The saints have sometimes spoken of it; of the awful burning of the Fire of Love, the flame of living charity that burns to heal, or the agony of the heat that purifies our desire, cleanses the thoughts of the heart, scorches and kills self-esteem. This is the real fire that burns on the altar, and into which the living sacrifice must be plunged. Outward trials, pains, renunciations, temptations, revolts are only the matter of this sacrament: appropriate to the creature, but not necessary to God. All that is needed for His purpose of consecration is the impact of the Eternal Charity in its transforming power upon the soul, that it may 'receive the diadem of beauty from the Lord's hand'.

This august sequence, which is yet one single act of consecration, has its close parallel in the secret experience of the soul; for all the aspects under which the Godhead has revealed Itself must have a part in the creature's sanctification. Here too we are first led out to the adoration which shall express the total Godward temper of our life; the awed and delighted contemplation of Reality, which includes, penetrates, and transforms all action. Then within this worship we are called to the perpetual remembrance and the faithful study of a pattern of sacrificial love, placed within our own order and subject to our own conditions; the bit by bit imitation of Christ and slow incorporation into the mystery of Christ. For the work of sanctification as experienced by us in time is successive, as the consecrating action in the Eucharist is successive. God the Sanctifier is simultaneous and eternal; but man the sanctified is ever subject to the law of growth and change. Nor does this growth and this change lie within his own capacity. Having offered himself to the Transforming Love, he has done what he is able to do. It is the Spirit, the Lord and Giver of life, coming to rest upon the offering, which sanctifies and changes by His deep mysterious action that humanity which of itself is nothing, and yet is capable of all.

Often it seems to the soul as if nothing happens. It is weak, finite, ineffective as before. So the victim on the Cross showed no marks of victory; nor does the bread upon the altar know it has become the matter of a sacrament, when it is taken up, broken, and made an instrument of self-imparting life. Thus the soul giving itself to the Eucharistic Action is seldom aware of all the implications of its destiny. Neither can it always recognize under earthly disguises the consecrating touch of the 'holy and venerable hands'. It has given itself to become part of that total sacrifice, the worship which creation offers to its Origin; a worship summed up in Christ, presented at His altar, and perpetuated in His Church. What its particular part in that solemn oblation may be, is not for it to choose or ask to know.

4.

COMMUNION

It is only those who have accepted the long, exacting discipline of preparation, who have offered themselves in oblation, given themselves to intercession and finally surrendered all to the triune consecrating Power, who can enter into the depth and fullness of that mysterious communion in which man feeds upon the self-given Divine life. Communion, then, must ever be thought of as the completion, the fruit of sacrifice; having, indeed, no meaning or reality without sacrifice. We spread out in time the successive phases of our Eucharistic worship and celebrate them one by one, because we live in time, and are bound to succession. But in those depths of the soul where Eternity is present, all are brought forth simultaneously as part of the single creative action of God; transforming and reconciling the world and each soul in the world to Himself by the besetting action of His Spirit, and making each soul a partaker of the divine nature.

Communion, the sacred act in which the Eucharistic sacrifice finds its consummation, reminds us above all of the completeness of our dependence on God. It was instituted, not merely as a memorial of something once accomplished; but as a necessity for those to whom is confided the continuance of Christ's redeeming work. As the Eternal Logos entered history to disclose to the world as much as it could bear of the awful mystery of Absolute Love; so the aim of sacramental communion is to make each soul subdued to His besetting action a better channel for the pouring out of that Absolute Love. For we receive the very life and light of the Eternal Wisdom, the shining forth of the splendour of the Father; yet a life and a light manifest in time, and disclosed to man and united to man by the very limitations of humanity. A life which could respond to God and reveal God, alike in the solitude of the wild mountain, and in the jostle, squalor, worldliness and poverty of the lakeside town; and fulfilled itself at last in an entire and loving sacrifice, an intensity of bewildered loneliness, which was yet the occasion of the most perfect self-abandonment. In the sacred mystery of communion the Christian accepts membership of the Body which continues in time this sacrificial life of Jesus; and with that membership a total dependence on the Supernatural Life of God, by which it is informed.

Two movements merge in the real act of communion. First, the creature's profound sense of need, of incompleteness; its steadfast desire. Next a humble and loving acceptance of God's answer to that prayer of desire, however startling, disappointing, unappetizing it may be; bread that seems hard, stale and tasteless, the wine of eternity given in a common or ugly cup. It is not only at the visible altar or under the sacred traditional symbols that the soul receives the 'rich bread of Christ'. God, who comes to each in the 'sacrament of the present moment' gives also in that sacrament the sustaining energy by which the present moment can be faced. Therefore that which the Church does here, each repeated presentation of the theme of creation under liturgic forms, must be done again by each of her members hour by hour, in and with the homely stuff of circumstance. All must be given again and again; not only at the visible altar, but at the invisible altar, on which man is to lay the oblation of his love and will, that it may be hallowed and made the medium of new life. Here, by and in every event and experience, the poor soul and the rich God meet, and their mysterious and life-giving communion does or can take place. By this unceasing giving and receiving the whole of life is to be eucharisticized; this is the Christian task. It is to be offered, blessed, and made the vehicle of that infinite self-giving, of which our small reluctant self-giving is the faint shadow on earth.

CORPUS CHRISTI

Come, dear Heart!
The fields are white to harvest: come and see
As in a glass the timeless mystery
Of love, whereby we feed
On God, our bread indeed.
Torn by the sickles, see Him share the smart
Of travailing Creation: maimed, despised,
Yet by His lovers the more dearly prized
Because for us He lays His beauty down –
Last toll paid by Perfection for our loss!
Trace on these fields His everlasting Cross,
And o'er the stricken sheaves the Immortal Victim's crown.

From far horizons came a Voice that said,
'Lo! from the hand of Death take thou thy daily bread.'
Then I, awakening, saw
A splendour burning in the heart of things:
The flame of living love which lights the law
Of mystic death that works the mystic birth.
I knew the patient passion of the earth,
Maternal, everlasting, whence there springs
The Bread of Angels and the life of man.

Now in each blade
I, blind no longer, see
The glory of God's growth: know it to be
An earnest of the Immemorial Plan.
Yea, I have understood
How all things are one great oblation made:
He on our altars, we on the world's rood.
Even as this corn,
Earth-born,
We are snatched from the sod;
Reaped, ground to grist,
Crushed and tormented in the Mills of God,
And offered at Life's hands, a living Eucharist.

THE UNIVERSAL CHRIST

Grant, O God, that when I draw near to the altar to com-
municate, I may henceforth discern the infinite perspectives
hidden beneath the smallness and the nearness of the Host in
which You are concealed. I have already accustomed myself to
seeing, beneath the stillness of that piece of bread, a devouring
power which, in the words of the greatest Doctors of Your
Church, far from being consumed by me, consumes me. Give
me the strength to rise above the remaining illusions which
tend to make me think of Your touch as circumscribed and
momentary.

I am beginning to understand: under the sacramental
Species it is primarily through the 'accidents' of matter that

You touch me, but, as a consequence, it is also through the whole universe in proportion as this ebbs and flows over me under Your primary influence. In a true sense the arms and the heart which You open to me are nothing less than all the united powers of the world which, penetrated and permeated to their depths by Your will, Your tastes and Your temperament, converge upon my being to form it, nourish it and bear it along towards the centre of Your fire. In the Host it is *my life* that You are offering me, O Jesus.

THE UNKNOWN GOD

One of the crowd went up,
And knelt before the Paten and the Cup,
Received the Lord, returned in peace, and prayed
Close to my side; then in my heart I said:

'O Christ, in this man's life –
This stranger who is Thine – in all his strife,
All his felicity, his good and ill,
In the assaulted stronghold of his will,

'I do confess Thee here,
Alive within this life; I know Thee near
Within this lonely conscience, closed away
Within this brother's solitary day.

'Christ in his unknown heart,
His intellect unknown – this love, this art,
This battle and this peace, this destiny
That I shall never know, look upon me!

'Christ in his numbered breath,
Christ in his beating heart and in his death,
Christ in his mystery! From that secret place
And from that separate dwelling, give me grace.'

PART III

The Prayer of Meditation and Contemplation

1. Entry Prayers

For use in the Prayer of Meditation and at other times

Serene Light, shining in the ground of my being,
draw me to Yourself!
Draw me past the snares of the senses,
out of the mazes of the mind.
Free me from symbols, from words,
that I may discover
the Signified,
the Word Unspoken,
in the darkness that veils the ground of my being,
Serene Light!

This verse may be used alone or the following may be added:

Serene Light, burning in the ground of my being,
draw me to Yourself!
Draw me past the snares of Time's memories,
out of my yesterdays.
Free me from grieving, from tears,
that I may discover
the pulse of joy –
rhythm of the Eternal –
in the darkness which veils the ground of my being,
Serene Light!

May quietness descend upon my limbs,
My speech, my breath, my eyes, my ears;
May heart and mind wax clear and strong;
May God show Himself to me.

A beggar, Lord, I ask of Thee
More than a thousand kings would ask.
Each one wants something which he asks of Thee.
I come to ask Thee to give me Thyself.

Thou hast made us for Thyself, O Lord, and
our hearts are restless until they find
their rest in Thee. My heart is restless,
Lord. Lead me into Thy rest.

2. Mantras

THE GREAT MANTRA OF BUDDHISM*

Om mani padme hum.

THE GAYATRI MANTRA

Om. Bhūr bhuvah swah: Tat savitur varenyam bhargo devasya dhīmahi; Dhiyo yo nah prachodayāt. Om.

Om. We meditate upon the glorious radiance of the Supreme Source of the universe. May He [*or* That] enlighten our hearts and direct our understandings. *Om.*

THE EIGHT-SYLLABLE MANTRA
OF THE SUPREME BEING

Om namo Nārāyanāya.

In the presence of God Most High, I adore and invoke the Lord Jesus Christ as True God and True Man; and I place myself within His Risen and glorified life, that through inner participation in that Life I may be made one with Him.

THE MANTRA OF THE HEART SUTRA

Om. Gatē, Gatē, Paragatē, Parasamgatē. Bodhi Svaha.

Gone, gone, gone beyond, gone altogether beyond. Oh what an awakening! All Hail.

---

* This and the following are some of the well-known mantras. Each must discover, either by himself or with the aid of a director, the mantra or mantras suited to his temperament and need. Many sacred sentences may be used as mantras, for instance, 'I am the Light of the world', or 'I am the Power within you'. The first of these may be given a better mantric resonance if said in Latin: '*Ego Lux mundi sum*'; the second: '*Ego Potestas in te sum*'.

THE KYRIE MANTRA

Kyrie eleison. Christe eleison. Kyrie eleison.
Lord have mercy. Christ have mercy. Lord have mercy.

THE PAULINE MANTRA

Christo sunestaurōmai: ouketi ego: en emoi Christos.
I am crucified with [*or* in] Christ. I still live; but it is no
longer I [my phenomenal ego] which now lives. It is the
Christ who lives in me.

Another form of this Mantra is:
Christ in me and I in Him.

THE MANTRA OF INNER SILENCE

Be still and know.

3. The Womb of Silence

'I do not require of you to form great and curious considerations in your understanding. I require of you no more than to look.' (St Teresa.)

Not in the whirlwind, not in the lightning, not in the strife of tongues or in the jangling of subtle reasoning is He to be found, but in the still, small voice speaking in the womb of Silence. Therefore, be silent.

Let the past be silent. Let there be no vain regrets, no brooding on past failures, no bitterness, no judgement of oneself or of others. Let all be silent.

Let the senses be still and the vain clamour of thoughts cease. 'By love may He be gotten and holden, by thought never.'

Be still and know. Be still and look. Let the eyes of the mind be closed, so that you may see what otherwise you would not see, that you may hear what otherwise you would not hear, that you may know what otherwise you would not know.

Abandon yourself to Him in longing love, simply, holding on to nothing but Him. So you may enter the Silence of eternity and know the union of yourself with Him.

And if in the Silence He does not answer, He is still there. His Silence is the silence of love. 'When the servant is ready, then is the Master present.' Wait then in patience and in submission. It is good to wait in silence for His coming.

> And all shall be well;
> And all manner of thing shall be well
> When the tongues of flame are in-folded
> Into the crowned knot of fire
> And the fire and the rose are one.

4. The Light Meditation

Jesus said, 'I am the Light of the world.'*

> Christ as a light
> Illumine and guide me!
> Christ as a shield o'er shadow and cover me!
> Christ be under me! Christ be over me!
> Christ be before me, behind me, about me!
> Christ be the Light within and without me!

O Light of Light, who dost illumine the obscurity of non-being with the splendour of Thy Light, make Thy Light the lamp of my subconscious being and of my mind and of my soul and spirit and heart and of all of me and each part of me, till I shall be only light and flooded with the Light of Thy Unity.

Divine Light, proceeding from the splendour of the ineffable
   Godhead,
I worship and adore Thee!
Lead me from the unreal to the real;
Lead me from darkness to light;
Lead me from death to immortality.

Serene Light, shining in the ground of my being,
draw me to Yourself!
Draw me past the snares of the senses,
out of the mazes of the mind.
Free me from symbols, from words,
that I may discover
the Signified,
the Word Unspoken,
in the darkness which veils the ground of being.

* Alternatively, the phrase, 'Ego Lux mundi sum', may be recited as a mantra.

5. The Divine Lover

FLIGHT

I fled Him, down the nights and down the days;
I fled Him, down the arches of the years;
I fled Him, down the labyrinthine ways
Of my own mind; and in the midst of tears
I hid from Him, and under running laughter.
Up vistaed hopes I sped;
And shot, precipitated,
Adown Titanic glooms of chasmèd fears,
From those strong Feet that followed, followed after.
But with unhurrying chase
And unperturbed pace,
Deliberate speed, majestic instancy,
They beat – and a voice beat,
More instant than the Feet –
'All things betray thee, who betrayest Me.'   (1)

> O ruthless One! Disturber of my peace,
> Derider of my comfort! Mockingly
> You taunt my little hopes and miseries,
> My small ambitious dreams, frustrated plans,
> Compelling me to unknown dreaded ways.
> O ruthless Lover! Never can my heart
> Find rest until I find my rest in You.   (2)

Why then do I fly from You whom I so desire? Why do
You pursue me when I try to flee from You?

SUBMISSION

The Lover: I am the One in whom alone you may find rest
and fulfilment. I am the heart within your heart

and you are a portion of my Heart Divine. Even
if you wished, you could not resist the magnet
of my attraction and my love; for at the centre
of your soul there is a celestial spark which is
perpetually drawn to the Fount from which it
came.

Did I not first draw you, you could not come
to me. Did I not first love you, you could not
love me, my beloved.

I am Alpha and Omega, the Beginning and the
End.

The Beloved: I can flee no longer. The armour of my self-love
You have taken away. I am utterly defenceless
in the face of Your love, O ruthless Lover. I
would be lost and found in You.

The Lover: You need not seek me here or there. You need
not call to me from a distance. I am closer to you
than you are to yourself. I am waiting at your
door. Your opening and my entry are but one
moment.

The Beloved: My Lover, my door is open. Come.

FULFILMENT

O night that was my guide!
O darkness dearer than the morning's pride,
O night that joined the lover
To the beloved bride
Transfiguring them each into the other.

Within my flowering breast
Which only for himself entire I save
He sank into his rest
And all my gifts I gave
Lulled by the airs with which the cedars wave.

Lost to myself I stayed
My face upon my lover having laid
From all endeavour ceasing;
And all my cares releasing
Threw them amongst the lilies there to fade.   (3)

6. On the Self

'You must know that the spirit, i.e. of man according to its essence, receives the coming of Christ in the nakedness of its nature ... In its inmost and highest part it receives without interruption the impress of its Eternal Archetype, and the Divine Brightness; and is an eternal dwelling place of God in which God dwells as an eternal Presence, and which He visits perpetually, with new comings and with new instreamings of the ever-renewed brightness of His eternal birth ...

By means of the brightness of its Eternal Archetype which shines in it essentially and personally, the spirit plunges itself and loses itself, as regards the highest part of its life, in the Divine Being; ... and it flows forth again, through the eternal birth of the Son, together with all the other creatures, and is set in its created being by the free-will of the Holy Trinity ...

This essential union of our spirit with God does not exist in itself, but it dwells in God, and it flows forth from God, and it depends upon God, and it returns to God as to its Eternal Origin. And in this wise it has never been, nor ever shall be, separated from God, for this union is within us by our naked nature ...

But our nature, forasmuch as it is indeed like unto God but in itself is creature, receives the impress of the Eternal Image passively.'

Then, a saying of the Lord Jesus, followed by a number of passages from the Upanishads:

Jesus said: 'God is Spirit and those who would come to Him must come in spirit and in truth.'

'The Self is one. Unmoving it moves; is far away, yet near; within all, outside all. The Self is everywhere. He lives in all hearts.'

'Pure eternal Spirit, living in all things and beyond whom none can go; that is Self.'

'The Self is the Lord of all; inhabitant of the hearts of all. He is the Source of all; creator and dissolver of all beings.'

'In this body of mine, in this town of Spirit, there is a little house shaped like a lotus, and in that house a little space. There is as much in that little space within the heart as there is in the whole world outside; everything is there.
What lies in that space does not decay when the body decays, nor does it fall when the body falls. That space is the home of Spirit. Every desire is there. Self is there, beyond decay and death.'

'Self is God. Therefore one should worship Self as love. Who worships Self as Love, his love shall never perish.'

'My son! Though you do not find that Being in the world, He is there. That Being is the seed, all else but His expression. He is truth. He is Self. You are That.'

These passages from the Upanishads may be followed by the spiritual exercise* known as 'Passing through the Bodies'.

* This spiritual exercise may be used on its own.

7. Passing through the Bodies

I am not the body.
I am not the senses.
I am not the mind.
I am not this.
I am not that.
What then am *I*? What is the Self?
It is in the body.
It is in everybody.
It is everywhere.
It is the All.
It is Self. *I* am It. Absolute Oneness!

8. Jane's Meditation

When the body is seen for what it is,
Layer upon layer of protective tissue
Hiding the soft parts where arises its strength,
A blind empty structure, intent on its own business,
Then the mind can be free from the five lower senses
To discover knowledge about itself.
Gradually it unfolds,
Each state more peaceful than the last,
But none lasting more than its conditioning allows,
Until at its apex
It opens into a golden flower.

The petals close.
The mind grows heavier with each accumulated part.

The results of karma carry on,
But the senses are dull and unresponsive.
However these journeys have not been in vain.
The gentle young Ring Dove lies needlessly slain,
Wisdom quenches the rising hatred and pain,
For nothing was killed, only form and name.

These hairs are not me, they are not mine, they are not myself.
This skin is not me, this is not mine, this is not myself.
This flesh is not me, this is not mine, this is not myself.
These bones are not me, they are not mine, they are not
    myself.

But what is this? There is something strange here.
A serene indifference is growing in the heart;
A coolness rises up through all the activity of the mind,
Which trembles and dies down.
The breath gently laps at the edge of this sweet consciousness,
Which pervades the whole being with its tender concern.

Meaning and purpose have returned;
Each moment has a crystal clarity.

For this is not me, this is not mine, this is not myself.

This meditation was composed by one of my Buddhist friends. It is based on actual inner experience while practising the Buddhist meditation called the Contemplation of the Thirty-two-fold Nature of the Body. The objective of this practice is to eliminate delusion with regard to the nature of the physical body, a delusion regarded by Buddhists as the root cause of that sensual craving, which is what the Buddha meant by 'desire'. It has affinities with the meditation on the Self and with the spiritual exercise of 'Passing through the Bodies', printed above. It also, so it seems to me, though it stems from a different religious tradition, has affinities with one of Emily Brontë's poems, which can also be used in meditation:

THE PRISONER

But first a hush of peace, a soundless calm descends;
The struggle of distress and fierce impatience ends;
Mute music soothes my breast; unuttered harmony
That I could never dream till earth was lost to me.

Then dawns the Invisible, the Unseen its truth reveals;
My outward sense is gone, my inward essence feels
Its wings are almost free, its home, its harbour found;
Measuring the gulf it stoops and dares the final bound!

Oh dreadful is the check, intense the agony,
When the ear begins to hear and the eye begins to see;
When the pulse begins to throb, the brain to think again,
The soul to feel the flesh and the flesh to feel the chain!

Yet I would lose no sting, would wish no torture less;
The more the anguish racks the earlier it will bless;
And robed in fires of hell, or bright with heavenly shine,
If it but herald death, the vision is divine!

9. Christ in the Universe

With this ambiguous earth
His dealings have been told us. These abide:
The signal to a maid, the human birth,
The lesson, and the young Man crucified.

But not a star of all
The innumerable host of stars has heard
How He administered this terrestrial ball.
Our race have kept their Lord's entrusted Word.

Of His earth-visiting feet
None knows the secret, cherished, perilous,
The terrible, shamefast, frightened, whispered, sweet,
Heart-shattering secret of His way with us.

No planet knows that this
Our wayside planet, carrying land and wave,
Love and life multiplied, and pain and bliss,
Bears, as chief treasure, one forsaken grave.

Nor, in our little day,
May His devices with the heavens be guessed,
His pilgrimage to thread the Milky Way
Or His bestowals there be manifest.

But in the eternities,
Doubtless we shall compare together, hear
A million alien Gospels, in what guise
He trod the Pleiades, the Lyre, the Bear.

O, be prepared, my soul!
To read the inconceivable, to scan
The million forms of God those stars unroll
When, in our turn, we show to them a Man.

10. On the Dharma of the Lord Jesus

Thus spake the Lord Jesus:

'Blessed are the pure in heart; they shall see God.

Blessed are the humble-minded; theirs is the kingdom of heaven.

Blessed are those who know sorrow; they shall find consolation.

Blessed are those who claim nothing; the whole earth shall be theirs.

Blessed are those who hunger and thirst after holiness; they shall be made holy.

Blessed are the compassionate; to them compassion shall be shown.

Blessed are the peacemakers; they shall be called the children of God.

Blessed are those who forgive; they shall themselves be forgiven.

Blessed are those who return good for evil; they shall destroy the power of evil.

Blessed are those who love; they shall also be loved.

Blessed are those who lose their lower selves; they shall find their true selves.

Blessed are those who suffer in the cause of truth; theirs, too, is the kingdom of heaven.'

'I take refuge in the Lord Jesus Christ, Revealer and Revelation, Life and Giver of Life, Pathway and Guide.

I take refuge in the Dharma [or, if the term is alien, in the Pattern of true life, the cosmic order] which He revealed.

I take refuge in those who followed the Dharma [or, this Pattern, the cosmic order], the blessed community of the saints in life.'

11. The Jewel in the Lotus

A meditation on the indwelling Christ

In the beginning was the Word; and the Word was with God; and the Word was God.

And the Word was made flesh.

In You, Jesus, the Eternal Word, which was with the Father from the beginning, became incarnate in time and history. You were born; You spoke of truth; You were crucified; You rose again; You ascended into the Radiance of the Eternal.

And now I know that in ascending You at the same time descended. You are still here, still dwelling on this earth, always and everywhere present, living in my heart. Now all hearts which open to You have become Your Bethlehem, Your Galilee, Your Calvary, Your Resurrection garden.

An invocation of the indwelling Christ follows:

Thou who livest within my heart,
Awaken me to the immensity of Thy spirit,
To the experience of Thy living presence!
Deliver me from the bonds of desire,
From the slavery of small aims,
From the delusion of narrow egohood!

Enlighten me with the light of Thy wisdom,
Suffuse me with the radiance of Thy love,
Which includes and embraces the darkness,
Like the light which surrounds the dark core of the flame,
Like the love of a mother that surrounds
The growing life in the darkness of the womb,
Like the earth protecting the tender germ of the seed.

Let me be the seed of Thy living light!
Give me the strength to burst the sheath of selfhood,
And like the seed which dies in order to be born,
Let me fearlessly go through the portals of death;*
So that I may awaken to the greater life,
To the all-embracing life of Thy love,
To the all-embracing love of Thy wisdom.

*This invocation may be used in conjunction with the above meditation,
or separately.*

> Thou, Mighty One
> Thou who art knocking
> at the portals of my heart,
> Thou art a ray of wisdom and of love,
> illuminating those
> whose minds are ready
> to receive Thy message.
>
> Do I not meet Thee
> everywhere I go?
> Do I not find Thee dwelling
> in my brothers' eyes?
> Do I not hear Thee speaking
> in the earth's sad voice?
> Do I not feel Thee
> in a mother's loving care?
>
> Thou Light!
> Whose ray transforms and sanctifies
> even our weaknesses,
> turning death's poison
> into the wine of life ...
>
> Wherever in the sea
> of hate and gloom
> a ray of wisdom
> and compassion shines,

* This is not the death of the physical body but the dying unto self, the
mystic death.

there I know Thee,
O Mighty One!
whose radiant light
leads us to harmony,
whose peaceful power
overcomes all worldly strife.

O Loving One!
take this my earthly life
and let me be reborn
in Thee!

12. The Mystery of the Child

A meditation on the mystery of Christmas

I

The immensities of space, glittering
With innumerable stars, moving
Silently, coldly, each in its predestined path,
Aeon on aeon, aeon on aeon,
Crushes me. I am afraid.
There is no compassion in the stars.

Time. Stretching back and back,
On and on, backwards and forwards!
And I and you and all of us are
Imprisoned for a brief span
In time and space, for a brief span,
For a brief span,
And then we are known no more.
There is no compassion in time.

Men are born,
Love, beget children, make friends,
Strive for mastery or fame,
Or simply go on living.
To each in his turn comes the unavoidable ending,
Death,
The ultimate solitude which no one can share.

There is comfort in the little room, by the fireside;
In the clasp of a hand, in a smile of understanding,
In the laughter of children, in friendship, in work.
For a time it is possible to forget
The loneliness of the universe, the loneliness of life,
The final loneliness of death.

Is there no place, somewhere, secure and quiet,
Where a man may place his hands
In the hands of a God his mind can compass,
Compassionate, caring for human frailty?

We cannot endure nothingness, a journey which leads no-
    where.
We can only grasp the universal in the particular.
Our hearts faint before infinity.

Out of the deeps we call to Thee.
Out of the deeps.

O show Thyself to us, O God, who can only
Know Thee in our own image – as a Man.

2

It didn't happen as one might have expected.
One would have anticipated something more spectacular;
Something which looked like a revelation.
But there was only
A weary man and a yet more weary woman
Trudging along a dusty highway; and when
They got to Bethlehem, the inn was full.
A child was born; but after all
Babies are born every day. It was all very normal.
No one saw the angels except the shepherds.
No one realized that anything had happened.
The life of the inn went on as usual.

Yet this was the Advent of the Eternal Child.
This was the fulfilment of the Promise of the Ages.

And as at the dawn of creation
The Morning Stars sang together
And the Sons of God shouted for joy,
Now Angels and Archangels sang
The wonder of this latter mystery.

The Christ has passed through the gates of birth;
   A baby smiles in a mother's face;
And Heaven has tumbled down to earth.
   Hail, Mary, full of grace.

The simple know the simple thing;
   A babe on a truss of hay is laid;
And wise men bring their offering.
   Hail, Mary, favoured Maid!

God is diminished to a span;
   A child to a woman's bosom pressed;
And the seed of Heaven is sown in man.
   Hail, Mary, Mother blessed!

Manhood is taken into God;
   Christ walks the earth for a little space;
And Angels' pinions brush the sod.
   Hail, Mary, full of grace!

But Mary held the Child to her breast,
Like any other mother, rejoicing in her maternity.
It was warm in the stable among the animals,
And there was a sweet scent of hay, and Joseph
Was kind and attentive to her needs.
Now that the journey and the pains of birth were over,
She was very content, in a pleasant lethargy,
Gazing at the baby in her arms and musing dreamily
On what the Angel had said: 'Hail, Mary, full of grace!'
Wondering what he had meant. But at the moment
It did not matter very much. The heartbeat
Of her child was against her own. That was enough.
She sang softly, rocking her baby.

      Rest, my baby, dear one, rest,
        Lullaby, lullaby.
      Soft and warm against my breast.
        Lullay sing lullay.

He is such a little thing.
    Lullaby, lullaby.
Far too frail for Heaven's king.
    Lullay sing lullay.

Just like other babes is He.
    Lullaby, lullaby.
Son of God? How can He be?
    Lullay sing lullay.

Never mind, I feel the beat
    . Lullaby, lullaby
Of your heart, my son, my sweet.
    Lullay, sing lullay.

Over you my watch I'll keep.
    Lullaby, lullaby.
Sleep, my baby; baby, sleep!
    Lullay, sing lullay.

3

There was silence over all the earth
As Mary sang her cradle song.
Still was the night and still the air
In wonder at this holy birth.
And birds and animals, marvelling, gazed
On the baby Jesus, so bright, so fair,
And, in its manner, each one praised,
In a song of joy and a hymn of mirth,
The King of Glory, sleeping there.

The quiet oxen, kind and mild,
Leaned their heads o'er the Holy Child,
And gently murmured: Moo.

A donkey rose from his bed of straw
And marvelling greatly at what he saw,
He carolled: Hee-haw, Hee-haw.

Some sheep came too their Lord to greet
And look on the Lamb of God, and bleat:
Baa, Baa.

And an owl in the rafters, old and wise,
Solemnly blinked his sleepy eyes
And said: Too-wit, Too-woo.

While a tiny puppy, O so small,
Gambolled gaily into the stall
And barked: Wow-wow, Wow-wow.

Through the window a cuckoo flew.
Where he came from nobody knew.
And he sang: Cuckoo, cuckoo.

And though it was night-time, Chanticleer
Flapped his wings and, loud and clear,
Crowed: Cock-a-doodle-doo.

*O magnum mysterium et admirabile sacramentum ut animalia
viderint Dominum natum jacentem in praesepio.*

4

Those who work in the countryside,
In the open air, in the forests,
On the high hills, are closer to the nature of things
Than those who live in cities.
They know the rhythm of the seasons,
The falling and quickening of the grain,
The annual mystery of death and resurrection.
Theirs is the wisdom of simplicity,
Of truth directly apprehended
Without the complications of thought.

There were shepherds on the hills above Bethlehem,
Simple men, minding their own business,
Watching over their flocks in the night-time,
Not expecting anything unusual to happen.
They were surprised when the angel appeared

And the hillside glowed with a strange radiance.
Indeed they were very frightened till the angel spoke to them.

Shepherds, what saw you on that night
   In the dim lantern's light?
Only a child, a woman tired and wan,
Some cattle poking their heads across the stall,
Some travellers' donkeys, rather woe-begone?
   Was that all you saw?
Or did you somehow faintly understand
   That from this tangled straw
Shone out the mystery of God made man;
And she, leaning o'er Him, touching the small hand
   That groped between the bars,
Was clothed with the sun and diademed with stars?

They were only simple men;
They hardly understood what they saw;
The meaning was not fully clear.
But they understood enough to know
That this was no ordinary birth,
But something very different, a holy thing,
Which forced them to their knees
And filled them with a great joy.
Though it did not look at all like that,
A baby lying in straw among the cattle,
This child was a king and a Saviour.
They were quite content with that knowledge.
They did the natural, spontaneous thing;
They offered Him their simple gifts.

A Shepherd: Look 'e, darling, what I bring 'e,
               A little coat to keep 'e warm.
               Hold 'e up and let I wrap it
               Snugly round your tiny form.
               From my own sheep's wool I made it;
               Right good workmanship it be.
               When the wind blows cold in winter,
               Wear it and remember me.

A Young   Just a little pipe I give 'e,
Shepherd: No fit present for a king.
               But I have naught else to offer;
               It's the best that I can bring.
               Will 'e take it? Hark, I play it
               To 'e. When 'es feeling sad
               And the days seem long and lonesome
               It will make 'e blithe and glad.

Old Shepherd: I am old and getting feeble;
               Three score years and more I be.
               Long I've led my sheep to pasture.
               Few more days I'm like to see.
               Take the shepherd's crock I've carried
               All my life and borne it true.
               'Tis the sign of Thine own calling.
               Men shall call 'e shepherd too.

And so they went away, wondering.
They were very happy.

5

Pale clouds in a pale sky
And a blue-green sea, whose waves
Lap gently on the shores of a quiet garden
In a still land.

I knew a garden once.
There was an apple tree there, shining.
I ate the fruit thereof, and died;
Or say I am asleep, and dream
Of the garden and the apple tree.

I wish I could go back.

There is no going back. An angel guards the gates
With a sword of fire. There awaits
Another garden, by the shores
Of a quiet sea in a still land.

The apple tree is there.

I do not know the way.

I am weary of seeking, weary of wandering.
There are so many ways. But who shall say
Which way leads to the garden?
There is so much to know, so much worth knowing.
But who shall say which knowledge
Will lead me to the garden
By the quiet sea in the still land?

I wish I could awake again.

6

There is a way of simplicity, of unclouded seeing;
Children and the pure in heart know it,
But for the learned it is hard to find
Except after much searching
And an unknowing of all their knowledge.
The shepherds had no difficulty in finding the stable;
For them the way was clear and easy;
They arrived there very quickly.
For the Wise Men it was very different;
Their journey was long and arduous.
But all ways lead to the same place in the end.
There is only one place to lead to.

We follow an arduous way
In travail of heart and mind,
Hoping at last to find
The ultimate secret of things.
We may not linger or stay:
Always we hear the distant bell and the rustle of hidden wings.

Gaspar: The Heavenly City stands serene,
            Divinely fair.
            I have glimpsed it dimly through the gleams which
              screen

Its turrets high in air.
O that I were there!
About its walls the healing water flows,
And at its heart is the Rose.

Melchior: I have sought the place where the sacred Spring
Flows out; and the Snake is curled
About the roots of the Tree of Life
In the Wood beyond the World.

Balthazar: The steps of a secret stair
My bleeding feet have trod,
The way of emptiness,
And the darkness of God.

Obscure the night and shrouded is the earth
Through which we journey onward to our goal,
To know the mystery of death and birth,
To know the final destiny of the soul.

We have known power, riches, knowledge, fame.
They fade away as mists at dawn of day.
Though all things change, yet all remains the same.
Is there no quiet place where we may lay
Our burden down at last, and find release,
The end of heart's desire, the certain ground of peace?

The Wise Men had no vision of angels.
That was not the sort of vision
Which comes to those who follow
The way of knowledge, and the emptying of knowledge.
They saw a Star.
And the Rose, and the Tree, and the secret stair
Were all gathered in the Star.

So they followed, and came to Bethlehem.
It was a long way, a tedious journey.
They came to a stable, the same stable
To which the shepherds had come
By a shorter, easier way.

They found a Mother and a Child
Among the cattle and the donkeys.

But to them it all looked different,
For the Rose, and the Tree,
And the end of the secret stair –
Or was it the beginning? –
Were in the Child.
And the Child and the Star were one.

Wondering, very quietly, very humbly,
They offered their presents.

They were very precious.

'We have known earthly power. We are kings.
Our power corrupts and fades; but Your power
Neither corrupts nor fades; it rests secure
In the safe casket of Your humility.
You are the King of Love. We hail You King of kings.
We offer Love the gold of royalty.

'We have sought wisdom, questing on towards
The boundary stone of earthly knowledge.
We have known the hidden wisdom, which obscurely lies
Beyond the encircling bounds of sense.
You are the eternal font of wisdom,
The ending and the beginning
Of all our searching.
Incense we offer You, Incarnate Deity.

'We know the transience of life, and sorrow's wounds,
And the final sorrow of death, and the tainted breath
Of corruption after death.
You, dying, will know sorrow, but Your sorrow
Will blossom in joy, and in death's ending.
We offer You myrrh, who, dying, will conquer death.'

7

So they went away. It was very quiet
In Bethlehem, in the stable,
When the Wise Men had gone.
The cattle lay still, chewing the cud.
And Mary held Jesus in her arms,
Dreaming about all that had happened,
Wondering what it had all meant.
But now it did not matter very much;
She was very happy.

Virgin Mother, maiden peerless,
Crowned with stars and clothed in gold.
Woman chosen from all others
In thine arms the Christ to hold.
Thou the loom on which the Spirit
Wove the Incarnate's robe of flesh,
Human woof and warp of Godhead,
Joined within a wondrous mesh.
Mystic union! a strange conjuncture!
Immanent transcendency!
Lo, the One thine arms upholdeth
In His arms upholdeth thee.

Heavenly Word, the Son Eternal,
Whom the Father bore, and bears
Always, in His timeless Being,
Now in time and flesh appears.
Christ, Revealer, Revelation;
Thou the Pathway, Thou the Guide;
Thou the Life and the Life-giver;
Gate of Heaven thrown open wide!
In Thy longed-for Incarnation
Starry sky meets flowery sod.
Now has God to earth descended.
Now is earth drawn up to God.

How shall mortal tongue extol Thee,
God of God and Light of Light,
Brightness of celestial splendour
Stooping from the heavenly height,
That in Thee lost man's redemption
Might in time accomplished be,
That in Thee, in human pattern,
God's own image he might see.
Linked are Anteros and Eros,
Joyful manger, bitter cross.
Glory be to Thee, Ischyros,
Agios, Athanatos.

8

Most strange, incredible mystery! Behold,
The King of Glory leaves His heavenly throne
And in the fashion of a mortal babe,
Assumes our human nature; and from afar
The wise, the rich, the powerful draw near
And join with humble shepherds from the downs
To kneel before this wondrous interchange.

O rich humility! that God should stoop
And thus reveal Himself, so men might learn
The awful loveliness of Absolute Love.

O luminous diaphany! in which the ray
Of the divine out-flowing thus streams through
The universe, and makes all parts transparent,
Bathed in light, bound firmly each to each
In one rich, marvellous, theophany.

O blessed night, more lovely than the day!
O sacred marriage, linking earth and heaven!
No longer weep we passing loveliness
Or earthly beauty falling to decay.
Nothing is lost; the sweep of daffodils,
Gilding the fresh, green carpets of the Spring,

And moon-kissed flowers, scenting summer nights,
The golden rustle of autumn leaves, the slow
Deliberate fall of snow, laughter and mirth,
Friendship and love, High thinking, brave endeavour,
All human things, splendid and lovely, new
Are taken with our manhood into God
And so become eternal.

Holy Light
Which fills the universe illumine us.
And as on that far night in Bethlehem
Men bowed the knee before the Light of Light,
So may we, too, in adoration bow.

13. The Victor-Victim

A meditation for Passiontide

I

In the beginning was the Word;
And the Word was with God;
And the Word was God.

Through Him all things came into being;
And without Him nothing came to be.
And that which came to be through Him was Life;
And the Life was the Light of men.

And the Word was made flesh,
And the Glory of the Eternal shone forth on earth.

The light shone in the darkness,
And the darkness rejected the light;
For such is the nature of darkness.
The Incarnate trod the ways of men;
But men rejected the Incarnate One;
For such is the nature of the world.
He spoke words of truth;
His words were like fire which burns and illumes.
But men fear the truth, or do not understand it.
Truth penetrates the dark places and changes the shape of
    familiar things;
But men cling to the familiar things, thinking that they are the
    real things.
Therefore, they persecute the prophets and slay those whose
    words are strange.
Hardly can light conquer darkness, truth triumph over
    illusion.
Truth must be denied that men may find truth;
Wisdom must be crucified that men may learn wisdom.

2

Jesus, the Word Incarnate, now,
His earthly mission near its end,
Goes forth from Pilate's judgement-hall,
    A criminal condemned.

With crown of thorns upon his head,
With wounded body and labouring breath,
He slowly drags a shameful cross
    Along the way of death.

By friends deserted, all alone,
In cruel, mocking ignominy,
He treads, amid a jeering crowd,
    The road to Calvary.

This is the hour.
The hour of blinded eyes,
The hour of the thing not understood, the hour of truth
    unrecognized.

This is the hour.
The hour of the closed mind,
When the ignorant turn on the wise
And the crowd cries out for blood,
The hour of fear and hate, the hour when the irrational
    triumphs.

This is the hour.
The hour of doom, when the pillars of the earth fall,
And the Prince of this world is judged.

This is the hour.
Poised between time and eternity,
The image of hours endlessly repeated,
The hour of betrayal, the hour of rejection.

Unthinkingly, unfeelingly,
The soldiers nailed Him to a cross.
He uttered no curse, no taunt, no judgement;
Only from His twisted lips there came a prayer,
An incredible prayer, reversing all values:

'Father, forgive them; they know not what they do.'

If this were all it were enough indeed;
The Holy One rejected, tortured, slain.
Alas, it is not all; His wounds still bleed,
And every day He is crucified again.
We are Thine executioners. It is we
Who, blind or wanton, pierce Thy flesh anew
And bind Thee to Thy cross eternally.
O Christ forgive; we know not what we do.

Sun quench your light; let heaven veil its face;
And let this noon be darker than the night;
To hide the darkness of the mind of man
And shroud the sin which crucifies the Light.

The Light of Light is dying in the dark.
His tortured body droops, a gasping breath
Passes His lips; His brow is dank with sweat.
The Light is nearing the dark gate of death.

Let it be dark; no darkness is too dark.
Let it be darker yet, that none may see
The Light Incarnate dying in the dark,
The Son of God dying upon this Tree.

Out of the dark there comes a cry,
A cry of unimaginable despair;
    the ultimate dereliction:
'My God, My God, why hast Thou forsaken Me?'

I can endure no more.
    Designer Infinite,

Why hast Thou made man thus,
  A creature blind of sight,
  Fettered to sin?
Why hast Thou put immortal longings in us
  And the bright seeds of love,
If we must crucify the Prince of Love?
Why is our human destiny
  Always to slay
The good, the wise, the true;
  To do the thing we inly hate,
Knowing not what we do;
Or, bitterest of all, knowing the good,
To do the ill, knowing the truth,
  To follow falsehood?
Why must Thou suffer thus, deserted One?
Why have we broken Thee, pitiful, ruined Love,
  Who on this Tree
Art dying? Word Incarnate, sole-begotten Son
Of God, why hast Thou put Thyself
  Beneath the feet of Thine own creation,
  That it might trample Thee?
Answer, O sharer and victim of our destiny.

Be still and know. Here is a Mystery,
Not to be understood save in the darkness
Which is the darkness of God.
Here is an Act without ending or beginning.
  Luminous, mysterious, unpriced,
Co-mingling with another, timeless, incomprehensible,
Where Love attains the apogee of love,
And God bows down before God sacrificed.
Wait then in silence and in submission.
  On Calvary
  All is silent now;
Silent the weepers, the mockers silent,
The soldiers silent, watching, still.
  There is no motion.
And, breaking the silence, the answer,

If the answer is understood:

'IT IS ACCOMPLISHED'

'Father, into Thy hands I commend My spirit.'

3

It seemed to be all over.
Faith and hope were dead;
Only love still lived.
Nearby there was a garden and an empty grave.
There they laid the body of the Beloved;
There was nothing more to do now.
They could not know
That this was only the beginning.

Rest awhile in timeless waiting,
Wounded body, tired with pain.
Thou hast triumphed, Victor-Victim;
Sleep awhile to wake again.

Thou hast known in fullest measure
Man's inevitable tragedy;
Shared, obedient, submissive,
All his bitter destiny.

Scorned, rejected, broken-hearted,
All is finished; quiet keep.
Till the hour of resurrection
Sleep, Victorious-Vanquished, sleep.

Still was the dawn when the Christ arose,
And still the sky and still the trees.
There was dew on the blossom and dew on the grass
And a waiting hush in a waiting breeze.

The waiting birds held back their song
As His pierced feet pressed the dew-drenched grass;
And small timid things came out to see
The risen Lord through the garden pass.

The morning woke, and the waiting birds
Broke into song; and a quivering breath
Passed over the earth, as, with quiet eyes,
The Christ came out through the gates of death.

Now is the time when midnight turned to noon;
When what seemed true proved false, what false proved true;
When greatest crime begat the greatest boon;
And losing all things gained all things anew.

Divine enigma! on an evil tree
The fruit of Paradise most strangely grows;
Amid the dung of death triumphantly
Burn the bright petals of the Mystic Rose.

                    Alleluya.

        Sing ye together, morning stars,
        And shout for joy ye sons of God;
        A glory flames along the path
        The Crucified has trod.

        A new creation now is born,
        A lovelier shape, a fairer birth
        Than that which seraph choirs proclaimed
        When God first made the earth.

        The winter of the world is past;
        The rain is gone. A song undreamed
        Wells up within the heart of man,
        The song of Man redeemed.

                    Alleluya.

                    4

Faintly I strive this Thing to understand;
Humbly I bow before the Mystery.
Eternal Wisdom, lead me by the hand.

O Truth, O Love, O Grace, too great for me,
Within Thy pitiful heart encompass me;
My Lord, My God, My Life, remember me.

Alleluya.   Amen.

14. Meditations and Prayers of a Poet-Mystic

Heart of the Universe, O Sacred Heart,
In You our birth, our being, our destiny.
Each soul, a glowing spark of Primal Fire,
Life of Your Life, sings, gathering into flame:
'Heart of Your Heart am I . . . and I . . . and I . . .'
So chant the souls of men, as crimson life-buds they
Course on within Your Heart through night to day.

Ocean of Light and Life from whom my being stems!
In whom I breathe and feel and think and move:
Your gift to me the world wherein I dwell:
Your gift the lowliest task of mind and hand.

Spring daffodils unfold You and returning day
Resolving night. Your voice is heard through pain:
Felt deep in love of furred and feathered tribes:
You, Friend of friends, in heart of every friend!

Through man-made threats of war, prevailing gloom,
And ugliness extolled, what should I fear?
You hold the worlds secure. My little world
No chance betides. It, too, is in Your Hands.

The seasons turn with time: Wheel turns through youth to
    age:
Beyond, death waits, Your gift, the gift of rest,
The consummation of a journeying
Through one of many days. So, welcome Death!

Beyond the scarlet splendour and the gold,
And rise and fall of age-old cloistered chant,
The Centre is, unnamed, unnamable;
Unseen, unspoken, challenging a quest.

Beyond the beauty of the manifest
And shadow of the truth no form may hold
The Centre is, remote from shape and shade:
Unseen, unspoken, calling for a quest.

Beyond the teacher and beyond the taught,
The shifting knowledge of the wisest men,
Abides the Centre, goal of every quest,
Where silence leads and darkness folds her in.

Beyond the gate, the signpost and the chart,
The written word, the footprint of a guide
The Centre is for man's eternal quest;
Where day is not nor flow of any tide.

Amid mankind's vast nebulae of thought
Shine hieroglyph and sign;
Eternal symbols of the Signified.

Immovable, as pillars, they stand firm;
Bear witness to immortal verities
Man knew and lost.

They point the pathway to the Signified.
Deluded, most have eyes but for the sign,
Adore and sleep beneath its pointing hand.

But some can see and follow where the sign
Still points, as wise men trod the Way in ancient days
And found the Signified.

As a garment awaiting the wearer
May I be.
Robe of gossamer, cloak of down and battle array
Wait in the world's vast presses, await the wearer –
So shall I wait.

As a pen awaiting the writer
May I be.
Innumerable His pens, scattered over every land,
They await their hour –
So shall I wait.

As a canvas awaiting the artist
May I be;
Empty, colourless, of no apparent purpose,
Field of a masterpiece to come –
So shall I wait.

All that I ever shall be that am I,
The Golden Tree that from an acorn sprang,
The man grown wise through foolishness and fear,
A Cornerstone within the House of God;
All that I ever shall be that am I.

Poised steep above the inner stair, the Door –
Half-opening Door from out the brevity
Of day and night, of seasons come and gone.
The cluttering robes of earth-life lie forgot.
I gather me in stillness. As the son,
Weary of exile, sees afar
The vision of the Father's House
In distant splendour set, so do I seek.
Joyful the prodigal to whom the Door is opening,
Though but one brief glance be given
Of future freedom, largening liberty!

Narrow the gate that leads through death* to Life;
Only the dying-to-self may enter there.
Empty the cup must be ere it is filled.
Through winter cold and darkness sprouts the bulb.
Bliss of the Christ-filled Cup – the opening Flower!
Through agony to bliss! The dispossessed
Alone shall know the Spirit's ecstasy!

Within an upper room enshrined
Your Presence waits unbreathing, still:
Below the warfare wages on.
Transcending self at last I seek

* The mystic, not physical, death is meant.

The inner stair;
Ascend on wings of will
To find that You are there!

O ruthless One! Disturber of my peace,
Derider of my comfort! Mockingly
You taunt my little hopes and miseries,
My small ambitious dreams, frustrated plans,
Compelling me to unknown dreaded ways.

O ruthless Lover! I may not withstand
Your call to arms against my littleness,
Your summons from sweet dalliance with Time
To tryst upon the everlasting Hills,
Compelling me to far unfathomed ways.

O ruthless Lover! Never can my heart
Find rest until I rediscover You.
Through this world's wilderness I take my road,
The earth a highway, never more a home.
I come – and now Your shining lights my way.

Shepherd of Ages, guiding to far hills
The earth-bound race. Way, Truth and Life,
Through You we ask, seek, find. Through You
Our bonds are severed and we see, hear, walk.
Through You we die and rise; are born again
As Sons of the Most High.
Thus each becomes the Way, himself the shining Truth,
And one with Life, the heart and pulse of Love.

Seek not His gifts, the more to be
Made one with Him who gives to thee:
No gift can fill the heart as He.

And when no light illumines prayer,
Then through the darkness grope and dare
Unseeingly to find Him there.

Clear shining Star, your Light has beckoned me
From tangled ways that bind the world without.
With empty hands I press along the road
That long ago was planned for me to tread.
My sight is sure. No longer can I doubt
For now I see. No man-made god nor creed
May dim your Light nor hold me still in thrall.
Clear shining Star, your Light has guided me
Through faith to dawning knowledge – Vision of the All!

My books are closed and every image veiled
That thus Your Light may enter full and free,
Draw inward all my being. Inward far
You summon me to dwell, in silence wait
Your Will. No book may longer speak
Nor image. Finding, wherefore should I seek?

Clear-seeing eyes! No longer can they shed
Tears for the stricken sorely suffering self.
Quick to perceive the pain of other men,
The saint, impervious to his miseries,
Eyes purified to envisage naught but truth,
Looks out with vision on God's universe:
Himself a world through suffering grown wise;
Eternal peace is mirrored in his eyes.

15. The Spiritual Adventure

To name the Nameless
Is to limit the Limitless.
And yet, how else should I
Tell you of my Father?
And so, because of my limitations,
The Infinite becomes Finite;
The Omnipotent is robbed
Of some of His Fire-Power;
The Omniscient, at times,
Goes unknown and unheard;
The Omnipresent, too often,
Is unrecognized.

Let us seek Him in
Your heart and mine
And in the hearts of
Our friends and enemies,
For He is everywhere.
Our limitations,
The Path of Darkness,
Conceal the invisible Light.
For He is the Whole,
The Unknowable,
Far greater than the sum,
Unrestricted by time
Or place.

In all religions,
And their varying sects,
There is much talk of love.
This is His nature.
The atheist and
The existentialist,
Groping in the desert,

Unknowingly walk
Towards His Love and Light.
The way up and the way down
Are one and the same;
And all shall be well,
And all shall be well,
And all manner of thing shall be well,
For synne is behovabil.

In my heart, His Voice
Whispers, 'Be still, My son,
Utterly still, for we meet
In the silence of
The Timeless Moment.
Let your everyday self,
The everchanging,
Phenomenal self,
Stand aside that I may
Fill your heart with my Presence.
That you may know the depth
And breadth of my love.

'With your intellect
You cannot know me.
Your very efforts draw
A veil between us.
In all people and
All things am I,
For I speak to you from
Within your true Self.
Know then the unity
Which binds us together
With cords of light and love
In the oneness of Life.

'Invisible Light, Unmanifest,
Ever becoming visible Light.
The Two and the One.
Hear! My music sounds

Throughout the spheres. Dance
And sing to my rhythm.
Man's self-punishment,
Lacking charity,
Is a bitter thing.
Who are you that you
Judge yourself and others?

'I have given you Life and Love,
Perfect, unpossessive Love.
Your antics on the stage of life
Have been no better and no worse
Than those of your fellow men.
You have walked the Path of Darkness,
Suffering, as all men suffer,
Until they find my Light and Love.
Seeking, asking, knocking, man finds
Acceptance. Perfect charity.
Accepted, he accepts himself.
Accepting, gives acceptance.'

16. The Man Born Blind

The long poem of nearly 500 lines, sections of which are used in this meditation, opens with the Gospel story of how the man, born blind, recovered his sight by washing, at the command of Jesus, in the pool of Siloam. Now that he is no longer blind, he finds himself in a strange, new, puzzling world. He longs for darkness and with the night darkness comes. But not the darkness he once knew. For the first time he sees the night sky and, as the clouds roll away, the moon shines forth, 'undimmed, serene, in royal loveliness'.

I

First wonder held
Him as he gazed on her, and then a knowledge
Of sure tranquillity, a peace beyond
All that his life had known; freed of all thought
And memory, scarce conscious of himself,
He yielded all his being to that flood
Nor even knew he yielded, wholly stilled
Within the candent spell of her enchantment.
Borne on her light he knew at length the stars,
Turning his gaze on this side and on that
To search their company, until his eyes
Rested in contemplation on one fire
That influent by his new found sight attained
His inmost spirit, so that thus fulfilled
He was no more, but seemed only to be
One with that light. Clean of his finite self,
As Siloam's pool had washed his eyelids clean
Of sealing clay, stripped naked and alone,
His soul participated in that life;
Not whelmed, not separate, but as a note
Has its place in the chord thus heard complete,

Nor is itself the less but, no more single,
Shares in a deeper life, a brighter flame,
Knowing fulfilment in that harmony . . .

                    He who was blind,
Joined of that fellowship though unreleased
Of his still body, had no more concern
To live or feel or know: neither the world
Which wrapped that body nor the misty paths
His daily thought surveyed. Free of desire
Or dream, untrammelled of his very self,
Unmoved, he rested in the contemplation
Which was his soul's ascent, gazing upon
The truth, as light made manifest in light
Of which that light is part, perceptible
Of its one radiance, perfect in itself,
Unbarred by shadow, broken by no change,
Deflect not even by transparency
Of purest crystal, wholly luminous
And thereby formless, as deep water known
Through its own depths. Nor did that glory burn
As other than himself but apprehended
Within his single being, correlate
With that which merged in it, his very soul
Made present to the vision by response
Of likeness unto likeness, and identic
With that towards which it yearned in virtue of
Only that yearning. Thus the soul, enlarged
Of finite grasp and speculative toils,
May contemplate the living truth and know
Its light a radiance of the one perfection,
Sole source of truth, of beauty and of grace . . .

                    Bathed in that light at length he knew the earth
Transfigured and adorned; not as before
Strange and perplexing to his sight, but now
A covenant of beauty whose design
Embraced himself and every humble life
That trod her ways. Hills, waters, fields and city

Were vested in a splendour whose array
Remembered and foretold the radiance
Of heaven that had but now received his soul
To its communion; and the earth transformed
In a like harmony before those eyes,
Which had been blind but now touched by her clay
Were blind no more, spoke with him and declared
That there is naught of nature, neither life
Apparent nor those still lives unperceived,
Which does not contemplate the light of God,
A finite reflect of the infinite.
And while he looked and mused his first seen dawn
Drew her bright webs across the eastern sky . . .

2

    Constrained by finite toils no mortal thought
May win beyond their grasp or disenfranchise
Itself of finite scope. However far
May stretch the fields of knowledge and man's view
Of strange horizons, thought's activity
Turns on the categories of this world,
And man, born blind to all that is remote
From mundane faculty, shall not attain
Things of the spirit till his eyes unsealed
Divine in spiritual light a world
Made present only through that light, and seen
But by the soul. To all in even measure,
Will they ensue it, that light shall reveal
The vision of a life whose radiance,
Surpassing all the loveliness of earth,
Embraces and transcends mortality . . .

    Man must at last
Affront that final barrier and renounce
The gift which brought him so far on his way,
For reason, meditating heavenly things,
Can but pronounce what they are not, proclaim

A realm its comprehension cannot serve
Directly, since that service manifest
In the distinctions and particulars
Proper to its own nature cannot be
Valid save for that nature . . .

        Though reason by instructed ignorance
Take refuge in such figures to denote
The substance of belief, these are but counters
Whose pious use disguises to man's heart
His thought's refusal. Here is Eden's wall
Construct of oppositions that the mind
Cannot admit except as integrals
Of an extraneous order: That which moves,
Itself unmoved; that which pervading all,
Transcending all, is present to each part
No less than to the whole; that which is other
And yet abides the same; that which is one
Made manifold, but manifold in one,
Apparent through the sole necessity
Of perfect essence, single, absolute,
And self-determined. Here arbitrament
Of time or space is meaningless, and all
Future and past, all width and depth and height
Are comprehended of unmoving vision
Persistent in a one eternal now.
Here the mind may not pass. Infinity
Rings round that garden, known of finite man
Only in virtue of his consciousness
That death supposes life, mortality
Immortal being. That beyond all name
Or concept or similitude or vision;
That which remains when all else is resolved
By thought, – that must remain because implicit
In thought's sole action which may not define
Or order knowledge save by recognition
Of knowledge unattained; – that which is known
Only in contradictories; an essence

Present to faith, inapprehensible
Of finite reason, is infinity:
A name to man, life's substance to his soul ...

                Infinity may never be conceived
By finite faculty, for God is known
Only of very God. That which is formed,
The primal matter of the universe,
Must needs ensue the shapes and the designs
Predicate by the limits of its nature.
So also sense may only reach the bounds
Imposed of its own faculty, and reason
Only may treat what is susceptible
Of its own measure. To the living soul,
That may not be content but meditates
Ever a final cause and dare not leave
That speculation lest she lose the pledge
Of her return from exile, faileth not
The presence of that spirit who inspires
Her life, in whom she has her being, of whom
She holds essential portion. But that spirit,
An emanation of the absolute,
Is yet distinct from God, a dyad nature
Perceiving in itself as separate
Its being, although itself perception; thus
Less than the absolute whose singleness
Alone is pure infinity. The source
Of grace and truth and beauty lies beyond
All revelation, yet from God proceeds
That Wisdom unto Whom may man approach
In contemplation, and therein be made
A living part of the all-seeing vision,
A flame of the eternal light, a star
Set in the glory of that plenitude
In whom all life is one.

Lord God, set Thy sweet clay upon these darkened eyes
That healed they may perceive the light of Paradise.

17. The Oblation of the World

Let my mind be still, emptied of all thought of self, that in quietness and humility I may bring before You, my Lord, the totality of the life of the earth.

May my heart, cleansed by Your transforming Fire, be a pure altar on which I may offer to You all the labour and sorrow of mankind.

On the paten of my heart I would place, O my Lord, the purposeful action of men, their aspirations, their achievements, their work. Into my chalice I would pour the sorrows, the failings and the pain of every living being.

Into this oblation of the whole world I would gather, first, those closest to me, those whose lives are bound up with my own personal life, those known to me, especially those whom I love.

With these may I unite those more distant and unreal to me, the whole anonymous mass of humankind, scattered in every corner of the globe. In sympathy and imagination I would unite myself with the ceaseless pilgrimage of mankind, with its joys and sorrows, its hopes and fears, its successes and failures, that I may be one with it all.

Let every sentient being be placed upon the altar of my heart, that I may raise them all up to You.

And not only the living would I gather into this oblation, but also the dead, that they too may be incorporated into the material of my sacrifice.

It is not enough. I would draw into it every form of life, animals and birds, reptiles and insects, trees, flowers, and all the kindly fruits of the earth. Let these too be laid upon this inner altar, that they too may be offered to You.

And yet the oblation is incomplete. Into it I would draw the very fabric of the earth itself, the material substance of which it is composed, that I may present nothing less than everything to You who are the All-in-all.

Creative Power, shining, deathless Spirit, wherein lay hidden the earth and all its creatures, so infuse this Your world with Your attraction that it may more and more be led back into You from whence it sprang.

Timeless Word, outpouring of the essence of the mysterious ineffable One, made flesh for us in the Lord Jesus, You who are ever moulding this manifold, phenomenal world so as to incorporate it more and more into Your divine life, You who are ever plunging Yourself into its depth and totality so as to touch us through everything within and without us, breathe into it now, Your transforming might. You who are Life and Giver of life.

May all life, past, present and future, that which was, that which is, and that which is to come, be now elevated at the altar to my heart, that in and through You, O eternal, cosmic Christ, it may now be presented, a holy sacrifice, in the secret place of the Most High, that all may be hallowed and consecrated unto that great Day of the final redemption of the whole creation, when this corruptible shall put on incorruption and this mortal shall put on immortality, and all things shall, in and through You, be brought back into the One from whence they came.

Now over the whole earthly pilgrimage of mankind (and over me, over us) pronounce Your revealing, consubstantial words, words of consecration, and also the annunciation of the ultimate mystery of the universe and of ourselves:

THIS IS MY BODY
THIS IS MY BLOOD

It is done. The oblation and the consecration are made. Grant us Your Peace.

18. The Radiation of Love

Jesus said: 'A new commandment I give unto you, that you love one another even as I have loved you.'

'God is love; he that dwells in love, dwells in God, and God is in him. Let us love one another; for love is of God; and everyone who loves is born of God, and knows God. But he who does not love knows not God; for God is love.'

Jesus said: 'Judge not that ye be not judged. For with what judgement ye judge, ye shall be judged; and with what measure ye mete, it shall be measured to you again.'

'What does it matter to thee whether another be guilty or guiltless? Come, friend, and look to thine own ways.'

'Canst thou destroy divine Compassion? Compassion is no attribute. It is the law of Laws – eternal Harmony, a shoreless, universal essence, the light of everlasting right and the fitness of all things, the law of Love eternal.

The more thou dost become one with it, thy being melts into its Being; the more thy soul unites with that which is, the more thou wilt become Compassion Absolute.'

Therefore:

'As a mother at the risk of her life cares for an only child, so let us diffuse boundless love towards all beings. Let us radiate thoughts of love, of compassion, of sympathetic joy, of equanimity and peace, over the entire world, above, below and all around, freed from all ill-will and enmity towards anyone, untrammelled by any thoughts of self.'

One then proceeds to gather into one's thought, radiating love, etc., over each in turn:

– those whom one definitely loves or likes, relatives, friends, etc.;

- those whom one knows, towards whom one's attitude is
  neutral or indifferent;
- those whom one dislikes, or even hates, with whom one
  feels oneself to be at enmity.

*During these first three love-radiations definite people may be named.
The last one may be at first difficult to do sincerely. One may feel that
one is being hypocritical. One must, however, do it as a deliberate act
of intention and will; gradually it will become more and more real.
One then spreads the radiation of love, etc., wider and wider to
include:*

- all mankind;
- all departed souls;
- all forms of life;
- the whole universe.

These radiations may be done silently or verbally:

'I gather into my thoughts all these whom I love and like,
my relatives and friends. I suffuse each one with thoughts of
love, compassion, joy and peace.'

And so on for each in turn.
Finally the Act of Love ends with this invocation:

'May the love of God fill the entire world in benediction,
peace and joy.'

19. On Detachment

The Disciple: I know, Master, that earthly existence is impermanent and insubstantial, a little span between birth and death, in the midst of infinite space and infinite time. I know that the world is full of suffering, sorrow and frustration. All is fleeting, nothing endures.

Though I may now be happy and serene, my body healthy, my mind sound, with worthwhile work to do, with friends and loved ones about me, I know that at any moment I may be struck down by disease of mind or body; those I love may die, my friends may fail me; the work to which I am dedicated destroyed. How, Master, may I be freed from the burden of this discord at the heart of things? How may I attain detachment and dispassion?

The Master: Thus, my son, spoke one who knew the Way:

In order to arrive at having pleasure in everything,
    Desire to have pleasure in nothing.
In order to arrive at possessing everything,
    Desire to possess nothing.
In order to arrive at being everything,
    Desire to be nothing.
In order to arrive at knowing everything,
    Desire to know nothing.
For in order to arrive at that wherein thou mayst find
    lasting joy,
    Thou must go by a way in which there is no joy.
In order to arrive at that which thou dost not yet know,
    Thou must go by the way of unknowing what thou
    dost know.
In order to arrive at that which thou desirest to possess,
    Thou must go by the way of dispossession.
In order to arrive at that which thou art not,
    Thou must go through that which thou art not.

The Disciple: This, I know, is the royal way, the way of the saint. But Master, I am not a saint: this way is too hard for me. I am not capable of such detachment. My life is in the world, the life of action. And, Master, I am puzzled. If all were to follow this royal way, how would the work of the world be done? Most men work because they desire something. It may be only money and possessions; it may be reputation, or the joy of achievement, or the desire for fame. Desire is the driving force of human action. Is there no worth in human action, in the aspirations and labour of mankind?

The Master: Listen, my son, this is wisdom. The world is imprisoned in its own activity except when that activity is placed in something higher than itself. Therefore, you must place all your actions in God and not claim any merit or reward. If you have dedicated all your actions to God, they are no longer yours but His. It will be He who works through you. Have no concern for results. Devote yourself to Him and then work, but for the work's sake only.

This is the way of detachment for those whose work is in the world. This is their way to eternal life.

But, remember always, my son, that in order to find the true life, you must die unto life; in order to find your true Self, your lower self must die. Your real Self is hid with Christ in God, who is your true Self. Have Self as a lamp, Self as a refuge, and no other refuge. Through Self you must urge on the self, for Self is the Lord of the self.

The Disciple: Now, Master, I understand and know what I must do. Each day and throughout the day I will dedicate myself to God and place everything I think or say or do in Him. And, if I can do that in complete sincerity and utter abandonment of myself, nothing will be mine any longer; everything will be His. Let this be my prayer:

My Lord and my God, take from me all that blocks my way to Thee;

My Lord and my God, give me all that speeds my way to
   Thee;

My Lord and my God, take this my-self from me and give
   me as Thine own to Thee.

Not I but Thou. Not mine but Thine.

20. The Meditation of the Silent River

Jesus said: 'Peace I leave with you, my peace I give unto you. Not as the world giveth give I unto you.'

Floating, floating, like a white bird on the water, floating unresisting, effortless — between the real and the imagined, between what comes to me from outside and from what wells up from deep, deep down within me — floating, unresisting, without effort, on the surface of the great flowing river of life — smooth, silent river, flowing so still, so silently, that it seems to be asleep, not flowing at all — still, sleeping river, flowing irresistibly.

Flowing inevitably; silently, irrevocably, into an ever fuller life, into a living peace, so profound, so rich, because in it all my strivings, all my sorrows, are taken into its own stillness and peace.

It is into that stillness, into that peace, that I am now moving — floating — just floating — not doing anything — just letting go — just allowing myself to be carried along — just letting this irresistible, sleeping river take me where it is going; and knowing all the time that it is going where I want to go, where I have to go — into more life — into reconciliation — into wholeness — into a living peace.

A period of silence, then:

It is very quiet now. Everything is so fresh, so pure, so charged with life — with real life — no longer imagined — so still, so restful — stillness — rest — into more life — into reconciliation — into wholeness — into the deep, deep peace of God.

21. On Old Age and Death

Dear, beauteous death; the jewel of the just!
Shining nowhere but in the dark;
What mysteries do lie beyond thy dust;
Could man outlook that mark!   (1)

What happiness to be able to die. That is the land for which
man must really yearn, the land of death, the holy land.

For in death we are caught up again, invaded, dominated
by the divine power. Death surrenders us totally to God; it
is there we must at last be united fully with Him. Let us
surrender ourselves to death in absolute love, absolute trust,
absolute self-abandonment. There is no need to fear. In death
there is peace, fulfilment, joy. To die will be a great adventure.

There is a place, the certain ground of peace,
The land of heart's desire, serene and lone,
Where stormy souls shall find at last release,
And walk with God, knowing as they are known.

Lord, in that secret place where ever flow
The quiet waters of the timeless sea,
Grant I may know the truth I longed to know
And be at last the one I wished to be.   (2)

For one who is ready to die there is no terror in death.
But men grow old; and with age there may come sickness,
pain and weariness. For many old age may become a burden,
difficult to bear.

Let this, therefore, be my faith; let this be my prayer:

After having perceived You as He who is 'a greater myself',
grant that I may recognize You under the species of each
alien or hostile force that seems bent on destroying or uproot-
ing me. When the signs of age begin to mark my body (and

still more when they touch my mind); when the ill which is to diminish me or carry me off strikes from without or is born within me; when the painful moment comes in which I suddenly awaken to the fact that I am ill or growing old; and above all at that last moment when I feel that I am losing hold of myself and am absolutely passive within the hands of the great unknown forces that have formed me; in all those dark moments, O God, grant that I may understand that it is You . . . who are painfully parting the fibres of my being in order to penetrate to the very marrow of my substance and bear me away within Yourself . . .

You are the irresistible and vivifying force, O Lord, and because Yours is the energy, because of the two of us, You are infinitely the stronger, it is to You that falls the part of consuming me in the union that should weld us together. (3)

> No end to suffering until
> We grasp it with awakened will,
> Inhale its perfume gratefully,
> At length discovering it to be
> No foe but friend, a light to see
> A brother's heart with charity,
> To understand and to forgive.
> Through suffering alone we live.
> Only through suffering men grow wise.
> Whom suffering speeds to joy arise.   (4)

O Lord may the end of my life be the best of it; may my closing acts be my best acts; and may the best of my days be the day when I shall meet Thee.   (5)

Support us, O Lord, all the days of this earthly life, till the shades lengthen, the evening comes, the busy world is hushed, the fever of life is over and our work is done. Then, in Thy mercy, grant us a safe lodging, a holy rest and peace at the last.

> In the hour of death, after this life's whim,
> When the heart beats low, and the eyes grow dim,

And pain has exhausted every limb –
  The lover of the Lord shall trust in Him.

When the will has forgotten the lifelong aim,
And the mind can only disgrace its fame,
And a man is uncertain of his own name –
  The power of the Lord shall fill his frame.

When the last sigh is heaved, and the last tear shed,
And the coffin is waiting beside the bed,
And the widow and child forsake the dead –
  The angel of the Lord shall lift his head. (6)

O Master, who payest not by time,
Take the thanks of Thy servant,
O Captain, receive my sword;
O Hands, O wounded Hands,
Reach and resume my soul.
Into Thy hands, Thy hands.
In manus tuas. (7)

Notes to the Prayer Book

Part I

1 ADORATIONS AND INVOCATIONS

(1) A generalized version of the Divine Praises, used by the Roman Catholic Church in the service of Benediction. (2) Part of the song of praise sung by the three young men thrown into a fiery furnace by King Nebuchadnezzar for refusing to worship the golden image he had set up. It is found in the Apocryphal, but not the Authorized, Version of the Book of Daniel. (3) A free translation for singing or reciting of a passage in Chapters 7–8 of the Book of Wisdom in the Apocrypha. This book was probably written by a Greek-speaking Jew of Alexandria about 100 B.C.

2 THE RADIATION OF LOVE

What I call the Radiation of Love is inspired by the Buddhist spiritual exercise of the Four Sublime States (*Brahma Viharas*). It is printed in the Anthology of *Mysticism* (third edition), Section 5.

This spiritual exercise is of great value in the transformation of personality, resulting, in the one using it, in an increase of clarity and the elimination of hatred. It should be used daily, particularly if one is inclined to dislike or hate anyone. A much longer form is included among the meditations.

3 NEW EVERY MORNING

Morning Meditations

(1) Bishop Ken 1637–1711. (2) John Keble 1792–1866. (3) George Herbert 1593–1632.

A Busy Man's Morning Devotion

(1) Part of Mrs Alexander's translation of St Patrick's Breastplate. I have changed a few words. (Mrs Alexander – 1823–95 – wrote many well-known hymns, including 'There is a green hill far away' and 'Once in royal David's city'.) (1a) Two verses from another

translation by J. C. Maugan 1803–49; the heading of this translation
is given as 'St Patrick's Hymn before Tara'. St Patrick (372–466)
brought the Christian Faith to Ireland. (2) The well-known prayer
of Robert Louis Stevenson. (3) From the Sarum Primer, 1532.
Since the Heart Centre is regarded as the seat of contemplative
intuition the word 'knowing', is the sense of spiritual awareness,
may be a better one than 'thinking', as in the original.

A Morning Thanksgiving

Many of the short 'offices' included in this Prayer Book were originally composed for use in the service, with which each day started,
of the Chapel of Bishop Wordsworth's, Salisbury, during my
headmastership of that school, 1928–60. This one, written as it was
for boys still at school, is particularly suitable as a corporate devotion for young people. The hymn 'Now thank we all our God', is
made up of the first and last verses of a seventeenth-century hymn,
'Nun danket alle Gott', translated by C. Winkworth. Another one
can be substituted if desired.

Another Morning Thanksgiving

The hymn, 'Praise the Lord' is made up of the first and last verses
of a hymn, the first verse of which is dated 1796, the last by E. Osler
(1798–1863). The concluding hymn, 'To Him from whom all
splendour springs', I wrote myself for the Commemoration of the
Faithful Ones, printed below.

Additional Morning Prayers

(1) Composed by The Right Reverend George Snow, Bishop of
Whitby. (2) Yet another version of St Patrick's Breastplate. (3) From
the Ambrosian Breviary.

   The remainder of the prayers in this section are of unknown
source. Some may be my own. During the course of my life I have
collected, written or adapted many of the prayers in this Prayer
Book.

A Morning Recessional Hymn

I wrote this hymn for use at the conclusion of the morning service
in the Chapel of Bishop Wordsworth's during my headmastership
of that school. The original tune, written for it by J. McN. Milne
and included with his permission, based on the song theme in the
second movement of Schubert's great C Minor Symphony, is

printed in this Prayer Book. Later I adapted the hymn for individual use. Both versions are printed here.

4 AT EVENTIDE THERE SHALL BE LIGHT

A Night Meditation

Three verses from a poem, 'The Night', by the seventeenth-century poet, Henry Vaughan.

An Evening Office

(1) Two translations of one of the oldest hymns of the Christian Church, used at the lighting of the lamps. The first version is a literal translation of the original Greek hymn, the second a verse translation by Father John Keble, one of the leaders of the Oxford Movement, which has had so great an influence on the Anglican Church. I have changed the last line of Keble's translation so as to make it a more exact translation of the original. (2) A seventeenth-century prayer, which was first brought to light by Father John Henry Newman, later Cardinal, in one of his sermons.

Evening Prayers

(1) This lovely night prayer is printed in that brilliant piece of research, Constance Padwick's *Muslim Devotions* (Student Christian Movement Press) from which I quoted so freely in Chapter 5 of the Study. I have omitted one phrase and changed another so that the prayer may be more suitable for present day use. (2) Both these prayers are in the Authorized Daily Prayer Book of the United Hebrew Congregations of the British Empire.

5 FORMS OF CONFESSION

Intended for use at any appropriate time. They are gathered from various sources. One I wrote myself.

6 MATINS AND EVENSONG

This shortened form of Matins was originally drawn up for use in the Chapel of Bishop Wordsworth's, so as to last not more than a quarter of an hour. The music of the responses used was composed by William Byrd. (1) This translation of the *Te Deum* is by my friend, the late Professor Edward C. Radcliff. The concluding versicles are omitted. (2) The well-known Prayer of St Chrysostom. I have altered one phrase, so that it conforms more closely with what Jesus actually said. At the end I have printed the General Thanksgiving from the Book of Common Prayer.

7 LITANIES

1 *A Litany based on the Litany of the Book of Common Prayer*

When I was a boy the Litany was more often said or sung than it is nowadays, and I used to find it very tedious. Except when sung in procession I still do. I was, however, much attracted by Tallis' five-part musical setting and since the Choristers of the Chapel of Bishop Wordsworth's School were of high standard, I composed this shortened form for use in that Chapel. In addition to shortening it, I 'modernized' it, if that is the right word, in several ways, for instance, by changing 'Have mercy upon us, miserable sinners' to 'Have mercy upon us when we call upon thee'; and rewriting and adding to the petitions. Well sung, it is a compact devotion of great beauty.

This and the other litanies which follow may be used privately or corporately.

2 *A Litany of the Good Life*

This litany was also composed for the Chapel of Bishop Wordsworth's. The two verses of the hymn I wrote to a tune I heard long ago on the radio and managed to get hold of a copy. I do not think the tune has ever been published. The second group of petitions were inspired by those in one of the litanies used by my own public school, Rydal, but are not an exact copy.

3 *A Litany for all men*

Some of the prayers in this litany are well known; the rest I wrote myself.

8 MEMORIALS OF OUR LORD JESUS CHRIST

1 *His Incarnation*

(1) Two verses of a seventeenth-century hymn by Henry Moore. (2) 1928 Prayer Book, based on a prayer in the Roman Mass. (3) From the Roman Missal; I cannot find the precise reference. (4) One of my own hymns, suggested by the eighteenth-century Latin hymn, '*Veni, Veni, Emmanuel*' ('O come, O come, Emmanuel').

2 *His Passion*

(1) and (6) Part of the well-known hymn, '*Pange lingua gloriosi proelium certaminis*', by one of the greatest of medieval hymn writers, Venantius Fortunatus, 530–609. I have followed the translations in the *English Hymnal* (95 and 96) by P. D. and J. M. Neale, except for one verse in (1) which is by A. F. (*Songs of Praise* 129). (2) There are several versions of the well-known hymn, 'O sacred Head', all based on the Latin hymn, '*Salve caput crucutatum*' of St Bernard, which was translated into German by P. Gerhardt, in the seventeenth century, and used by Johann Sebastian Bach. (3) A completely new version of a Lenten Prose; a good many Proses exist. (4) Four verses from a seventeenth-century hymn by Samuel Crossman. (5) From the Roman Missal. The symbolism is of particular interest. The Tree symbol is much older than Christianity. Its use in Christianity I tried to express in the following verses:

> In the Garden, Eve, the Mother
> Of our race, our race betrayed;
> Shut the paradisal portals
> Till another choice was made
> By the second Mother, Mary.
> In a crib the Child was laid.

> Consummation. In the darkness
> Of the hill of Calvary
> Hung the timeless Victor-Victim
> That upon another Tree
> He who by the Tree had conquered
> By this Tree should vanquished be.

The first Tree is the Tree of Knowledge of Good and Evil which, in the Genesis myth, was situated in the midst of the Garden of Eden. Tempted by the Serpent, Eve eats the forbidden fruit and Adam and Eve are expelled from the Garden. The second Tree is the Tree of the Cross, the 'one and only noble Tree', of the hymn of Venantius Fortunatus (6). Note also in these verses the symbolism of the 'Two Women', Eve and Mary.

3 *His Resurrection*

(1) From my verse sequence, 'The Victor-Victim', included among the meditations in Part III of this Prayer Book. (2) See I Corinthians, Chapter XIX from which these sentences are taken. It is interesting to compare the teaching of St Paul on the spiritual man and the

natural (or psychical) man with that contained in the Yoga Sutras of the Hindu sage, Patanjali, which has been called 'The Book of the Spiritual Man'* written more than a thousand years earlier. Though in different idioms, there are very close affinities between the two. (3) The last verse of Charles Wesley's Easter hymn, 'Love's redeeming work is done'.

9 OFFICE OF THE HOLY SPIRIT

Compiled from several sources. (1) Three verses of a thirteenth-century Latin hymn, '*Veni, sancte Spiritus*', translated J. M. Neale.

10 COMMEMORATIONS

1 *Commemoration of the Faithful Ones*

My own composition, except for (1) the version of '*Justorum animae in manu Dei sunt*' ('The souls of the righteous are in the hands of God'), arranged for singing, from the Book of Wisdom in the Apocrypha, Chapter 3; and the prayer, 'We give thee most high praise . . .' from the Book of Common Prayer. In the Chapel of Bishop Wordsworth's it was used not only on certain Saints' Days, but also to commemorate such 'Faithful Ones' as great artists, musicians, explorers, etc. It may be so used in churches, etc.

2 *Commemoration of the Departed*

(1) A Prayer of John Wordsworth, Bishop of Salisbury. (2) Cardinal Newman's 'Support us, O Lord, all the days . . .' put into verse form for a 'Requiem for an Unknown Soldier', which I wrote and which John Carol Case, my old pupil, set to music while he was still in the Army. So far as I know, it has only been performed twice, both times under his conductorship.

When this Commemoration of the Departed is used as part of a funeral service or immediately after the death of someone 'Go forth upon' is used instead of 'Pass on'.

11 DEDICATION

1 *An Office of Dedication*

This office was originally written for a Federation of Companies of Service which I formed during the Second World War. The Federa-

* A good translation and interpretation is that of Charles Johnston: *The Yoga Sutras of Patanjali* (John M. Watkins).

tion, which never had any firm roots, quickly faded out at the end of the War. The Office, however, continued to be used by Bishop Wordsworth's.

The Dedication Hymn, John Carol Case set to music. His tune is printed in this Prayer Book with his approval. The prayer, 'Make us, O Lord', was inspired by the prayer of St Francis of Assisi, included among the prayers of some Christian Saints in Section 14.

2 *A Simple Act of Dedication*

This little devotion is composed for use when a short Act of Dedication is needed, for instance at midday.

12 A SOLEMN LITURGY

This was, as already stated, composed for a special service in Salisbury Cathedral. A considerable amount of original, as yet unpublished, music was used. The music for the opening, 'In the beginning God created the heaven and the earth', and for the versicles and responses, 'In the beginning was the Word', was composed by Peter Evans, at one time one of my music masters, now Professor of Music at the University of Southampton; those for 'The first Adam was made a living soul', by John Carol Case. Items printed in other places in this Prayer Book are incorporated in this solemn Litany. It can be used in its entirety or parts, for instance, the prayers, 'Praise be to Thee', and 'Brightness of the glory', as well as the 'Prayer of Completion', of which I have written several variations, may be used separately.

13 CREDO

This is an attempt to draw up a declaration of fundamental belief, which can be used by those who find more elaborate creeds, such as the Nicene Creed, alien or difficult to understand. The first two clauses would, I think, not be alien to most Moslems, Hindus and Buddhists; the third is essentially Christian. In composing this Credo I was influenced by the statement of his own faith by Professor Arnold Toynbee in his autobiography, *Experiences*. I trust he will not mind my using some of his actual phrases.

14 AN ANTHOLOGY OF PRAYERS IN PROSE AND VERSE

Prayers from the Ancient Liturgies

(1) Liturgy of the Nestorians. (2) Roman Breviary. (3) Sarum Missal. (4) Sarum, based on Gelasian. (5) Gallican Liturgy of Alcuin. (6) Leonine Liturgy.

The Nestorian Church is one of the branches of the Eastern Orthodox Church. The Liturgy of the Roman Church developed gradually through the sixth-century Leonine, the seventh-century Gelasian and the eighth-century Gregorian, Sacramentaries, eventually supplanting the French medieval Gallican and Spanish Mozarabic Liturgies. Medieval England had several Uses, the most famous of which was the Sarum Use, which Cranmer used in making his Book of Common Prayer.

Prayers of some Christian Saints

(7), (8) and (9) St Augustine. (10) St Benedict. (11) Thomas à Kempis. (12) John Scotus Erigina, ninth-century Irish. (13) St Ignatius Loyola. (14) Nicholas van der Flües, the Swiss mountain saint. (15) St Francis of Assisi.

Prayers from various Sources

This section is made up partly of prayers I have collected in the course of a lifetime, but the sourceso f which I am unable to trace (some may be from the ancient liturgies, or have been composed by Christian saints); partly of prayers which I have written or adapted myself; partly of prayers composed by or sent to me by friends.

The Masonic Prayer at Lodge Closing (1) was composed by the late W. L. Wilmshurst. It is printed in one of his well-known books on Masonry which has sold freely to the general public as well as to Freemasons. For drawing my attention to it and getting permission for me to use it I am indebted to my friend, Brian G. Moorhouse.

The first of the two prayers for animals (2) has an interesting history. It was sent to me by my friend, Major Harold Mead, of Southampton University, who told me that it came to him quite spontaneously one morning and he wrote it down just as it came.

Prayers in Verse Form

Most of these prayers are well-known hymns, which lend themselves for use as prayers. Prayers in verse form have been found to be congenial to many people who find their rhythmic quality helpful. They will be found in many hymnals. The last two are my own.

(1) John Greenleaf Whittier, the American poet (1807–92); three verses only. (2) Oliver Wendell Holmes (1809–94). (3) Edwin Hatch (1835–89); three verses only. (4) J. E. Bode (1816–74). (5) Father F. W. Faber, a Jesuit missionary to India (1814–63). (6) Four verses of a hymn by Father Pusey, one of the leaders of the Oxford Movement. It is based on a seventeenth-century hymn, '*Christe du Beistand*'. So as to make it more personal and general I have printed 'children's' for 'Church's' in the first verse and changed three words in the last verse. (7) One of the several translations of '*Jesu, dulcis memoria*', possibly the best known of the Jesus hymns of St Bernard of Clairvaux, eleventh century. (8) Charles Wesley, brother of John Wesley, the founder of Methodism. He wrote many well-known hymns. I have printed three verses only of a much longer hymn for use as a prayer at a time of spiritual perplexity and doubt. (9) The first verse of a hymn or poem by H. C. Beeching (1859–1919), which I have called, 'The Prayer of a Boy'. (10) I wrote this hymn for the baptism of my son, David, in Salisbury Cathedral in the Spring of 1936, when it was sung to the tune, 'Welwyn'. It may be used for its original purpose or as a parent's prayer for a child. (11) I wrote this as my own epitaph. By changing the first person singular pronouns in the last two lines of the second verse to the third, it may be sung at a funeral to the tune composed by J. McN. Milne for the Morning Recessional Hymn, which is printed in this Prayer Book.

15 THE PRACTICE OF THE PRESENCE OF GOD

With the exception of one prayer, which I wrote myself, all these prayers of Recollection in daily life were written for me by my friends. It is possible for anyone to compose similar prayers to suit his or her own needs. It is important to make Acts of Recollection as frequently as possible in the course of one's daily duties, so that all actions are taken into God and every action becomes a prayer. It is sufficient simply to say 'Christ in me and I in Him' at intervals throughout the day.

Part II

THE HOLY EUCHARIST

PRAYERS FOR USE IN THE HOLY EUCHARIST

These prayers are drawn from various sources. Most are taken directly or adapted from prayers in the ancient Liturgies, for instance, 'Behold us, Lord Jesus', from the Liturgy of St Chrysostom; 'Grant, O Father', from the Liturgy of St Basil; 'Cleanse our consciences' from the Gelasian Liturgy; 'Most merciful God', from the York Missal.

The hymn, 'Let all mortal flesh keep silent', was translated or, rather, adapted, by E. Moultine from the Liturgy of St James.

The Liturgies of St Chrysostom and St Basil, the two chief Liturgies of the Eastern Orthodox Church, are combined in the present Rite. The Liturgy of St James is the ancient Liturgy of Jerusalem.

SIMPLE PRAYERS AT THE CONSECRATION AND COMMUNION

In the course of compiling this Prayer Book I found these simple prayers on some sheets which I had stuck into a prayer book I used many years ago and felt that they might appeal to some who may find more elaborate prayers alien. I regret that I do not know the origin of the little paperback from which I tore the sheets.

A PRAYER OF THANKSGIVING

I cannot recall the source. I may have written it myself for a special purpose as long ago as 1930.

THE HYMN OF THE OBLATIONS

I wrote this hymn for use at the Great Entrance in the Chapel of Bishop Wordsworth's. The original tune to it was composed by J. McN. Milne and is printed in this Prayer Book. It is intended to make articulate the nature of the Oblation, i.e. the presentation of the bread and wine by the people, and to allow the congregation to share in it.

A COLLECTION OF EUCHARISTIC HYMNS

(1), (2) and (3), translations of three of the widely used Feast of
Corpus Christi hymns of St Thomas Aquinas. (4) H. Bonar 1808–80.
(5) Two verses of a hymn by the late Colonel W. H. Turton. To
make the prayer more universal, I have changed the words, 'For
all Thy Church', to 'For all mankind', in the second verse. (6)
W. H. H. Jervios, 1852–1905.

THE EUCHARISTIC ACTION

This is reprinted from a Prism Pamphlet entitled *A Cosmic Eucharist*,
now out of print, which opened with an introduction on the evolution of the Eucharistic Liturgy. In this reprint I have made a number
of changes from my original version. Liturgists will notice the influence of the Liturgy of St Chrysostom and St Basil, and also of the
Eucharistic Liturgy of Hippolytus. The Great Adorations are an
extension of Hippolytus' doxology. For the introduction of a Communion of the World to replace the individual communion of the
celebrant and of a corporate Act of Love I take responsibility; they
will not be found in any other Liturgy. In order that the reader may
understand this Cosmic Liturgy more clearly, may I refer him to
Chapter 4 on Christian Prayer in The Study.

MEDITATIONS ON THE HOLY EUCHARIST

The Pattern of the Eucharistic Action

This was compiled by making a mosaic of passages from Evelyn
Underhill's *The Mystery of Sacrifice* (Longmans, Green & Co.), the
most beautiful book on the Eucharist I have ever read. I am indebted to Mrs G. A. Wilkinson for permission to print this meditation and for the poem, 'Corpus Christi', also by Evelyn Underhill
included in her volume of poems, *Immanence* (J. M. Dent and Co.),
which follows it.

The Universal Christ

I wish to acknowledge with thanks my indebtedness to Messrs
Collins (and to Harper and Row) for permission to print this passage from Teilhard de Chardin's *Le Milieu Divin*.

The Unknown God

Similarly, for permission to print Alice Meynell's lovely poem, 'The Unknown God', I should like to thank her Executors and her granddaughter, Mrs Sylvia Mulvey.

Part III

In the Introduction to this Prayer Book I divided the Prayer of Meditation into two main types, rational-reflective, the Prayer of the Head, and intuitive-contemplative, the Prayer of the Heart. I then sub-divided it into seven types, primarily reflective, i.e. 'mental' prayer, through reflective-contemplative, to the Meditation of Pure Silence. A combination of reflection and contemplation seems, in my experience, to be the most suitable for the majority. The objective of the practice of the Prayer of Meditation, whatever means (spiritual exercises) are used for the purpose, should be, for everyone, to pass from the sphere of thought to the sphere of contemplation. So to this section I have given the title 'The Prayer of Meditation and Contemplation'.

No one who has read the prayers of Recollection of the Presence of God in active life, written by my friends, or the last Chapter of the Study can accuse me of regarding the Prayer of Meditation as a retreat from the world in order to revel in spiritual delights. If in the practice of contemplation one is taken up to the Mount of Transfiguration it is only to come down again to the dusty market place to pursue better the life of dedicated service to one's fellow men. 'Seek ye first the Kingdom of Heaven,' said Jesus, 'and all the rest will be added unto you.' In this age, when so much of the emphasis is on action, too little on the necessity of making 'The Journey Inwards' (for the Kingdom of Heaven is within one), in order effectively to lead the life of action, it is necessary to emphasize this. 'It is as futile to concentrate on adoring the ONE and ignoring the Many, as it is to lose oneself in the Many without finding the ONE'.*

The 'meditations' contained in this section on the Prayer of Meditation and Contemplation are of different types and are arranged as follows:

1. Entry prayers, mantras and 'The Womb of Silence'.

2. A group of two meditations, The Light Meditation *and* The Divine Lover.

3. Meditations on the Self.

4. A long group of Meditations on the Christ.

* A. Graham Ikin: *The Great Awakening.*

5. A group of three meditations in verse, all by poets known to me. The first two have never appeared in print before, the last is from a long verse sequence, To His Blind Mistress, *long out of print. I have given them the titles of* Meditations and Prayers of a Poet-Mystic, The Spiritual Adventure *and* The Man Born Blind.

6. A group of meditations on the Active Life, The Oblation of the World, The Radiation of Love *and* On Detachment.

7. The Meditation of the Silent River. This 'deep' meditation, which has proved in practice to have a marked psycho-spiritual effect, stands alone from all the rest. It is essentially an inward movement of heart and mind into a state of stillness and quiet.

8. On Old Age and Death *brings this collection of meditations to an appropriate ending.*

The material for these meditations, or better, spiritual exercises, is gathered not only from Christian sources, but also from all the higher religions and from none. In a meditation with a group recently, without any intention of doing so, I found that I had used elements from Christian, Islamic, Hindu Vedanta and Buddhist sources. If you desire an apologia, it will be found in the last chapter of The Journey Inwards, *entitled 'All May be One'. The last sentence of that chapter read: 'For one of the greatest graces which can come from the sincere practice of spiritual meditation is to know better that infinite compassion, which lived in Him who, on the Eve of His Passion, prayed that "they all may be one, as Thou, Father, art in Me and I in Thee, that they also may be one in Us".'*

MANTRAS

On the nature and use of mantras I have written fully in Chapter 13 and need add little more here. I thought that it would be useful, however, to gather together the chief Eastern and Western mantras in The Prayer Book.

The repetition of mantras is very useful in keeping the attention fixed during a period of silence. Since some at least are 'words of power' they must be used with care. It is best for the beginner in the practice of meditation to use mantras such as 'Be still and know' and Christian mantras such as the *Kyrie* and the Pauline ones and to avoid the Eastern ones until he is ready for them.

THE WOMB OF SILENCE

Inspired by the Rules of Silence of Taizé, a copy of which was given to me by one of my friends. It is suitable for use with a meditation group, but more especially for private meditation. An excellent method of private meditation is to start by saying 'The Womb of Silence' and then to remain silent for a quarter of an hour at least, repeating a mantra to keep the mind quiet and receptive. Never has better advice been given than that which St Teresa gave to her nuns, with which 'The Womb of Silence' opens.

THE LIGHT MEDITATION

This meditation is not only a favourite with my meditational group but is also interesting on account of the elements of which it is composed.

It opens with a saying of the Lord Jesus. This is followed by a piece from St Patrick's Breastplate, turned into a light meditation by a small change in the last line. Then comes Ahamad-at-Tijāni's 'inward prayer of light', which is Islamic. 'Lead me from the unreal to the real . . .' is from the Hindu Upanishads. The meditation ends with Phyllis Campbell's 'Serene Light'.

THE DIVINE LOVER

(1) The first stanza of Francis Thompson's 'The Hound of Heaven'. (2) One verse of a poem by Phyllis Campbell. The last two lines are my own. (3) Three verses from Roy Campbell's translation of 'Upon a gloomy night' of St John of the Cross (Penguin Books). The whole poem is printed in the Anthology of *Mysticism*.

ON THE SELF

The teaching of the Blessed John Ruysbroeck in the opening passage from his *The Adornment of the Spiritual Marriage* has close affinities with that in the passages from the Upanishads which follow; the last words, 'You are That' are the basic Hindu formula of faith, *Tat twam asi*. I have incorporated it into the first clause of the Credo printed earlier: 'the Dweller in the innermost spiritual sanction of a human being, which is his real Self, is of the same essence as that spiritual Reality which men call God, which is within, behind and beyond the universe.'

PASSING THROUGH THE BODIES

This is a spiritual exercise designed to assist in an inner realization of the nature of the real Self. It is used both in Buddhist and Sufi devotion. The one printed here is the Sufi form. Jane's Meditation is a meditation on the Self of a different type.

CHRIST IN THE UNIVERSE

For permission to print this beautiful poem of Alice Meynell I am indebted to her granddaughter, Mrs Sylvia Mulvey, and to the Executors of Alice Meynell. It speaks for itself and needs no comment from me.

THE DHARMA OF THE LORD JESUS

I regard this meditation as of great importance. It is the teaching of all religions that progress in the spiritual life is based on the cultivation of the moral and social virtues. But what moral and social virtues? These vary from age to age and from culture to culture; they are not absolute. Is there a moral law which is independent of time and place, a Cosmic Law, a law of the universe, timeless, inviolate, unalterable? I believe that there is and that all the great religious leaders revealed it in different ways. To me, who in my old age am more a Christian than ever, yet am compelled in the light of the truth that is me, to stand like that modern saint, Simone Weil, at the intersection of Christianity and everything that is not formally Christian, the Lord Jesus is indeed very God and very man. I do not need to believe this, I *know* it to be true. His commands are, for me, absolutely binding. I know that I shall fail to keep them, and fail badly, but I must try to show that faith in my life.

In that collection of sayings, grouped together in the so-called Sermon on the Mount and in others of his sayings scattered throughout the Gospels, the Lord Jesus revealed this Cosmic Law. They are not vague, impractical idealism but an acute social, ethical and psychological analysis of things as they really are. What He is saying is something like this: 'There is a moral law of the universe, a pattern or texture of things as they really are, whether you, silly little men, realize it or not. You did not invent it; it simply *is*. It has its origin in God, the Source of everything. I declare to you what this Cosmic Law is. You can identify yourself with this pattern of things as they really are and frame your actions thereon. If you do you will have the backing of the law inherent in the universe on your side. The stars in their courses will fight for you. You cannot fail. You must, however, make your choice, and take the consequences of that choice; they are inevitable.'

PRAYER AND MEDITATION

Let these sayings of the Lord Jesus be meditated on and a real
effort be made to live them in ordinary life; they are a statement of
the pattern of the only true, and so the only happy, life. They are
followed by a Christianized version of the Buddhist devotion of the
Three Gems (see page 78) with which it is customary for many
Buddhists to begin a meditation.

The word, *Dharma* (Pali, *dhamma*) is used in the Buddhist scriptures with three interconnected meanings; first to designate the one
Ultimate Reality; next in the sense of the supreme moral law of the
universe, the cosmic order, which is the expression of the nature of
the one Ultimate Reality. It also has a secondary meaning; a body
of teaching or doctrine of this universal Law. In the Sermon on the
Mount and in other of his sayings Jesus enunciated this supreme
universal Law of the cosmos (see Chapter 17 of The Study). In this
meditation on the Dharma of the Lord Jesus I have turned some
of these other sayings into Beatitudes. In the interests of clarity I
have used a number of different translations.

In the last of these Beatitudes I have translated the word which
the Authorized Version translates as 'righteousness' as 'truth'. It
is a difficult word to translate in a way which brings out its true
meaning. The medieval Latin word is *justitia*, justice. Its subtle
meaning is seen in the following passage from Ruysbroeck, printed
in the Anthology of *Mysticism*:

> The justice of the spirit desires to pay every hour which is demanded
> of it to God. And, therefore, at each irradiation of God, the spirit turns
> inward in action and in fruition; and thus it is renewed in every virtue,
> and is more deeply immersed in fruitive rest. . . . Thus the man is just. . . .
> He dwells in God, and yet goes forth towards all creatures in universal
> love, in virtue and in justice.

THE JEWEL IN THE LOTUS

The title of this meditation on the indwelling Christ is based on the
Great Mantra of Buddhism. *Om mani padme hum* (or *Om*). *Mani* is
the Radiant Jewel; *padme* the lotus which, rooted in mud, grows
upwards through the water and opens its petals in the light of the
sun. The lotus is the symbol of the enlightened consciousness. In
Christian theology the Incarnate Christ is the Radiant Jewel, mani-
festing in time and history the enlightened consciousness in its
supreme form. The Invocation, a perfect invocation of the indwel-

ling Christ, is not Christian but Buddhist in origin. Composed by the Lama Anagarika Govinda and printed by his permission, it is addressed to Amitabha, the Buddha of Infinite Light, 'who is meditated upon while facing the setting sun, when the day's work is over and the mind is at rest'. It is printed in *The Way of the White Clouds* (Hutchinson). The second invocation, addressed to Maitreya, 'the Buddha who is to come', beginning 'O Mighty One', is also by the Lama Govinda. I have ventured to make some small changes in his text.

THE MYSTERY OF THE CHILD

The next two meditations are two of my own verse sequences. The first, a meditation for the season of Christmas, was written at the request of John Gardner, who has set it to music. It has not, as yet, been published or performed. I have omitted some of the lyrics, which are more suitable for singing than for meditation.

The verse sequence falls into eight sections, each of which can be regarded as a separate meditation. Section 1 is a Prologue. Section 2 treats of the Advent of the Eternal Child, the *puer eternus*. I might have omitted Section 3, 'The Adoration of the Animals', an ancient Christmas legend. It was, however, great fun to write it and it appeals to children. Section 4, 'The Coming of the Shepherds', the simple, unsophisticated ones, who find their way to the Manger very quickly, contrasts with Section 6, 'The Coming of the Magi', the intellectuals for whom the Way is long and hard. Section 5 is an interlude dividing Sections 4 and 6. The two 'apple' trees are respectively the Tree of the Knowledge of Good and Evil in the Garden of Eden in the Genesis myth, (by eating of the forbidden fruit the parents of the human race are expelled into the phenomenal world of polar opposites); and the Apple Tree in the Garden of the Hesperides in Greek mythology. It is here used as the symbol of the Tree of Life. Having been expelled from the Garden of Eden, the garden of primal innocence, man is called through the sufferings of the earth-life to find his way back, but to another garden, the garden of spiritual maturity, of eternal life.

The origin and evolution of symbols is of great interest. Several of them have a double meaning. For instance the Serpent is both the symbol of evil and destruction and also of healing and redemption, cf. 'As Moses lifted up the serpent in the wilderness so shall

the Son of Man be lifted up.' It appears again in a different form in
Section 6:

> . . . the Snake is curled
> About the roots of the Tree of Life
> In the Wood beyond the World

The Tree is another such symbol, cf. 'Behold the salvation of the
world is set upon the Tree of the Cross. . .' in the second of the
memorials of our Lord Jesus Christ.

Whether the apple is a true symbol I do not know; I am doubtful.
It is interesting that, though there is no scriptural authority, the
Tree of Knowledge of Good and Evil came to be thought of as an
apple tree, as in the medieval carol 'Adam lay ybounden':

> And all for an apple
> An apple that he took,
> As clerkès finden written
> In their book.
>
> Ne had the apple taken been,
> The apple taken been,
> Ne never had our Lady
> A-been heavenè queen.
>
> Blessed be the time
> That apple taken was.
> Therefore we moun singen
> *Deo gratias!*

In Section 6 'The Coming of the Magi', which is celebrated in the
Feast of the Epiphany at the end of the Twelve Days of Christmas,
I have used symbols lavishly, the City, the Rose, the Tree, the Star,
etc. I shall not attempt to explain them; neither shall I write of the
meaning of 'the way of unknowing'; I have done so in other parts
of this trilogy. The image of 'the secret stair' is taken from St John
of the Cross.

Section 7. Throughout this verse sequence I have tried to picture
a very human Mary. In this section a transformation takes place.
She becomes the Queen of Heaven, 'crowned with stars and clothed
in gold', the *Theotokos*, the Bearer of the Incarnate Word.

The hymn to our Lady merges into a hymn to the Incarnate
Christ, ending with his three great titles, *Ischyros, Agios, Athanatos*,
the Strong, the Holy, the Immortal.

The Epilogue (Section 8) sums up the whole sequence. It is
itself a complete meditation on the Mystery of the Incarnation.

THE VICTOR-VICTIM

The story of this verse sequence on the Passion may be of interest to the reader. At the end of the Second World War I had written a 'Requiem for an Unknown Soldier', which my old pupil, John Carol Case, set to music. It was performed by the Choral Society of Bishop Wordsworth's under his conductorship. A composer who heard it said to me after the performance, 'You seem to be able to write librettos. Will you write me a Passion?' I replied that I could not write this sort of thing to order, but that I would see if the inspiration came. For some reason the idea gripped me, not in the form of what the composer wanted, a simple Passion suitable for a Church choir, but at a deeper level. Sibelius has said of the composition of his Fifth Symphony that he seemed to be composing under the influence of a power which was not himself. So it was with me. The verses simply came, though not in an orderly sequence. I seemed to be writing automatically. Polishing was rarely called for. Some pieces, however, gave me a lot of trouble. I do not know how many times I have re-written the section beginning, 'Be still and know'. In this version of the sequence Part 1, the Prologue, is much shorter than the original one; Part 2, the Passion, is, except for the last section, as it was originally written. So is Part 3, the Resurrection, except that the first verse, 'It seemed to be all over', was added later.

MEDITATIONS AND PRAYERS OF A POET-MYSTIC

I am very glad to have this opportunity of presenting, for purposes of meditation, this anthology of the mystical poems of Phyllis Campbell, as yet unpublished, to a wide public. They were sent to me as a result of my writing *Mysticism*, the first volume of this trilogy. The anthology fits perfectly into the pattern of this section of the Prayer Book. In this meditation I have not included 'Serene Light', perhaps her best poem. It is included in the Entry Prayers and in The Light Meditation.

Phyllis Campbell, now in her late seventies, is the daughter of a member of the Calcutta High Court. From the age of seventeen she lived for two and a half years in India, where she came into contact with the teaching of Hinduism. She returned to England to study at the Royal College of Music and for some years was a professional musician, specializing in violin/piano and viola/piano sonatas. Since 1920 she has lived in Australia as the wife of a Senior Lecturer, now retired, in Electrical Engineering at the University of Sydney. Of the composition of her poems she writes:

I am neither a scholar nor a poet, but from time to time I have experienced an opening up of consciousness. I become intensely aware of certain ideas and rhythms which possess me until I have woven them into permanent forms. Sometimes this has happened when meditating, or at night, or during illness. As I have little or no contact with people interested in such matters, the poems have for some years been relegated to a shelf and there they have remained. Actually when I have looked at them at rare intervals, I cannot believe they came through my pen.

In fitting the poems together for meditational purposes I have, with Mrs Campbell's permission, built the collection of poems into a sequence, sometimes printing a whole poem, sometimes a single verse or a couple of verses. The pattern of the sequence stands out very clearly, moving from the universal through a series of illuminations, vividly described, to the intensely personal, and culminating in the last two poems, which bear the titles of 'The Mystic' and 'The Saint'.

Also, with Mrs Campbell's consent, I have altered some of her punctuation, removed a good many capital letters – her use of capitals is seventeenth- and eighteenth- rather than twentieth-century – and very occasionally altered a word.

THE SPIRITUAL ADVENTURE

This poem was sent to me from South Africa by Leslie G. Machin with a charming inscription, 'With deepest gratitude to Dr F. C. Happold for having written *Mysticism*.' It bore the title, 'Meet my Father', which, though a vivid one, I did not really like. I have called it 'The Spiritual Adventure'. Though, perhaps, difficult at first reading, its meaning will soon become clear. It shows considerable spiritual insight. It should be meditated on in a mood of quietness, of looking and waiting.

THE MAN BORN BLIND

The author of this poem, whom I am honoured to call a friend, has had a distinguished career. He is also at the same time a poet, a polished Classical scholar and an intellectual mystic of the type of St Augustine and Nicholas of Cusa. This meditation is not suited to everyone. Unless one has some acquaintance with mystical theology and the literature of mysticism it may be incomprehensible. To understand its profound meaning, it is necessary to read it several times, pondering on each section, even on each line, until the meaning becomes clear. Those who have read and understood my *Mysticism* may find it comparatively easy. It will, I think, help the reader if I analyse the different parts.

Section 1 describes the *pan-en-henic* experience, the sense of the all in the One and of the One in the all, i.e. the co-inherence of the material (phenomenal) and the spiritual (noumenal, ultra-phenomenal) worlds. With 'Constrained by finite toils . . .' the meditation moves into a section on the limitation of human reason to apprehend ultimate truth, the 'quiddity' of things, and so to the need of entering 'the Cloud of Unknowing' (see the Sections in the Anthology of *Mysticism* on 'The Divine Darkness', in first and second editions, no. 9, in third, no. 11; and 'God may well be Loved but not Thought', in first and second editions, no. 19, in third, no. 22). The passage beginning, 'Though reason by instructed ignorance . . .' is an elaboration of the teaching of Nicholas of Cusa on '*docta ignorantia*' and 'the coincidence of contradictories' (see Section no. 22 in first and second, no. 25 in third edition, of the Anthology). The last passage, 'infinity may never be conceived . . .' passes through the urge of man to find 'the uncaused Cause', to the oneness in essence of God and man, *Tat twam asi* (Thou art That), and then to the doctrine of *Sancta Sophia*, Holy Wisdom.

The meditation ends with a prayer:

Lord God, set Thy sweet clay upon these darkened eyes
That healed they may perceive the light of Paradise.

The next three meditations are meditations of the active life, of the sort which in *The Journey Inwards* I called 'coming-out' meditations.

THE OBLATION OF THE WORLD

This meditation was inspired by, but not copied from, Teilhard de Chardin's 'Mass of the World', printed in *Hymn of the Universe* (Collins). It falls into two parts: (i) a gathering together of all mankind, both the living and the dead, of all life, even of the material substance of the universe as the offering to be consecrated; (ii) the Consecration, beginning, 'Creative Power, shining, deathless Spirit', inspired by the insight of the Hindu *Vedanta*, and then passing into the Christian insight of the Incarnation of the Eternal Logos, the Cosmic Christ and of the *Pleroma* towards which the whole creation moves.

The meditation ends with the words used at the high moment of consecration in the Holy Eucharist, 'This is My Body; this is My Blood'. At this moment there is a double movement, inward and upward, outward and downward; there is an echo, as it were, of the words uttered by the celebrating priest, in the revealing, consubstantial words of the Cosmic Christ, 'You, the very earth itself, are My Body and My Blood.'

THE RADIATION OF LOVE

This meditation is a form of the Buddhist Brahma Viharas meditation, the radiation of the Four Sublime States, benevolence or loving kindness (*metta*), Compassion (*Karuna*, the Christian virtue of *agapē*, love), sympathetic joy and equanimity (or peace of mind); see the Anthology of *Mysticism*, third edition, Section 5, for the full text.

The opening sentences are partly Christian, partly Buddhist in origin.

ON DETACHMENT

This meditation is in the form of a dialogue between the Master and his Disciple. The group of sayings beginning, 'In order to arrive at having pleasure in everything', are from St John of the Cross: *The Ascent of Mount Carmel*. The passage, 'The world is imprisoned in its own activity . . .' is from the Hindu scripture, the *Bhagavad Gita*. The concluding prayer is by the Swiss mountain saint, Nicholas van der Flües.

The next two concluding meditations are of an entirely different sort.

THE MEDITATION OF THE SILENT RIVER

This is definitely a 'deep' meditation, which has proved in practice to have a marked psycho-spiritual effect. It is a movement of heart and mind into a state of stillness and rest. Further, it seems to have a therapeutic quality, a quality of spiritual healing. It should be said very slowly, with frequent pauses.

It was inspired by a passage in Aldous Huxley's novel, *Island*, from which I have, by permission of Chatto and Windus, borrowed some of the phrases used.

ON OLD AGE AND DEATH

(1) One verse of a poem by the seventeenth-century poet, Henry Vaughan. (2) One of my own poems. (3) From Pierre Teilhard de Chardin's *Le Milieu Divin* (by kind permission of the publishers, Messrs Collins, and of Harper and Row). (4) Another poem by Phyllis Campbell, not previously quoted. (5) An Islamic prayer. (6) The first three verses of an anonymous poem '*Dominus Illuminatio Mea*', printed in Q's *Oxford Book of English Verse*. (7) Inscribed on the memorial to 'Q' (Sir Arthur Quiller-Couch) on the cliffs at Fowey.

MORE ABOUT PENGUINS
AND PELICANS

Penguinews, which appears every month, contains details of all the new books issued by Penguins as they are published. From time to time it is supplemented by *Penguins in Print*, which is a complete list of all books published by Penguins which are in print. (There are well over three thousand of these.)

A specimen copy of *Penguinews* will be sent to you free on request, and you can become a subscriber for the price of the postage. For a year's issues (including the complete lists) please send 30p if you live in the United Kingdom, or 60p if you live elsewhere. Just write to Dept EP, Penguin Books Ltd, Harmondsworth, Middlesex, enclosing a cheque or postal order, and your name will be added to the mailing list.

Two Pelicans by F. C. Happold are described overleaf.

Note: *Penguinews* and *Penguins in Print* are not available in the U.S.A. or Canada

F. C. HAPPOLD

Mysticism

A Study and an Anthology

Mysticism is concerned with spiritual knowledge – the knowledge of truths we cannot understand with our minds. Most books on mysticism are difficult to follow without acquaintance with the writings of the mystics themselves, and the latter are hard to come by and too extensive for the ordinary reader.

This new book offers an original and effective solution of the difficulty. In it the author has combined both a study of mysticism, which makes its own contribution to the literature of the subject, and an anthology of mystical writings. Covering a wider field than previous selections, this anthology has been compiled to illustrate and complement the study. Its twenty-seven sections (each with an introductory note) are taken from the work not only of Christian mystics, but also from the *Upanishads* and the *Baghavad Gita*, from Plato and Plotinus, and from the Sufi mystics of Islam.

Religious Faith and Twentieth-Century Man

Religion, it is easy to believe, has been blown sky-high by the discoveries of modern science. But millions of people are undoubtedly waiting for the pieces to fall. When they do, what new pattern will they form?

In *Religious Faith and Twentieth-Century Man* Dr Happold examines and analyses the major influences which must determine a modern picture of reality. Whatever new worlds have been charted by quantum physicists, radio astronomers, and depth psychologists, the great mystical experiences of individual men cannot be excluded from any total view of the universe. Dr Happold's search for a satisfactory synthesis leads him to a religio-philosophy of the mystical as a way out of the spiritual dilemma of modern man. From this develops an entirely fresh attitude towards the world – an attitude he terms 'Intersection'.